Welcome to the EVERYTHING® series!

These handy, accessible books give you all you need to tackle a difficult project, gain a new hobby, comprehend a fascinating topic, prepare for an exam, or even brush up on something you learned back in school but have since forgotten.

FACTS
Important sound bytes of information

You can read an *EVERYTHING®* book from cover-to-cover or just pick out the information you want from our four useful boxes: e-facts, e-ssentials, e-alerts, and e-questions. We literally give you everything you need to know on the subject, but throw in a lot of fun stuff along the way, too.

Essentials
Quick handy tips

We now have well over 100 *EVERYTHING®* books in print, spanning such wide-ranging topics as weddings, pregnancy, wine, learning guitar, one-pot cooking, managing people, and so much more. When you're done reading them all, you can finally say you know *EVERYTHING®*!

ALERT
Urgent warnings

QUESTIONS?
Solutions to common problems

THE

EVERYTHING®

Series

Dear Reader,

If demographic projections hold true, the community of American non-Orthodox Jews may disappear in fifty years. Moreover, in absolute numbers, there are fewer Jews in the United States now than there were when I was a kid growing up in the fifties! Though I am not a very "observant" Jew, I am proud of being Jewish and feel an overwhelming sense of loss as our community diminishes.

One way to keep Judaism and Jewish culture alive is through knowledge. We cannot reject Judaism without first trying to know and understand it, and we have to give the same opportunity to future generations. The Talmud says that whoever teaches his son also teaches his son's son—and so on, to the end of generations. We owe it to our grandchildren's grandchildren not to leave them uninformed about Judaism.

Jews are called the People of the Book because for 4,000 years they have venerated learning. *The Everything® Judaism Book* is an opportunity to share in this knowledge. If, along the way, it will help some of you fortify your Jewish identity, all the better.

THE
EVERYTHING®
JUDAISM
BOOK

A complete primer to the Jewish
faith—from holidays and rituals
to traditions and culture

Richard D. Bank

Adams Media Corporation
Avon, Massachusetts

EDITORIAL
Publishing Director: Gary M. Krebs
Managing Editor: Kate McBride
Copy Chief: Laura MacLaughlin
Acquisitions Editor: Gary M. Krebs
Development Editor: Julie Gutin
Production Editor: Khrysti Nazzaro

PRODUCTION
Production Director: Susan Beale
Production Manager: Michelle Roy Kelly
Series Designer: Daria Perreault
Cover Design: Paul Beatrice and Frank Rivera
Layout and Graphics: Colleen Cunningham,
Rachael Eiben, Michelle Roy Kelly, Daria Perreault

An Everything® Series Book.
Everything® and everything.com® are registered trademarks of F+W Publications, Inc.

Published by Adams Media, an F+W Publications Company
57 Littlefield Street, Avon, MA 02322 U.S.A.
www.adamsmedia.com

ISBN: 1-58062-728-5
Printed in the United States of America.

J I H G F E D C B

Library of Congress Cataloging-in-Publication Data
Bank, Richard D.
The everything Judaism book : a complete primer to the Jewish
faith–from holidays and rituals to traditions and culture /
by Richard D. Bank.
p.   cm.   —(Everything series)
Includes index.
ISBN 1-58062-728-5
1. Judaism. I. Title. II. Series.
BM561 .B27   2002
296—dc21   2002008429

Illustrations by Barry Littmann.
Photos courtesy of © 2001 Brand X Pictures and Joshua Marowitz.

*This book is available at quantity discounts for bulk purchases.
For information, call 1-800-872-5627.*

Visit the entire Everything® series at everything.com

In Memory of
Sophie and Ludwig Frank
David and Celia Bank

Contents

Acknowledgments

The daunting task of doing a book covering everything about Judaism was made possible only with the invaluable help of my consultants, Rabbi Robert S. Leib and Rabbi Jacob Rosenthal. Credit for the birth of this concept belongs to my editor, Gary Krebs, and my gratitude, as always, goes to Carol Susan Roth, my literary agent, who brought me to the project. It was a pleasure to work with Kate Epstein, of the editorial staff, who always answered my questions and made everything seem to work.

Introduction

Despite the fact that Jews comprise 0.02 percent of the world's population, Judaism has made an indelible impact on world history over the past several thousand years. Judaism introduced the concept of monotheism, the belief in one God, and served as the foundation for Christianity and Islam. Given its long history, its endurance, and its amazing ability to survive while remaining true to its essence, Judaism merits study.

Regardless of whether you are Jewish, you will find something of interest in Judaism. Perhaps you are a Gentile (a non-Jew) who has fallen in love with someone who is Jewish. Maybe your son or daughter has married a Jew and you would like to know more about Judaism. Maybe you are a Christian or Muslim who is interested in learning more about the origins of your own religion.

Then again, perhaps you consider yourself a Jew but know next to nothing about Judaism. If this is the case, you have no reason to be embarrassed. Today, many of those who identify themselves as Jews are unaffiliated with any Jewish institution. Possibly, you grew up in a household where being Jewish was defined in terms of what you didn't do, like not celebrating Christmas or not going to church. Conceivably, you may not have attended Hebrew school or participated in the rites of passage like bar or bat mitzvah.

Or you may have had a Jewish education when you were young but would like to revisit your studies with a mature mind. Another possibility is that you may be active in Jewish communal life but do not know much about the "religious" aspects of Judaism. Finally, you may be concerned about your children or grandchildren who are growing up uninterested in Judaism, and you want to be in a position to speak intelligently to them about it. If any of the above rings true (and, clearly, the list is not exhaustive), *The Everything® Judaism Book* is a great place to start.

This book is a guidebook for anyone interested in learning about Judaism, including Jews and Gentiles alike. It will not attempt to define Jewishness, a subject of much debate and controversy, but it will define "Judaism" and its relationship to "Jew." Think of it this way: Everyone professing "Judaism" is "Jewish," but not all Jews practice "Judaism." While there are those who might disagree and argue that every Jew embraces Judaism to at least some extent because it is more than a religion or system of belief—because it also encompasses a people's language, culture, history, and traditions—there are those who proudly call themselves Jews but just as adamantly eschew any identification with Judaism. Better to err on the side of inclusiveness by acknowledging that one need not embrace Judaism to be a Jew.

Judaism is a religion, but one that touches upon the daily lives of its adherents. Hence, this book addresses the more "religious" aspects of Judaism as well as the holidays, traditions, and a bit of Jewish culture. As you continue to read through the rest of the book, keep in mind that there is more than one way to practice Judaism, and there is always room for inquiry and independent thought in the Jewish tradition.

CHAPTER 1
What Is Judaism?

Judaism is more than just a religion. Jews have been regarded as a "people," a "nation" (though, for most of its existence, one without a homeland), a "race," and a "culture." Consequently, it has never been clear who is a Jew nor what exactly defines "Judaism."

Who Defines Judaism?

Should Jews allow others to define them, or should they take this responsibility upon themselves? Throughout much of history, non-Jews often took this role upon themselves. Motivated by anti-Semitic beliefs, they did not limit their concept of the Jews to those who professed the faith of Judaism and complied with its tenets. In some cases, people who did not consider themselves to be Jewish, who looked upon Judaism with disdain as an archaic religion, were labeled Jews and practitioners of Judaism just the same.

FACTS

In April, 1933, the German Third Reich decreed that a person was Jewish as long as he or she was descended from at least one Jewish parent or grandparent. This is a more inclusive interpretation than the traditional Orthodox requirement, which stipulates that one must be born of a Jewish mother to be Jewish. Of course, the Nazis had their reasons to expand the delineation!

Clearly, Jewish people should take it upon themselves to define the concepts of Jew and Judaism. In fact, Jews have been considering this subject for centuries, and today it remains a point of argument and controversy among Jews. As mentioned in the introduction, it is beyond the scope of this book to decide who is Jewish and who is not, but we will attempt to examine the definition of Judaism.

A Religion for a People

First and foremost, it must be remembered that Judaism is the religion of the Jewish people. Though over the centuries Jews have dispersed among the nations, a strong sense of kinship has remained among them. Some Jews like to think of themselves as "the tribe"; for instance, the Yiddish word *landsman* (countryman) is used fondly to refer to another Jew. If you are not a religious Jew, you might still identify with this sentiment of belonging to the Jewish people.

This explains why some Jews feel a connection when introduced to someone who is also Jewish, feel a sense of pride when a Jew is honored for a major accomplishment, or bear an inordinate sense of loss when learning something terrible befell a fellow Jew. As Amos Oz, an Israeli writer, observed, "To be a Jew means to feel that wherever a Jew is persecuted for being a Jew—that means you."

QUESTIONS?

What is the current world Jewish population?
It is estimated that at the beginning of the new millennium, there are thirteen to fourteen million Jews in the world. Of these, five million live in Israel and another five million in the United States. Two million Jews reside in Europe (including Russia); 400,000 in Latin America; 350,000 in Canada; 100,000 in Australia and New Zealand; 60,000 in South Africa; and 50,000 in Asia.

The "Chosen" People

Judaism teaches that God made an eternal covenant with the descendants of Abraham, Isaac, and Jacob (Israel), and that every Jew participates in this covenant as one of the Chosen People.

However, being "chosen" by God does not in any way impart a notion of superiority. In fact, according to one rabbinic interpretation, the Hebrews were not the first to be offered God's covenant and to receive the Torah—this took place only after all the other nations turned it down!

ESSENTIALS

Don't go looking for the word "Judaism" in the Bible or in early rabbinical literature—you won't find it! Hellenized Jews introduced this concept in the second century B.C.E. to describe their religious practice.

Judaism is a living religion that functions in terms of many relationships: between God and the Jewish people; between God and each individual Jew; and among all humans. Judaism is not practiced in a cloistered environment—it is a religion of the community. This is why, as you shall see in Chapter 7, prayer takes place in groups of ten or more (a *minyan*), and holidays are celebrated in the home, where family and friends gather together.

The Canons of Judaism

Exactly what Jews believe, or are expected to believe, is not clear. Nor is there one accepted definition of Judaism acknowledged as absolute dogma. (For an overview of various branches of Judaism, see Chapter 2.) However, Judaism does encompass certain tenets that all religious Jews adhere to. Maimonides, a twelfth-century influential Jewish thinker, outlined these tenets as the Thirteen Principles of Faith.

FACTS

Maimonides, also known as Moses ben Maimon or Rambam (1135–1204), was a physician, scholar, and philosopher. Maimonides organized Jewish oral law into the *Mishneh Torah* and wrote *Moreh Nevukhim* (*A Guide for the Perplexed*), a great philosophical work.

1. God exists.
2. God is one and unique.
3. God is incorporeal.
4. God is eternal.
5. Prayer is to be directed to God alone and to no other.
6. The words of the prophets are true.
7. Moses was the greatest of the prophets; his prophecies are true.
8. Moses received the Written Torah (first five books of the Bible) and the oral Torah (teachings contained in the Talmud and other writings).
9. There will be no other Torah.

10. God knows the thoughts and deeds of men.
11. God will reward the good and punish the wicked.
12. The Messiah will come.
13. The dead will be resurrected.

The Nature of God

It is no small matter that seven of the Thirteen Principles of Faith set forth by Maimonides pertain to God. The Jews' relationship to God is fundamental to Judaism. The principal declaration of Jewish faith is the *Shema,* a prayer that begins with the following words: "Hear, O Israel: The Lord is our God, the Lord is one." This avowal affirms the belief in one God, a unity that encompasses everything.

Yet the Jews admit that comprehending God is beyond their ability. When Moses asked God for His name, he received the following enigmatic response: *"Ehyeh asher ehyeh"* (Exodus 3:14), which may be translated as "I am that I am," but literally means, "I will be what I will be," and has also been taken to mean "I am what I will be."

God Is the Creator

Nonetheless, Judaism does hold a number of concepts about the nature of God. Of course, the most important belief is that God is One. In addition, God is considered to be the Creator of everything. Even many nonobservant Jews have held to this belief.

Baruch (later Benedict) Spinoza (1632–1677) was a Dutch philosopher who belonged to the Jewish community that fled from the Inquisition in Spain and Portugal. Spinoza's most famous work, *Ethics,* reflects his deductive, rational, and monistic philosophy.

Baruch Spinoza, a Jewish philosopher who was excommunicated from the Jewish community for questioning the accepted nature of God, ultimately concluded that God "is the free cause of all things."

Albert Einstein, a nonobservant Jew, compared the universe to a clock, with God as the "clockmaker" who cannot be envisaged or understood.

God is also responsible for the creation of humans, which Judaism considers to be an unceasing process. The Talmud teaches that parents provide the physical form of every human being, but God supplies the soul. A prominent piece of Jewish liturgy repeatedly describes God as *Avinu Malkeinu,* "Our Father, Our King." Judaism purports that we are God's children.

Not a Bearded Old Man in the Sky

While God is often described with anthropomorphic features, such portraits are not designed to be taken literally. Instead, they are employed to help humans understand God's actions. The Jews know that God is incorporeal. He has no limbs nor parts, and He is neither male nor female. God is referred to in the masculine because Hebrew has no gender-neutral nouns. Indeed, there are occasions when feminine terms are applied to God. For instance, the manifestation of God's presence that fills the universe is called *shechinah,* a feminine word.

Should you have the occasion to correspond with an observant Jew, don't forget that Jews are not permitted to write out the word "God." To avoid offense, follow the common practice of observant Jews who eliminate the vowel and write "G-d."

Since God is incorporeal, Jews are forbidden to represent God in a physical form. (Such an act would be considered idolatry.) This admonition has been heeded in many ways, from the way Jews adorn synagogues to the prohibition of tattoos on the body. However, the prohibition to write the name of God has nothing to do with this commandment, nor with the commandment that prohibits Jews from taking the Lord's name in vain. The fact is, Jews may not write down the name of God because they are enjoined from erasing or defacing it.

Because no one can ever be certain what may subsequently happen to the paper (or any other medium) written with the name of God, avoiding writing it down in the first place ensures that it cannot be destroyed. The source for this practice is found in Deuteronomy 12:3, which recounts how God commands the Israelites to obliterate the names of all local deities, but not the name of God, when they take over the Promised Land.

God Is Eternal

Judaism holds that God is omnipotent (all-powerful), omniscient (all-knowing), and omnipresent (filling all places at all times). God is eternal. Past and future, here and now, are irrelevant in terms of God. Einstein attempted to describe this idea in more scientific terms: For God, "a thousand years and a thousand dimensions are as one."

Now, you may ask, if God is eternal and did act in history and intervene in human affairs in the past, why doesn't God continue to do so now? Where has God been hiding? While there is no single answer to this question, an important principle of Judaism does offer an explanation grounded in the notion that the relationship between God and people is reciprocal. One way this has been expressed is in the following Hasidic tale:

> "Where is the dwelling of God?" This was the question with which the rabbi of Kotzk surprised a number of learned men who happened to be visiting him. They laughed at him: "What a thing to ask! Is not the whole world full of his glory?" Then he answered his own question. "God dwells wherever man lets him in."

Martin Buber, the twentieth-century Jewish philosopher and scholar, used the phrase "eclipse of God" as a metaphor to demonstrate something that has come between people and God, a something that may well be within ourselves. Imagine you are standing under a bright glaring sun. You raise your hand and lift your thumb so it blocks the sun from sight. The sun is no longer visible. You cannot see it. Yet, it is there just the same. All you have to do to experience its existence is to remove your thumb. So it is with God. Before experiencing God, you must first remove the impediment you have erected.

It's a Way of Life

It is crucial to remember that Judaism is not merely a set of ideas about the world. Perhaps more importantly, it is a blueprint for a way of life. To follow Judaism means more than praying or contemplating, having faith or believing in a supreme being or an afterlife. Following the dictates of Judaism means taking action. Jews cannot excuse themselves from this requirement by claiming that one person cannot possibly make a difference in the world. Such an attitude is anathema to Judaism, which emphasizes the significance of the individual.

In the Talmud, the Jews are taught that every person is like a balanced scale—a person's deeds will tip the scale either toward good or toward evil. According to Elie Wiesel, a writer and human rights activist who survived Auschwitz, "A Jew is defined by his actions more than his intentions. It is his actions that bind him to his community and, through it, to the larger human community."

God holds people responsible for their actions and teaches us to follow His high standards of ethical behavior. His expectations apply to all human beings, even those who have lost contact with God. In Micah 6:8, it is written that God requires that we "do justice . . . love goodness and . . . walk modestly with . . . God."

Abiding by the Laws

How do the Jewish people know what model of ethical behavior to follow? First and foremost, there are the Ten Commandments. In the Halakhah, a collection of Jewish laws found in the Torah or instituted by Jewish scholars over centuries, you will find 613 *mitzvot,* or commandments, that Jews are expected to observe. (See Chapter 6 for more information on the Jewish Law.)

There are many laws to follow, but God doesn't expect humans to be perfect. There is room for mistakes, and God is both just and merciful.

Of the two names for God most commonly used in the Bible, one refers to His quality of mercy *(midat harachamim),* and the other to His quality of justice *(midat ladin).*

The singular for *mitzvot* is *mitzvah.* In Hebrew, the plural ending is *–ot* for feminine nouns and *–im* for masculine nouns—hence, for instance, the terms Ashkenazim (Ashkenazi Jews) and Sephardim (Sephardic Jews). You will read more about Ashkenazim and Sephardim in Chapter 2.

Waiting for the Messiah

Indeed, God has promised that perfect days lie ahead when the Messiah arrives. (See Chapter 19 for more on Jewish messianic beliefs.) On that occasion, a number of things will happen:

- The Messiah will ordain himself as king.
- He will achieve independence for the Jewish people in their own land (Israel).
- He will be an ideal king.
- The dead will be resurrected.
- Peace, justice, and brotherhood will be established for all the world.

Following 2,000 years of messianic reign, all humans will be resurrected and will spend the rest of eternity living in *Olam Ha-Ba* (the world to come), where the righteous are to be rewarded and the wicked are to be punished.

Knowledge Through Study

On what does Judaism rely to establish its basic tenets? How do you know what God wants you to do? Where did the Jews get the concept of the Messiah? The answers lie with the belief in the authenticity of the

Torah, the written work of Moses and the subsequent prophets. Although the degree to which the Jews take the Torah literally depends on the

Rabbi leading his congregation

Photo courtesy of © 2001 Brand X Pictures

branch of Judaism they belong to (see Chapter 2), the Torah is indeed the keystone of Judaism.

Many Jews have devoted their entire lives to the study of Torah, the highest calling. Yet the essence of Judaism is splendid in its simplicity. To illustrate their point, Jews tell a story about Hillel, a great Jewish sage. As the story goes, a man once approached Hillel and asked him to explain the essence of Judaism while standing on one foot. To this, Hillel responded, "What is hurtful to you, do not do to others. That is the whole Torah; the rest is commentary. Now, go and study."

FACTS

Hillel (around 30 B.C.E.–10 C.E.) was the great spiritual and ethical leader of his generation, who usually took a more liberal stance in the interpretation of the Torah. He is regarded as the forebear of the later sages who led the Jews of Palestine until 400 C.E.

CHAPTER 2
The Branches of Judaism

Perhaps you have heard the anecdote about the small town that had two Jewish residents and three synagogues. Though this story is a hyperbole, there is a grain of truth to it. Throughout history, various movements in Judaism have sometimes split up, like different branches growing from a trunk of the same tree.

Historical Movements Within Judaism

Before considering the contemporary movements of Judaism, an examination of the past should be useful. No one can say with any certainty when the first formal divisions within Judaism arose. However, the oldest records we have of an explicit difference of opinion took place during the time of the Maccabean revolt, in the second century B.C.E.

Hellenized Jews

During the period leading up to the Maccabean rebellion, the Jews lived under Greek occupation. The Greeks were an enlightened people and tolerant of their subjects. As a result, secular life was good and a number of Jews were attracted to Greek culture, known as Hellenism.

Hellenism, with its pagan joy, freedom, and love of life, stood in stark contrast to the austere morality and monotheism of Judaism. Those Jews who allowed themselves to be influenced by Hellenism were known as Hellenistic Jews; the Hasideans (not to be confused with Hasids) formed their conservative opposition.

Jews who no longer practiced Judaism became known as *apikoros,* a derisive term that may be translated as "heretic." Nevertheless, the majority of these unobservant Jews were proud of their Jewish identity.

While there was a great deal of animus between the two groups, sometimes even leading to violence, the situation resolved itself because, as fate would have it, the Greeks began to oppress the Jews. Faced with an external enemy, the Jews united in their fight for independence. (This part of Jewish history, commemorated by the holiday of Chanukah, will be covered in greater detail in Chapter 12.)

Essenes, Sadducees, and Pharisees

At a later period in history, when Rome conquered the land of ancient Israel, Judaism had split into three distinct sects. The

CHAPTER 2: THE BRANCHES OF JUDAISM

Essenes formed an ascetic and mystical order that consisted mostly of adult males who took an oath of celibacy. Ceremonial purity and the wearing of white garments were common. The members pledged piety toward God, justice to men, and adherence to the order and its doctrines.

The Essenes accepted the authenticity of several men who claimed to be messiahs. This ardent belief in the true messiah's imminent arrival may have played a role in the emergence of Christianity. However, the Essenes as a sect disappeared sometime in the second century C.E., due to the practice of celibacy and lack of new converts.

The Sadducees embraced some of the Hellenistic elements of Judaism. Their relatively small following was comprised of the priests and the upper class of Jewish society. The Sadducees did not believe in the oral Torah, and their interpretation of the written Torah was narrow and conservative. Since this movement consisted of so many priests, it is not surprising that the center of their worship was the Temple in Jerusalem. Consequently, when the Romans destroyed the Temple in 70 C.E., this sect disappeared.

ESSENTIALS

Because of their disagreements with the Sadducees, who had control of the Temple, the Pharisees developed the synagogue as an alternative place for study and worship. Their liturgy consisted of biblical and prophetic readings and the repetition of the *Shema* (Judaism's central prayer).

Pharisees formed the third and most powerful group among the Jews. The Pharisees believed that both the written and oral Torah came directly from God and were therefore valid and binding. In accordance with the Torah, the Pharisees began to codify the Halakhah (the Law), insisting upon its strict observance. However, they did encourage debate among scholars about the finer points of the law, and emphasized the individual's relation to God.

It should be mentioned that a fourth subgroup existed during the time of the Roman Empire. The movement of Zealots did not really represent

13

a division of Judaism. Rather, it was a nationalistic movement "zealous" in seeking independence from Rome. The members of this group did not survive the war with Rome and, like the Essenes and Sadducees, vanished after the destruction of the Temple and the suppression of the Jewish revolt.

The Pharisaic movement alone endured the rebellion against Rome. Until almost the end of the first millennium C.E., no separate movements within Judaism would emerge. Naturally, such a state of affairs could not be expected to last forever.

Karaites and Rabbinical Judaism

As you have seen, the major disagreement between the Pharisees and the Sadducees was the role and validity of the oral Torah—whether it had come directly from God or was merely commentary inspired by human minds alone. During the ninth century C.E., a movement in Persia again voiced skepticism of the validity of the oral Torah, rejecting rabbinical law as part of the Jewish tradition. The Karaites, or "People of the Scripture," believed in a literal reading of the Bible without rabbinical interpretation. The Rabbanites (Rabbinical Judaism) opposed this viewpoint.

It has been estimated that at one time, as many as 40 percent of Jews were Karaites. Until recently, a surviving Karaite community existed in Egypt. In 1967, after the Six-Day War between Egypt and Israel, most Karaites immigrated to Israel, Europe, or the United States. Today, the Karaite community is minuscule, but it retains its particular culture that developed during the centuries of its existence in Egypt.

Hasidim and *Mitnagdim*

Although some people see Hasidism as a branch of Judaism, it is really a spiritual movement that will be discussed in greater detail in the following chapter. It should be noted that the emergence of this movement represented a deep schism within Judaism during the eighteenth and nineteenth centuries. Those who opposed Hasidism became known as *mitnagdim,* or "opponents."

ALERT

While Hasidism certainly still has its detractors today, they are generally neither organized nor vociferous in their condemnation. This actually means that there are no longer any *mitnagdim.* The original *mitnagdim* who adhered to traditional rabbinical Judaism are now more or less at one with the Hasidim in their rejection of the liberal movements in Judaism.

Ashkenazic and Sephardic Jews

Today, most Jews either identify themselves as Ashkenazic or Sephardic. The difference is the result of history and geography. The Babylonian exile and later dispersions forced the Jews to live in the Diaspora (communities outside of Israel). Those who eventually ended up in Central and Eastern Europe became known as Ashkenazim, or Ashkenazic Jews (derived from the Hebrew word for "Germany," *Ashkenaz*). Those who resided in southern France, Spain, Portugal, North Africa, and the Middle East came to be known as Sephardim, or Sephardic Jews (derived from the Hebrew word for "Spain," *Sepharad*).

Most of the early Jewish settlers in the United States were Sephardic, as were the first Jewish synagogues (Shearith Israel, founded in New York in 1684, and Congregation Mikveh Israel, founded in Philadelphia in 1740). However, the majority of Jews living in the United States today are Ashkenazic. They are descended from Jews who emigrated from Germany and Eastern Europe from the mid–nineteenth through the early twentieth centuries.

The respective cultures of the countries in which the Ashkenazim and the Sephardim lived greatly affected these two Jewish groups in respect to their customs, language (see Chapter 4), and their mode of thinking. It has been said that perhaps Sephardic Jews place greater emphasis on intellectualism, though they also practiced the Kabbalah, a form of Jewish mysticism. Unlike the Ashkenazim, the Sephardim never split up into separate branches of Judaism. Today, Sephardim practice Orthodox Judaism, which is similar to the Orthodox branch of the Ashkenazim.

FACTS

One of the great mysteries in history has to do with the "Ten Lost Tribes of Israel," that made up the northern kingdom of Israel when it was conquered in 722 B.C.E. The vanquished Jews were transported to Assyria, and from that point on, their fate remains unknown. Speculation regarding their descendants has included such varied groups as the Ethiopian Jews, Native Americans, certain Indian sects of Hindus, Afghans, and even the English.

The Orthodox

During the last millennium and up until the nineteenth century, the Orthodox branch was by far the most prevalent. In most places, it was the only type of Judaism that existed. While there was some diversity within the Orthodox—between the Sephardim and the Ashkenazim (and, among the Ashkenazim, between the Hasidim and the *mitnagdim*)—the theology among the different groups was essentially the same. What ultimately did lead to divisions within Judaism was the same old controversy; that is, the difference of perceptions concerning the Halakhah and the Torah.

ALERT

The various branches within Judaism should not be referred to as "denominations." While there are differences in the respective philosophies of these movements, involving such things as custom, practice, and observance, the differences are not nearly as great as those among Christian denominations.

Orthodox Beliefs

The essential principle governing Orthodox Judaism is *Torah min Hashamayim*. This means that the Torah, both the written Law

(Scriptures), and the oral Law (rabbinic interpretation and commentaries), is conclusive. It is directly derived from God and therefore must be obeyed. Orthodox Jews lead a *mitzvah*-centered life. There is not much room for individual discretion regarding which *mitzvot* (commandments to be fulfilled) need to be obeyed or how they should be practiced.

Synagogue services are conducted in Hebrew, and men and women sit separately. Women are not ordained as rabbis, nor do they count in a *minyan* (the group of ten necessary for public prayer). While the synagogue is the domain of men, women clearly have dominion over the home. The tasks of following *kashrut* (dietary laws) and the *mitzvot* concerning *Shabbat* largely fall upon them. In addition, women are primarily responsible for ritual purity and for faithfully upholding the laws of *niddah* (separation laws, discussed further in Chapter 6).

Groups Within the Orthodoxy

Today, several different groups within Orthodox Judaism share common fundamental beliefs. The best known of these groups is probably the ultra-Orthodox, which includes the Hasidim. Its members are most visible because of their largely Hasidic mode of dress. The men wear *payees* (side earlocks), full beards, hats, and dark clothes. The women dress modestly, and married women must wear a head covering (a hat, scarf, or wig) in public. By contrast, the modern Orthodox are integrated in contemporary society while still observing halakhic laws.

Obeying Halakhah in a closed society, where the entire community follows the same observances and rituals, is not nearly as difficult as doing so when living in an open society, where the prevalent customs and habits are different. For example, it is easy to close your business on Saturday for *Shabbat* in a community where no business would be conducted that day in any event. If you live in an open society, however, you will have to close your business on a day when your nonobservant or non-Jewish competition keep their businesses open. This explains why many ultra-Orthodox communities, particularly the Hasidim, are insular. One can only look on in awe at the modern-Orthodox who must be consistently vigilant in maintaining a balance as they live and work in contemporary society.

Orthodoxy Loses Its Grip on Judaism

When Jews were segregated in ghettos or the "pale of settlement" (regions in Russia that were designated for Jews to inhabit), they had no access to the secular society of the "outside world." They therefore led their lives according to the customs that had been practiced for generations before them.

As the Enlightenment spread through Europe in the seventeenth and eighteenth centuries, many societies began to open at least some of their doors to Jews. Suddenly, particularly after the effects of emancipation in Germany in the nineteenth century, Jews had choices and alternatives. They now had access to new ideas and new occupations; the barriers that had encased their own closed society were broken down.

Strict observance of Halakhah made it difficult, if not impossible, to integrate into secular society. Moreover, many Jews incorporated aspects of the Enlightenment into their own way of thinking. The concept of divinely revealed commandments and the stress on ethnocentricity ran contrary to "enlightened" ideas. Such were the circumstances that brought forth Reform Judaism.

Reform Judaism

Reform Judaism (sometimes known as Liberal or Progressive Judaism) had its beginnings in Germany. German Jews used an insightful phrase to describe themselves: "German in the streets; Jewish in the home." This was not a matter of shame in being Jewish but merely reflected a desire to take advantages of the new opportunities afforded by an open and liberal society.

History of Reform Judaism

The first reforms introduced to Judaism did not occur in the home but in the synagogue. In the early nineteenth century, several congregations in Germany instituted fundamental changes in the service, including mixed-gender seating, a shortened service, use of the vernacular in the liturgy, single-day observance of holidays, and the inclusion of musical instruments and a choir.

American Reform Judaism was born when some of these reformers emigrated to the United States from Germany in the mid-nineteenth century. Under the leadership of Rabbi Isaac Mayer Wise, Reform Judaism became the dominant belief held by American Jews. By 1880, over 90 percent of American synagogues were Reform. This situation would change with the first waves of immigration of Eastern Europeans, who were predominantly Orthodox. Today, however, Reform Judaism is again the largest of the movements, with approximately 900 Reform synagogues in the United States and Canada.

FACTS

Some of the first Reform congregations in the United States were Beth Elohim in Charleston, South Carolina (1825); Har Sinai in Baltimore, Maryland (1842); Bene Yeshurun (I. M. Wise) in Cincinnati, Ohio (1854); Adath Israel (The Temple) in Louisville, Kentucky (1855); and Keneseth Israel in Philadelphia, Pennsylvania (1856).

Some American congregations went beyond the alterations instituted by the German Reform movement. In fact, a number of congregations became almost indistinguishable from neighboring Protestant churches, adopting such features as the use of organs, singing of hymns, the requirement that rabbis wear robes, and, in some cases, even holding *Shabbat* services on Sunday! However, by the 1930s, the Reform movement gradually turned back to a more traditional approach to Judaism.

Principles of Reform Judaism

The essential principle of Reform Judaism is that religion ought to be dynamic and that the essence of Judaism is found in its ethical teachings. In contrast to the Orthodox tenets, Reform Jews believe that while the Torah was divinely inspired, it was written by a number of individuals and then revised and edited. Therefore, while Reform Jews revere and retain most of the values and ethics of the Torah, each individual is free to follow those practices that are most likely to advance a meaningful and ethical life and enhance his or her relationship with God.

Along with the great deal of room it offers for individualism, Reform Judaism does have its fundamental principles, including the following beliefs:

- The Torah was divinely inspired but authored by humans.
- There is only one God.
- The reinterpretation of Torah is continuous and must be adapted for new circumstances and challenges.
- The moral and ethical components in the Torah are important.
- The sexes are to be treated equally.

Given its more egalitarian view of males and females, it should come as no surprise that Reform Judaism ordains female rabbis and cantors. Moreover, the emphasis placed by Reform Judaism upon the concept of equality has resulted in its involvement in social action for many worthy causes.

In recent years, Reform Judaism has experienced a movement toward spirituality and conventional ritual. In response, Reform has adopted a more traditional stance concerning certain practices such as allowing (and even encouraging) the wearing of both *kippot* (also known as *yarmulkes* or skullcaps) and *tallit* (ceremonial shawls worn by men at religious services) and bringing back Hebrew to its prayer books. And there hasn't been a *Shabbat* service on a Sunday in decades!

Conservative Judaism

Despite its many supporters, some Jews felt that Reform Judaism had admirable intentions but that it simply went too far. A more reasoned and less extreme break from Orthodox Judaism seemed more desirable. Out of this middle-ground movement came Conservative Judaism.

History of Conservative Judaism

It did not take many years for a breach to occur within Reform Judaism in Germany. In 1845, Rabbi Zecharias Frankel broke with the emerging European Reform movement when he insisted that the liturgy should be conducted in Hebrew. A decade later, Rabbi Frankel became the first head of the Jewish Theological Seminary of Breslau.

On the other side of the Atlantic, it took somewhat longer for reaction to mount against what were seen as the excesses of the Reform movement. The seeds of Conservative Judaism were sown in the United States with the founding of the Jewish Theological Seminary of America in 1886. However, Conservative Judaism did not really begin to expand until Dr. Solomon Schechter became president of the seminary in 1902. In 1913, Dr. Schechter organized the movement under the aegis of the United Synagogue of Conservative Judaism. Today, the Conservative Judaism movement is nearly as large as Reform Judaism.

Principles of Conservative Judaism

Like Reform Jews, Conservatives believe that the Torah was divinely inspired but authored by humans—that it does not come to us directly from God. Conservative Judaism parts with Reform in that it generally

Inside the synagogue

Photo courtesy of © 2001 Brand X Pictures

accepts the binding nature of Halakhah. However, Conservatives do agree that Halakhah is subject to change and that adaptations may be made to it based on the contemporary culture, so long as the Halakhah remains true to Judaism's values.

It is probably in the area of the synagogue service that Conservative Judaism has made its most notable accomplishment in providing a distinct middle ground for Jews who are not satisfied with either the Orthodox or the Reform approach. Hebrew is the predominant language of the liturgy, but the native language of the worshippers is used as well. In Conservative congregations, men and women may sit together, and many Conservative congregations have choirs and even organs.

Being in the middle, Conservative Judaism's positions vary between liberal and traditional. Since 1983, women have been accepted for training at the rabbinate. On the other hand, Conservative Judaism has reaffirmed matrilineal descent in determining who is a Jew. As for the individual, it is expected that *Shabbat* and dietary laws be observed, although many, if not most, Conservative Jews either do not adhere to these *mitzvot* or follow them only to a limited extent.

Remember, there is a great deal of variability among Conservative practices. You may find that some seem almost indistinguishable from Reform congregations and that others come very close to the Orthodox type of service.

Reconstructionism

Reconstructionism is another branch of Judaism, distinct from Orthodox, Reform, and Conservative movements for two reasons. First, it does not fit neatly along the spectrum of observance as do the other three branches; that is, it cannot be differentiated merely by degrees of adherence to the Halakhah. Second, Reconstructionism is a movement based on the teachings of just one man, its philosopher and founder, Mordecai M. Kaplan (1881–1983).

History of Reconstructionism

Reconstructionism took shape in twentieth-century America and is Judaism's youngest movement. In fact, although the Jewish Reconstructionist Federation was founded in 1955, it did not truly become the fourth branch of American Judaism until the late 1960s, when it was able to train its own rabbis with the establishment of the Reconstructionist Rabbinical College.

Reconstructionism germinated from an eloquent and momentous article written by Mordecai Kaplan in 1920, in which he called for a reinterpretation of Judaism in keeping with modern thought and the strengthening of ties with Jewish communities in Palestine. Two years later, as he became more vocal in urging economic justice and more critical of orthodoxy, he resigned from the pulpit of a Conservative congregation in Manhattan. Leaving with thirty-five families, he founded a congregation based on his philosophy of Judaism that came to be known as the Society for the Advancement of Judaism (SAJ).

During the first two decades of its existence, the SAJ remained affiliated with the Conservative movement. However, in 1963, when Kaplan retired from teaching at the Jewish Theological Seminary, a Conservative organization, the road was paved for the founding of an institution to train Reconstructionist rabbis. Five years later, the Reconstructionist Rabbinical College was established.

FACTS

In 1927, Rabbi Kaplan's own daughter, Judith, had the distinction of being the first bat mitzvah. In 1928, Rabbi Ira Eisenstein, who would later become Mordecai Kaplan's son-in-law, joined the movement; in 1945, he succeeded his father-in-law as the leader of SAJ and one of Reconstructionism's most prominent figures.

Kaplan had no desire to create a new branch of Judaism, but given its unique philosophy, this was inevitable. As of the 1970s, Reconstructionism has been recognized as the fourth branch on the Judaic tree. It remains the smallest movement, with 100 congregations worldwide, but its impact belies its numbers, given Kaplan's legacy and the philosophy developed by his followers.

Principles of Reconstructionism

Now, you may ask, what makes Reconstructionism so revolutionary? Consider the following. For starters, the notion that the Jews are God's "chosen people" is rejected. Each culture and civilization, Kaplan postulated, has a unique contribution to make to the greater human community. Judaism is only one of these cultures. There is nothing special or divine about it.

Furthermore, Halakhah need only be observed if one chooses to do so; if a person does follow an aspect of Halakhah, this is not because it is binding law from God but because it is a valuable cultural remnant.

In fact, the entire notion of a supernatural God acting in history is discarded. Instead, God is considered to be a process or power—an expression of the highest values and ideals of a civilization.

Kaplan taught that Judaism is more than a religion. It's an evolving religious civilization that incorporates traditions, laws, customs, language, literature, music, and art. While he believed in the need for all Jewish communities to thrive in the Diaspora, Kaplan foresaw a Jewish state as the hub of the Jewish wheel. Therefore, Zionism and the establishment of Israel have always been fundamental to Reconstructionism.

Although Reconstructionism's social ideas are very liberal, their services are more conservative. Except for the fact that men and women sit together and that women can be ordained, you might think you are *davening* (reciting Jewish prayers) in a modern-Orthodox *shul* (Yiddish for "synagogue"). While open to new forms of expression, Reconstructionists observe traditional practices, recognizing *kashrut,* the *Shabbat* and the holidays, the liturgy, and life-cycle events. There is an emphasis on learning that does not end with a bar or bat mitzvah but continues through adulthood.

FACTS

Although not considered a fifth branch of Judaism, the Jewish Renewal movement, which began in the 1970s with the socially conscious agenda of *tikkun olam* (the "healing and transformation" of the world), has both a religious dimension and its own rabbis. Another recent addition to the tree of Judaism is the Society for Humanistic Judaism, which has thirty congregations across the United States.

One point often puzzles those who learn about Reconstructionism. If it does not teach belief in a God who acts in history, why the prayers? After all, traditional liturgy is an important consideration in Reconstructionist services. The answer may be found in the Jewish concept of prayer. To learn more about the role of prayer in Judaism, you will have to read on to Chapter 8.

CHAPTER 3

Spirituality in Judaism

Jewish spirituality and mysticism are just as much a part of Judaism as devotion to the Torah and the keeping of all the laws prescribed by the Halakhah. This chapter will examine Jewish spirituality in general as well as the two most well-known spiritual traditions, Kabbalah and Hasidism.

Jewish Spirituality and Mysticism

What is life all about? Is there any meaning to it? Who am I? Will there be an afterlife, or is this all there is to human existence? Is there such a thing as a "soul"? Is something going on at a deeper level than my senses are aware of? And, if so, how do I go about finding out how to connect? These and similar questions are conundrums you probably considered when you were an adolescent or maybe in college. They may still vex you even now. Expecting answers from religion, you turn to Judaism, but you have your doubts that a theology with such an emphasis on laws and codes of behavior can possibly provide explanations for such cosmic concerns. You will be happy to discover that Judaism does, in fact, have a spiritual component that goes all the way back to its beginnings.

Ever Since Abraham

Actually, Jewish spirituality goes all the way back to Abraham, who is said to be the first kabbalist. The Torah contains numerous stories about angels, prophetic dreams and visions, and other mystical experiences. The Talmud (the collection of oral interpretations of the Torah) does not flinch from addressing the question of the "soul," and it suggests that a mystical school of thought was taught to advanced students. Later still, many mystical teachings were set down in books like the Zohar.

ALERT

Although spirituality and mysticism have a distinct place in Judaism, be aware that not all Jews recognize this to be the case. In fact, most Ashkenazic Jews either refrain from acknowledging this mystical component or tend to minimize its significance.

What makes Judaism's spirituality different from other types of spirituality? This is a good question. The answer lies in the fact that Judaism's spirituality, no matter what variation, is grounded in the basic doctrines of Judaism—holding fast to a belief in one God who is the Creator of all things. What is more, since God created the world, holiness is to be found by encountering the world, not withdrawing from it.

The Divine Sparks

If Judaism's spirituality and mysticism had to be summed up in one word, the closest word would have to be "sparks." What does that mean? Well, it all has to do with the way spiritual Judaism views Creation.

It is said that divine energy poured into the void, creating a seamless vessel of supernal light. But this God-energy was so intense that it shattered the vessel it was shaping, causing it to explode into a multitude of sparks. These sparks of holy light dispersed. Because they were disconnected from each other and in a state of alienation, each became obscured by a shell of darkness and unholiness. You can find a darkened spark of holiness in exile at the root of every soul, in each and every thing and act, and in every relationship.

The entire purpose of Jewish mysticism, whether Kabbalistic or Hasidic, is to gather the sparks and to bring them back into a holy whole. Obviously, this is not something one can do in seclusion or in "retreat" from the world. Hence, Jewish spirituality requires that a person go out into the world and engage with it and all therein in a concerted effort to release holy sparks from their imprisonment, gathering them so they are free to return to the divine light. At such a time, the world can become one in God and will have been redeemed.

A Soul Is a Divine Spark

The divine sparks are in all things, including humans. From the mystical viewpoint, a divine spark is what you might otherwise call the "soul," but it lies dormant within a person, encased by the body surrounding it. This soul, or transcendent self, has a burning desire to attach itself to God, but in order to even begin this voyage, a person's soul must become receptive and allow the surrounding light to enter it.

How does one receive the light? Where is it to be found? It is found in this world. Spiritual Judaism teaches Jews how to open themselves and absorb the world—in other words, to receive the light. This mystical school of thought in Judaism came to be known as Kabbalah.

Jewish Mysticism—the Kabbalah

The Kabbalah is a method through which you can address the questions raised at the beginning of this chapter—questions relating to human existence, the purpose of life, and so on. Kabbalah teaches how to empower yourself to reach the spiritual world by enhancing your "sixth sense." This sixth sense is also called the spiritual vessel *(kli),* and is independent of material reality. Ordinarily, *kli* is not sufficiently developed to make contact with the spiritual world. By studying Kabbalah, a person's soul will widen to the point of allowing the surrounding light to enter it.

FACTS

The word *Kabbalah* comes from the Hebrew verb *lekabbel,* which means "to receive" or "to accept." In Hebrew, this word does not have any of the sinister connotations that it has in English, where the word "cabal" refers to a clandestine band of conspirators.

The method of Kabbalah is like a mathematics of emotions. It takes the total of all feelings and desires, divides them, and then provides an exact mathematical formula for each and every circumstance. Kabbalah combines emotions and the intellect and infuses an element of spirituality to study.

History of the Kabbalah

Kabbalistic knowledge is said to have been passed down from Abraham and through the generations. As with Halakhah, Kabbalah evolved in this fashion by word of mouth, with each kabbalist leaving his own unique imprint.

Ultimately, the time came to memorialize this information in writing. Preserving this knowledge became pressing after the destruction of the Second Temple in 70 C.E. Following the failed revolt of Bar Kochba and the execution of Rabbi Akiva in the second century, Rabbi Shimon Bar Yochai (also known as the Rashbi, which is an abbreviation of his name) escaped with his son and went into seclusion for thirteen years. Emerging from the cave in which he had hidden, the Rashbi brought forth the Zohar, the pre-eminent Kabbalistic writing that provided a method of achieving spirituality.

The Zohar

Actually, the Rashbi did not write the Zohar. He worked it out in his head and later dictated his thoughts to Rabbi Aba, who transcribed the material in the form of parables. The Zohar is written in Aramaic. According to the Zohar, Aramaic is "the backside of Hebrew," its hidden side.

The Zohar teaches that human development progresses over 6,000 years. During this period, souls undergo a continuous process of growth, at the end of which all souls reach the highest level of spirituality and wholeness.

The Study of Kabbalah Through the Centuries

Subsequently, the Zohar mysteriously vanished, only to reappear again centuries later among secret groups of kabbalists who studied it as a holy text. In the sixteenth century, Rabbi Yitzhak Luria, known as the Ari, provided a basic system of studying Kabbalah and produced writings that for the first time presented the pure language of Kabbalah.

 **ESSENTIALS**

Rabbi Yitzhak Luria was born in Jerusalem in 1534. When he was still a child, his father died, and his mother took him to Egypt and raised him there. In 1570, Rabbi Luria arrived in Safed, Israel, where he taught Kabbalah, and his brilliance was immediately recognized. Although Rabbi Luria died only two years later, at the age of thirty-eight, his system of study is still practiced today.

In the sixteenth and seventeenth centuries, small groups of kabbalistic scholars continued to study the Zohar. Then, from the mid-eighteenth century until the beginning of the twentieth century (known as the great Hassidut period), the Zohar assumed a prominent position in Judaism. In fact, many prominent rabbis were involved in Kabbalism.

In the twentieth century, interest in the Kabbalah waned until it practically disappeared. Although currently the study of Kabbalah is gaining in popularity, and there are Kabbalah centers throughout the United States, Kabbalah remains an alien and esoteric subject for the vast majority of Jews.

You may not want to study Kabbalah until you are well versed in Torah. In the past, Kabbalah was not taught to anyone under the age of forty because it was believed that a comprehensive understanding of Judaism was necessary before learning Kabbalah. There was also a concern that receiving instruction in Kabbalah could prove harmful to the mental and emotional health of a young person.

The Kabbalistic Tree of Life

Kabbalah is a mysterious and complicated system of ideas. It is not easily accessible to all, and is certainly beyond the scope of this book (though other sources do exist if you would like to pursue the study of Kabbalah further). Just to give you a sense of the Kabbalah, this section will take a look at one of its more fundamental and better-known concepts, the Tree of Life.

In Judaism, God is believed to exist beyond time and space. Consequently, Kabbalah asks the question, "How can there be any interaction between God and humans, who are limited by the context of time and space?" The answer lies in the Tree of the Sefirot, also called the Kabbalistic Tree of Life.

Since the true essence of God, *Ein Sof* (without end), is so transcendent that it cannot have any interchange with the universe, contact is achieved by way of the ten emanations from God's essence, known as the Ten Sefirot. These Ten Sefirot correspond to the qualities of God. They are:

1. *Keter* (the crown)
2. *Chokhmah* (wisdom)
3. *Binah* (intuition, understanding)
4. *Chesed* (mercy) or *Gedulah* (greatness)
5. *Gevurah* (strength)
6. *Tiferet* (glory)
7. *Netzach* (victory)
8. *Hod* (majesty)
9. *Yesod* (foundation)
10. *Malkut* (sovereignty)

The Ten Sefirot are generally represented in a diagram that resembles a tree, and hence the schema is commonly called the Tree of the Sefirot or the Kabbalistic Tree of Life. These Sefirot are part of God, and yet they are capable of interacting with the universe, including human beings. The Sefirot experience the good and evil human deeds, which thus affect the entire universe and God.

Even the mystical aspect of Judaism emphasizes the reciprocal nature of the relationship between humans and God. Unlike most other forms of spirituality and mysticism, Judaism's unique interpretation stresses contact with the world. It is only through direct interaction with and involvement in the world that God can be experienced.

The Spiritual Side of Orthodoxy—Hasidism

Probably no group or branch of Judaism underscores the encounter with God in the world more than the Hasidim. So, who are the Hasidim? Most simply, they are practitioners of a form of mystical Orthodox Judaism.

Now, recall the point made earlier that while all followers of Judaism are Jews, not all Jews adhere to Judaism. The same rule of logic applies when considering the Hasidim. All Hasidim are Orthodox, but not all Orthodox are Hasidim. Far too many people, Jews and Gentiles alike, believe that all Orthodox Jews are Hasids, but this is simply wrong.

The Historical Setting

The Hasidic movement emerged from one of the darker pages of Jewish history, during the times of the Cossack massacres of 1648, which were led by Bogdan Chmielnicki. Thousands of Jews (about half the Jewish population of Ukraine and Poland) were murdered, and hundreds of Jewish communities were decimated. Following this bloody rampage and well into the eighteenth century, Eastern European Jewry suffered regular acts of violence and discrimination.

During such times, it is common for people to seek salvation and solace wherever they can find it. Many Jews came to prefer the spiritual nature of the Kabbalah to the legalistic approach of Orthodox Judaism. In reaction to this, rabbinic studies became even more focused on Halakhah and conventional Talmud rumination.

Another consequence of these trying times was a tendency to embrace "saviors." Hence, in the seventeenth century, many Jews flocked around the Turkish Jew, Shabbetai Zvi, believed to be a messiah. Later in the eighteenth century, Jacob Frank, a Polish messianic pretender, garnered a large following. As with all false messiahs, disillusionment ensued when Shabbetai Zvi adopted Islam and Jacob Frank converted to Christianity.

Since it was from the lower and less-educated classes of the Jewish population that these false messiahs drew their support and where mysticism (and even magic) was practiced, the educated classes grew more and more wary and intolerant of those who would not strictly adhere to traditional ways. A schism between the mystics and the traditionalists was in the works.

The Ba'al Shem Tov

Out of this schism emerged Rabbi Israel ben Eliezer, who became known as the *Ba'al Shem Tov* (Master of the Good Name). The Ba'al Shem Tov was born around 1700 in Ukraine. He was a simple man who roamed the countryside believing it was there that he could best commune with God (much like Abraham and the early nomadic Hebrews did in the desert). His appeal was widespread because he criticized the pedantic reiterations of scholars and the rabbinical emphasis on formal learning. His movement became known as Hasidism and his followers as Hasidim. To his credit, despite the fervent devotion of his followers, the Ba'al Shem Tov shunned any claim to being a messiah.

Ultimately, the Ba'al Shem Tov (also known by the abbreviation "Besht") settled in a remote Carpathian village where he supported his family by digging lime. Teaching in parables and recounting simple stories, the Besht gained widespread appeal, despite public denunciation from the rabbinical establishment that he was ignorant and irreverent. When he died in 1760, he left behind no written work of his own. However, the principles established by the Besht remain the core of Hasidism today.

The Hebrew word *hasid* means "pious" or "pious one." In classical Jewish sources, it designated anyone whose spiritual devotion extended beyond the technicalities of Halakhah. Over the last 200 years, "Hasid" has been used to describe a member of the Hasidic movement.

Hasidic Teachings of the Besht

One of the more revealing stories about the Besht and his teachings has to do with the time he refused to enter a house of prayer. "I cannot enter there," said the Besht. "The house is full to the brim of teaching and prayer." This puzzled his companions, since what the Besht said seemed to be a compliment. Seeing their bewildered faces, the Besht went on to explain: "During the day, the people speak here words without true devotion, without love and compassion, words that have no wings. They remain between the walls, they squat on the floor, they grow layer by layer like decaying leaves until the decay has packed the house to overflowing and there is no longer room for me in there."

When asked to explain Hasidism, the Besht replied: "Do you know the story of the ironmonger who wanted to become independent? He bought an anvil, a hammer and bellows and went to work. Nothing happened—the forge remained inert. Then an old ironmonger . . . told him, 'You have everything you need except the spark.' That is what Hasidism is: the spark."

From this Hasidic tale, you can glean the importance of sincerity in the hierarchy of Hasidic values. The moral here is that how one prays is more important than where one prays. Sincerity is required not only in prayer but in all of life's actions. And herein lies the essence of Hasidism as expressed by the Besht himself.

It's that same "spark" of the Divine presence within all of us, every living creature and every thing. It is the purpose of the Hasid to redeem these sparks. According to what the Ba'al Shem Tov taught, this is not accomplished through perfunctory prayer or asceticism but through *kavana* (pure intention), *devekut* (clinging, devotion to God's presence), joy in performing all deeds, and sincere prayer. The goal is to hallow life and thus awaken the holy reality in all things.

Tzaddikim

It is not surprising that after the Besht died, there was no formal framework for leadership. At first, his circle of disciples, each of whom was considered a *tzaddik* (a righteous one), exercised the Besht's authority. Since the average Hasid could not be expected to achieve full religious perfection, he would devote himself to a particular *tzaddik* and obtain vicarious fulfillment through him. The different Hasidic sects can trace their roots to a specific *tzaddik* and often to a town or city in Eastern Europe.

FACTS

In the mid–twentieth century, the philosopher Martin Buber translated numerous Hasidic tales that were subsequently published. Buber's own philosophy of "I and Thou" has striking parallels in Hasidism and Jewish mysticism. It is something you may want to consider investigating more deeply if you are looking for a more "secular" approach to Jewish spirituality.

Hasidism Today

Through the early twentieth century, the large Hasidic populations were largely confined to Eastern Europe. The devastation these communities suffered during World War II was unimaginable. Yet Hasidism survived, and new communities were established in the United States, Israel, Canada, and other parts of the world.

These communities are often identified by the name of the geographic locale where their forebears resided in Europe, and they are centered on their own *rebbe* or spiritual master. Some of these sects are fairly well known, such as the Lubavitcher (Chabad), Satmar, Breslov, and Modsitzer, but there are many more, each with its own customs, style of service, philosophy, and politics. Generally, however, Hasidic groups share much in common. They revere the Besht and other *tzaddikim*, and they have similar customs of dress. The men wear *payees* (side earlocks), full beards, hats, and dark clothes. Women wear modest dresses; married women wear scarves or other head coverings. (It is a common practice for married women to wear wigs.)

QUESTIONS?

What are those white strings hanging down over Hasidic men's pants?
The *tzitzit,* or white tassels, are attached to the *tallit katan* (a small prayer shawl), also known as *arba kanfot* ("four corners"). Hasidic men wear the *arba kanfot* throughout the day underneath their clothes. This mode of dress is required by the commandment to "make them fringes on the borders of their garments throughout their generations" (Numbers 15:38).

To some Jews the Hasidim are a strange breed, and elicit derisive snickers whenever they are mentioned. To other Jews, even many who do not agree with their teachings and beliefs, the Hasidim are respected for their adherence to their faith.

CHAPTER 4
The Languages of Judaism

Language is a body of words and systems that are common to a people, community, or nation. The Hebrew language, used for worship and religious study by Jews all over the world—in distant places like Yemen, Greece, and Poland—helped them to retain their sense of a nation. Moreover, Jewish communities in various countries developed their own dialects, such as Yiddish, to use in everyday life.

Hebrew—an Ancient Tongue

For thousands of years and without interruption, Hebrew has been the universal language of Judaism used for prayer and worship. Hebrew is one of the world's oldest languages, dating perhaps as far back as 4,000 B.C.E. The early Israelites conversed in Hebrew, a Semitic idiom of the Canaanite group that includes Arabic. The patriarchs spoke Hebrew as they made their way into the Promised Land, and it remained the language of the Israelites throughout the biblical period.

However, in the fifth century B.C.E., when Jews began to return to Israel from Babylon, where many had lived after the destruction of the First Temple in 586 B.C.E., most of the inhabitants of Palestine conversed in Aramaic, which gradually infiltrated into the language of the Israelites. A few centuries later, Hebrew had all but ceased to exist as a spoken language. It would not be re-established as such for two millennia.

If you would like to learn Hebrew, there are books and Web sites available to you and courses that you can take. As a matter of fact, there are intensive courses in conversational Hebrew of which you may avail yourself, should you be planning a visit or a stay in Israel and desire to be fluent in its vernacular language.

Writing in Hebrew

Hebrew is probably not the easiest language to learn. Should you undertake the task of mastering Hebrew, sometime during your efforts you will probably find yourself muttering, "This is all Greek to me!" And the truth is, there are similarities in the letter names and in the order of the alphabet between Hebrew and Greek!

Hebrew is read from right to left, just the opposite of reading English. You have to learn a new alphabet, which consists of twenty-two consonants, five of which assume a different form when they appear at the end of a word. And if this isn't enough of a challenge, how about the fact that Hebrew is generally written without vowel sounds!

The Hebrew Alphabet

mem sophit (final mem)	ם	aleph	א
nun	נ	bet	ב
nun sophit (final nun)	ן	gimel	ג
samech	ס	dalet	ד
ayin	ע	heh	ה
pei	פ	vav	ו
phe sophit (final phe)	ף	zayin	ז
tzadi	צ	chet	ח
tzadi sophit (final tzadi)	ץ	tet	ט
kuf	ק	yud	י
resh	ר	kaf	כ
shin	ש	khaf sophit (final khaf)	ך
tav	ת	lamed	ל
		mem	מ

The absence of vowels is common in Semitic languages. The convention dates back to the earliest days of Hebrew, when most people were fluent in the language and had no need for vowels in order to read it. However, literacy declined, especially after the destruction of the Second Temple when the Jews commenced their 2,000-year-long Diaspora. Sometime around the eighth century C.E., the rabbis came up with an answer to help increase the number of Jews who could become literate in Hebrew—the *nikkudim* (points), a system of dots, dashes, and lines that are situated just about anywhere (above, below, beside, or inside the consonants). Most *nikkudim* indicate vowels; when *nikkudim* appear in the text, it is called pointed text and is obviously easier to read.

While you will find *nikkudim* in prayer books and in many texts, especially books for children, you will see only the consonants in Torah scrolls or the parchment inside *tefillin* (see Chapter 8) and *mezuzot* (scrolls of parchment affixed to the doorpost). In fact, the entire style of writing in the sacred scrolls is different.

In contrast to the block print that is customarily seen in Hebrew books, sacred documents are written in a style that utilizes "crowns" on many of the letters. These crowns resemble crows' feet that emanate from the upper points. This type of writing is known as "STA'M" (an abbreviation for *Sifrei Torah, Tefillin,* and *Mezuzot*).

A more modern cursive form of writing is frequently employed for handwriting. Yet another style, Rashi script, appears in certain texts to differentiate the body of the text from the commentary. This kind of text, named in honor of Rashi, the great commentator on the Torah and Talmud, is used for the exposition.

QUESTIONS?

Why do some words that come from Hebrew have more than one spelling?
Hebrew words are spelled out in English letters according to a transliteration system, and there is more than one system to choose from. For example, the distinctive throaty Hebrew *h* is sometimes transliterated as *ch,* so the word Hanukah may be spelled as Chanukah.

Hebrew Letters Have Numerical Values

The Hebrew numerical system uses letters as digits in the same way that Roman numerals are letters of the Latin alphabet. In Hebrew, though, each letter of the alphabet has a corresponding numerical value. The first ten letters have values of one through ten; the next nine have values of twenty through 100, counting by tens; and the remaining letters have values of 200, 300, and 400, respectively.

Unlike the Roman numerical system where the order of the letters is important, in the Hebrew system the sequence of the letters is irrelevant. The letters are simply added to determine the total value.

Since every Hebrew word can be calculated to represent a number, Jewish mysticism has been painstakingly engaged in discerning the hidden meanings in the numerical value of words. For example, the numerical value of the Hebrew word *chai* (life) is eighteen. Hence, it is a common practice to make charitable contributions and give gifts, especially for weddings and bar or bat mitzvahs, in multiples of eighteen.

Modern Hebrew

Travel through modern Israel, and you will see the Hebrew letters that Diaspora Jews associate with prayer books filling the pages of newspapers and magazines, blaring messages on billboards, posted on cereal boxes and for-rent signs. Some visitors find this as nothing short of miraculous.

For most of the second millennium, Hebrew was rarely spoken other than during religious observances or by scholars studying Torah and other sacred tomes. However, in the nineteenth century, Hebrew underwent a renaissance. Thanks in large part to Eliezer ben Yehudah, who dedicated himself to the revival of Hebrew and introduced thousands of modern terms to the ancient language, Hebrew regained its status as a vernacular language.

Reinforcing Hebrew's rescue from near extinction as a spoken tongue, the Zionist movement made the decision that Hebrew should become the language of the modern State of Israel once the Jewish homeland was established. As a result, Hebrew was recognized as the official language of Jewish Palestine in 1922.

There is a difference between the Sephardic and Ashkenazic way of pronouncing several of the Hebrew vowels and one consonant. Because Israel has adopted Sephardic pronunciation for modern Hebrew, most Ashkenazim are adopting the Sephardic method of pronunciation.

Naturally, additional adjustments had to be made to Eliezer ben Yehudah's earlier efforts to bring Hebrew up to date. After all, the language had lain dormant for thousands of years. Much was new in the way of technology and devices, and the world was a very different place. Consequently, the Hebrew of worship and religious scholarship is not exactly the same as the modern Hebrew that was established as the official language of the new State of Israel, established in 1948.

Today, more than four and a half million people speak modern Hebrew. While Hebrew is the principal language for Israeli Jews, it is also a second language for many Israeli Arabs and recent immigrants. And, of course, Jews living outside of Israel may also be fluent in modern Hebrew.

Yiddish—the *Mame Loshen*

Yiddish has a long and colorful history; tens of millions of Jews affectionately called it the *mame loshen* (the mother tongue). Yiddish is primarily a language of Ashkenazic Jews, though even segments of this group have often avoided, and at times even snubbed, the language. Nonetheless, Yiddish holds a prominent place in the hearts and minds of millions of Jews the world over. An examination of the languages of Judaism would be incomplete without taking a look at Yiddish.

Jews do not speak "Jewish." Just because "Yiddish" means "Jewish" in the language of Yiddish, these words are not synonymous. "Jewish" is an adjective, while "Yiddish" is a noun that describes a particular Jewish language.

History and Development of Yiddish

Yiddish can trace its roots to the beginning of the second millennium C.E., when Jewish emigrants from northern France began to settle along the Rhine. These emigrants, who conversed in a combination of Hebrew and Old French, also began to assimilate German dialects. The written language consisted completely of Hebrew characters.

At the beginning of the twelfth century, after the horrific pogroms of the First Crusade, Jews migrated to Austria, Bohemia, and northern Italy, taking their new language, Yiddish, with them. When Jews were invited to enter Poland as traders, Yiddish incorporated Polish, Czech, and Russian language traits.

While it might seem that Yiddish is a hodgepodge of languages, this is not the case. In the end result, Yiddish came out to be composed mostly of Middle/High German, with a measure of Hebrew and touches of Slavic tongues and Loez (a combination of Old French and Old Italian).

Yiddish served the Jewish people well because it was an adaptable and assimilative language, absorbing some traits of the tongues spoken in the places Jews lived. Consequently, even English words and phrases made their way into Yiddish after the waves of immigration into the United States by European Jewry at the end of the nineteenth and early twentieth centuries.

Who Spoke Yiddish?

The Yiddish language was the chief vernacular of Ashkenazic Jews, but not all Ashkenazic Jews spoke Yiddish. For one thing, it was the vernacular not of scholars but of the ordinary people. The language for prayer and study remained Hebrew, although Yiddish was often used in yeshivas (religious schools) to discuss the texts. The fact that Yiddish had to do with the daily tasks of living is reflected in the language itself, and this is one of the factors that makes Yiddish such a unique and alluring language—one that is peculiarly Jewish.

FACTS

Since Jewish women were not taught Hebrew, they spoke Yiddish to their children, who, in turn, later spoke it to their own children. Thus, Yiddish became known as *mame loshen,* the "mother's language," as opposed to Hebrew, *loshen ha-kodesh,* or "the sacred language."

Yiddish is a very social language, replete with nicknames, terms of endearment, and more than a good share of expletives. You will find proverbs and proverbial expressions, curses for just about every occasion, and idioms reflecting the fears and superstitions of the times. To learn and know Yiddish is to understand the Jews who created and spoke the language hundreds of years ago.

The Rise, Fall, and Renaissance of Yiddish

In the first decades of the twentieth century, Yiddish was the daily language of an estimated eleven million Jews all over the world. A short time later, this number was reduced by more than half; by the middle of the twentieth century, the language could have been placed on the endangered species list.

Even at its apex in the early twentieth century, Yiddish had its detractors. German Jews, who were very much integrated in the greater German society, were embarrassed at what they considered to be a bastardized version of the sublime German language. In the United States, Sephardic Jews who had lived there for many generations were chagrined at the foreign tongue that their "greenhorn" compatriots used. Furthermore, Zionists rejected Yiddish in favor of Hebrew, which they wanted to revive as the vernacular of a new Jewish state.

However, the most important factor in the rapid decline of Yiddish was the *Shoah* (Nazi Holocaust), which destroyed entire communities of Yiddish-speaking Jews. When the survivors emigrated to Israel, they discovered that Yiddish was frowned upon as a language of the "ghetto" that reflected a subservient mentality.

However, in recent decades Yiddish has shown itself to be as stubborn and resilient as the Jewish people themselves when it comes to threats of destruction and extinction. In the United States, colleges and universities offer Yiddish courses, and special organizations and groups promote Yiddish both in the United States and in Israel, where there is now a greater acceptance for the language.

Yiddish Literature

Although it was born as a spoken language, Yiddish did eventually make headway in literature. Yiddish literature was produced mainly in Eastern Europe and later in the United States. Unfortunately, while Yiddish literature is rich and immensely attractive, with a multitude of stories, novels, poems, and essays, most of it has never been translated—and it is unlikely that it ever will be.

Given the nuances and uniqueness of the language, translations from the Yiddish are often found wanting. Yet even with these caveats, an exploration into Yiddish literature is most rewarding.

The Period of Preparation

Yiddish literature can be divided into three periods: the period of preparation, the classical age, and the postclassical period. The first of these, the period of preparation, is the longest, spanning seven centuries.

During this time, most Yiddish literature consisted of devotional works whose purpose was to make Judaism more intelligible to ordinary people. Perhaps the most noteworthy of these writings is the *Tz'enah ur'enah*, a liberal reworking of the stories from the Pentateuch (the Five Books of Moses), written by Jacob ben Isaac Ashkenazi.

However, there were also other modes of expression of Yiddish literature during this period. Beginning in the twelfth century, roving Jewish minstrels wandered through Germany reciting Gentile romances in Yiddish. By the fifteenth century, books of poetry, stories, and folktales appeared in Yiddish. In 1686, the first Yiddish newspaper was published in Amsterdam.

In the eighteenth century, Yiddish was the language used by the Hasidim in recounting the numerous tales and stories of the Ba'al Shem Tov and the ensuing masters of the movement. But it would take another hundred years for Yiddish literature to truly come into its own.

The Classical Age

The classical age of Yiddish literature was brief in duration but brilliant, bold, and beautiful in its bloom. This period in Yiddish literature lasted for a short interval, commencing in the late nineteenth century and ending fifty years later. While there were many distinguished writers of Yiddish literature during this time, three stood at the forefront: Sholom Jacob Abramowitz, best known as Mendele Mokher Sefarim (Mendele the Itinerant Bookseller); Sholom Rabinowitz, known as Sholom Aleichem; and Isaac Leib Peretz.

ESSENTIALS

You are probably familiar with the musical *Fiddler on the Roof,* but did you know that it was inspired by the collection of stories titled *Tevye's Daughters,* written in Yiddish by Sholom Aleichem?

These three luminaries of Yiddish fiction wrote about everyday life in the *shtetl* and in the pale of settlement in Russia, and each made a unique contribution to the body of Yiddish literature. Mendele Mokher Sefarim was the first to employ Yiddish as a vehicle for literary creation. Sholom Aleichem was perhaps unequaled in his ability to depict the authentic human condition of his day with humor, gentleness, and profound sadness. Peretz, trained as a lawyer and the most intellectual and sophisticated of the three, provided a thread of psychological finesse in his work.

The Postclassical Period

In the early part of the twentieth century, as a result of wars, revolutions, and persecutions, many Yiddish writers fled Eastern Europe for the United States. Consequently, New York became a Yiddish literary center almost equal to Warsaw in stature. Notable during this time were Abraham Reisen, who wrote poetry and short stories, and Sholem Asch, who, along with Israel Joshua Singer, helped perfect the Yiddish novel. Israel Singer's younger brother, Isaac Bashevis Singer, emerged as one of the most well known Yiddish writers of short stories and novels.

FACTS

Isaac Bashevis Singer won the Nobel Prize for literature in recognition of his writing, which preserved for posterity the civilization of Yiddish-speaking Eastern European Jews. His body of work is packed with fantasy, erotica, and themes of the Jewish faith, a depiction of humans with all their blemishes and frailties.

In the Soviet Union, Yiddish writers pursued themes of social realism. Among these writers, many of whom were murdered in the purge of Yiddish writers and poets during the Stalin era, were the poet Moshe Kulbak, the novelist David Bergelson, and short-story writer Isaak Babel.

Poetry, Drama, and Journalism

Yiddish poetry gained literary merit in the twentieth century. Like the Yiddish writers of fiction, many Yiddish poets emigrated to the United States and Israel, where their new milieu helped shape their work. For example, Morris Rosenfeld, who lived in the Lower East Side of Manhattan, wrote poetry protesting the inhumane conditions of the slums and sweatshops. Other notable poets were Simon Samuel Frug; Hayyim Nahman Bialik, who wrote in Hebrew and Yiddish; and Chaim Grade, whose poetry frequently dealt with the Holocaust.

Yiddish drama began to take hold with the establishment of theaters in Romania, Odessa, Warsaw, and Vilna toward the end of the nineteenth century. However, the Russian government closed numerous Yiddish theaters in the 1930s, sending actors scurrying for safer shores. With many of these thespians settling in the United States, New York soon became the hub for Yiddish theater.

Yiddish newspapers not only provided a way for Yiddish writers to make a living but also offered an outlet for their fiction. A number of Yiddish tabloids published stories and columns for readers who couldn't always afford books. In 1863, the weekly *Kol Mevasser* was founded in Odessa, and in 1865, the first Yiddish daily newspaper, *Yiddishes Tageblat,* began publication in New York City. Perhaps the most renowned of the Yiddish papers was *The Jewish Forward,* a Yiddish daily founded in 1897. It is still in publication today, although it is now a weekly, published in English with a special Yiddish edition.

Along with a recent resurgence of the Yiddish language, Yiddish literature has become more accessible, particularly with the publication of anthologies. How long this revival will last remains to be seen. Yiddish, unlike Hebrew, is not the holy tongue of Judaism, and is not shared by all Jews. As the demographics of Jewish communities change, there is less incentive for Jews to learn Yiddish, and with each generation less and less people know how to speak it.

Other Languages and Dialects

Yiddish is not the only language to have developed within Jewish communities in the Diaspora. Over the centuries, there have been and remain other languages, dialects, and vernaculars that Jews have used to converse amongst themselves. Sephardic Jews have their own international language known as Ladino or Judezmo, and many Sephardic Jews from Arab countries still speak a mix of Hebrew and Arabic.

Ladino is written in either Hebrew or Roman characters and is based upon Hebrew and Spanish. It made its appearance as early as the Middle Ages and it is still spoken in Turkey, North Africa, Palestine (Israel), Brazil, and other parts of South America.

CHAPTER 5

Judaism's Holy Texts

For centuries, Jews have been called the People of the Book. Religious study has always been greatly revered in the Jewish tradition, and there is much to study, such as the Torah, Talmud, the Midrash, and other important texts, which will be examined here.

The Torah

The Torah is inarguably the cornerstone of Judaism. The word "Torah" is sometimes translated as "the Law." It also means "a teaching," because it represents God's instructions regarding how Jews should live and what they ought to believe.

In its most limited sense, the Torah comprises the Five Books of Moses, also called the Pentateuch. However, in its broadest sense, Torah encompasses everything that follows the Pentateuch—the whole body of Jewish law and teachings.

Avoid referring to the Holy (Hebrew) Bible as the "Old Testament." What Christians call the "New Testament" is not part of Jewish scripture. Consequently, there can be nothing "old" about the Hebrew Bible!

The Torah is the first part of the Bible, which is sometimes called the Hebrew or Holy Scriptures. The Bible is also known by the acronym "TaNaKH" (or Tanach), formed from the first letter of the three sections of the Bible: Torah (Pentateuch), *Nevi'im* (Prophets), and *Ketuvim* (Writings).

The Written Torah

In its most general sense, the Torah is composed of two components. First, there is the Written Torah *(Torah Shebichtav)*, which in turn has three parts. The first part is the Pentateuch, also known as the Five Books of Moses or *Chumash*. The Pentateuch includes the following five books:

1. *B'reishit* (Genesis)
2. *Shemot* (Exodus)
3. *Vayikra* (Leviticus)
4. *Bamidbar* (Numbers)
5. *Devarim* (Deuteronomy)

The Torah
scrolls

Photo courtesy of Joshua Marowitz

The second part of the Written Torah is *Nevi'im* (Prophets), which contains the following eight books:

1. *Yehoshua* (Joshua)
2. *Shoftim* (Judges)
3. *Shmuel* (Samuel I and II)
4. *Melachim* (Kings I and II)
5. *Yirmiyahu* (Jeremiah)
6. *Yechezkel* (Ezekiel)
7. *Yeshayahu* (Isaiah)
8. *Trey Asar* (the Twelve)

FACTS

The last book in Prophets, *Trey Asar,* encompasses the remaining twelve prophets: Hosea, Joel, Amos, Obadiah, Jonah, Micah, Nahum, Habakkuk, Zephaniah, Haggai, Zachariah, and Malachi.

Finally, the third part of the Written Torah is the *Ketuvim* (Writings), which consists of eleven books:

1. *Tehillim* (Psalms)
2. *Mishlei* (Proverbs)
3. *Iyov* (Job)
4. *Shir Ha-Shirim* (Song of Songs)
5. *Ruth*
6. *Eichah* (Lamentations)
7. *Kohelet* (Ecclesiastes)
8. *Esther*
9. *Daniel*
10. *Ezra and Nechemiah*
11. *Divrei Ha-Yamim* (Chronicles)

In total, there are twenty-four books in the Written Torah.

The Oral Torah

In addition to giving Moses the written Torah, God also provided explanations that are called the *Torah Sheb'al Peh* or the oral Torah. These exegeses, which were not written down, were meant to be passed from teacher to student.

Perhaps you are beginning to wonder just how God imparted this rather immense amount of information. You may have heard it said that God whispered the additional 613 commandments into Moses' ear. It would serve you well to remember that anthropomorphic features are there to help you understand how God acted in history and communed with mortals. But who is to say what means of communication God really employed? Perhaps it's something akin to "inspiration" or "intuition" or "ESP."

The point is that God transmitted the Torah to His chosen people through Moses. Beginning around the year 200 C.E., the oral Torah was inscribed into a series of books called the Mishna.

Torah Is Eternal

It is axiomatic in Judaism that the Torah is everlasting and immutable. Since Torah comes from God and God is eternal, it follows that the Torah also shares this feature.

Undoubtedly, this is one reason Judaism takes upon itself the responsibility to be true to the Torah and to maintain it as part of the Jews' very existence. According to Judaism, God chose the Hebrews for the task of receiving and preserving the Torah, and this task cannot be abrogated.

Judaism is a vibrant and pulsating religion that deals with the application of the Law to everyday life. New thoughts, new questions, new ideas, and new answers are always taking shape as scholars study the Torah and its precepts are applied. This has given rise to other great works—this time written by men—that also play an integral role in Judaism.

The Talmud

In the years after the destruction of the Second Temple (70 C.E.), there was a danger that the oral Law, passed down from teacher to student, would be forgotten. In order to prevent this from happening, a group of scholars and jurists, led by Rabbi Yehuda Ha-Nasi, assembled a basic outline of the oral Law into the Mishna, which was completed around 200 C.E.

FACTS

Rabbi Yehuda Ha-Nasi was variously addressed as Rabbi, Rabbi Judah the Prince, and our Master the Saint. He was referred to as "Rabbi" because he taught the Torah; he was designated "the Prince" because he was elevated and made the prince and most honored of Israel; he was called "our Master the Saint" because it was said that his body was as pure as his soul.

But the students and scholars of Torah had far from completed their work. Over the next several hundred years, they continued to raise questions and seek explanations for the text and its laws. Once again, in order to keep the results of their efforts from being lost, Rav Ashi and

Ravina guided the compilation of the material into the Gemara. Together, the Mishna and Gemara form what we know as the Talmud.

The Talmud is a record of the way rabbis and scholars and jurists have applied the laws of the Bible to the life they faced. Consequently, it covers "all of life" because it encompasses everything that went on in those people's daily existence. Themes include the social and the private, urban and rural, civil and criminal, public and domestic, everyday and ritual. Virtually nothing was overlooked.

 **SSENTIALS**

There are actually two Talmuds—the Jerusalem Talmud and the Babylonian Talmud. Generally, when people speak of the Talmud, they are referring to the more comprehensive of the two, the Babylonian Talmud.

Organization of the Talmud

The Talmud is divided into six sections called *sedarim* ("orders"). Each *seder* contains several books called *masekhtot* ("tractates"); in total, there are sixty-three *masekhtot*. Although the respective *sedarim* seem to address rather specific and narrow topics, each *seder* in fact contains diverse and assorted subjects.

The six *sedarim* are the following:

1. *Zera'im* (seeds): This *seder* deals primarily with agricultural laws but also laws of prayer and blessings; it is comprised of eleven *masekhtot*.
2. *Mo'ed* (season): This *seder* addresses *Shabbat* and festivals; it includes twelve *masekhtot*.
3. *Nashim* (women): This *seder* deals with the laws of marriage and divorce; it contains seven *masekhtot*.
4. *Nezikin* (damages): This *seder* deals with civil law and ethics; it contains ten *masekhtot*.
5. *Kodashim* (holy things): Sacrifices and the Temple are considered in this *seder,* which includes eleven *masekhtot*.
6. *Toharot* (purities): This *seder* deals with laws of ritual purity and impurity, and contains twelve *masekhtot*.

A Work of Many Genres

The Talmud is an amazing and singular tome. It is the written product of discussions among a number of learned authors—but it is also so much more. Despite the fact that it deals with legalisms and extremely specific issues, it is not a code or catechism that lays down the law in summary, categorical form. In fact, the Talmud is filled with legend, folklore, parables, reminiscences, prayers, theology, and theosophy.

The Talmud is the end result of a process by means of which the law is made clear. Hence, the tensions, conflicts, and arguments of its collaborators come alive before the reader's eyes. What you see when examining a page in the Talmud is that a statement is quoted and then the scholars and sages immediately commence their exchange to explain the "text." These explications are the most important parts of the Talmud.

FACTS

Today, many observant Jews study a page of the Talmud every day. This practice, referred to as *daf yomi,* was started at the First International Congress of the Agudath Yisrael World Movement in 1923. Many synagogues organize less rigorous classes or informal sessions that allow participants to study the Talmud together.

As a result, engaging the Talmud can be both a fascinating and intellectual experience. It's not like reading a book of laws but rather coming face to face with a living, breathing people who left a little of themselves dispersed throughout the pages.

The Midrash

One might suppose that after receiving and studying the Torah—both the written and oral Torah—and then spending the first half of the first millennium promulgating the Talmud (the Mishna and Gemara), Judaism would have sufficient material to last the lifetime of even its most dedicated and erudite scholars. You would think ample questions had been raised regarding the text of the Bible and enough dialogue and answers developed. But, of course, there is always more. Between the

Jewish
religious texts

Photo courtesy of © 2001 Brand X Pictures

third and twelfth centuries, rabbis and religious scholars compiled their ideas and arguments in the form of stories that sought to explicate and probe even deeper the underlying truths and meanings of the biblical text. These stories, or *midrashim* (interpretations), eventually became known as the Midrash.

In the Midrash, each interpretive story is designed to expand on incidents in the Bible, to derive principles and laws, or to offer moral lessons. Moreover, because of their nature, *midrashim* can be used to gain a glimpse into the way the rabbis read the biblical text and into their thinking processes.

ESSENTIALS

The Hebrew word *midrash* translates as "commentary" or "interpretation." It is based on a Hebrew root meaning, "to investigate" or "to study." Midrash is a method used to inquire into what a biblical text might mean.

Some *Midrashim*

Many *midrashim* deal with the story of Creation. For example, when God was ready to create man, He said, "Let us make man." But who is "us"? Wasn't God alone? The *midrash* explains this by concluding that, indeed, God was not alone and that God consulted with the ministering angels.

In contemporary times, there is much controversy over the matter of capital punishment. But the issue is raised much earlier, in the biblical story of Cain killing his brother Abel. While the Bible does allow for capital punishment, God does not inflict this penalty upon Cain. Why not?

The *midrash* addressing this question suggests that since Cain had never witnessed death, he could not possibly have known how his physical assault on Abel would culminate. Therefore, it would not be just to have taken Cain's life—that's why he was sentenced to permanent exile instead. In modern legal jargon, this equates to American and English jurisprudence, where there is a distinction between involuntary manslaughter and voluntary manslaughter as well as among other degrees of murder.

QUESTIONS?

What is the difference between a *midrash* and any other analysis?
The *midrash* purports to penetrate the "spirit" of the material in question and reach a conclusion that is not necessarily obvious. There is no hesitancy to use poetic license, and the customary rules of logic are not always relied upon.

Or consider this example. In Exodus 4:10, the Bible portrays Moses as being a very poor speaker, but it doesn't say why this is so. Hence, a *midrash* provides an explanation that this goes back to when Moses was a child. It was decided that he be tested to determine if he harbored ambitious desires against Pharaoh's throne. The young Moses was to choose between sparkling jewels and hot coals placed before him. If he opted for the precious stones, it would mean he might prove a threat to Pharaoh. Naturally, his eyes focused upon the gems, but a divine interdiction guided his hand to the burning coals. After touching the hot embers, the young lad put his hand in his mouth to cool it off, resulting in a lifelong speech impediment.

As you might guess after looking at these examples, the Midrash has become a major literary component of Judaism. Yet there is even more. Still not completely satisfied, the rabbis and scholars wrote other great texts of Judaism. Let us consider some of these.

Shulhan Arukh

By the Middle Ages, volumes of text had been written to provide authority upon which the rabbis could rely in answering the questions that constantly arose in the daily lives of the Jews. But just as people today yearn for simpler and less cumbersome means to find the answers to their questions, several attempts took place to create definitive codes. We have already seen that Maimonides authored the *Mishneh Torah*, which was the best known of these codes, but another treatise has also gained eminence.

The *Shulhan Arukh*, written by Rabbi Joseph Caro in the sixteenth century, has its roots in his earlier work, the *Beit Yosef* (House of Joseph), and summarizes the conclusions reached in this prior text. In turn, the *Beit Yosef* was a detailed commentary of the *Tur*, by Rabbi Jacob ben Asher. The *Shulhan Arukh* is just one more example of how Jewish law evolved, and still does today, by examining and building upon previous work and text.

FACTS

Rabbi Joseph ben Ephraim Caro was born in Toledo, Spain, in 1488. Following the expulsion of the Jews from Spain, he wandered through Turkey, Bulgaria, and Greece, ultimately settling in Safed, Israel, where he died in 1575. His gravestone is intact and a frequent stop for visitors to Safed.

Since the *Shulhan Arukh* was a summary, a number of rabbis initially opposed it, preferring the method of going back to the original sources. However, the *Shulhan Arukh* rapidly gained acceptance in almost all Jewish communities. Today, the *Shulhan Arukh* has come to be regarded as a defining criterion of religious Orthodoxy and traditionalism.

The Responsa Tradition

In times past, the Jews often sought guidance from their rabbi on matters of everyday life, ritual, and tradition. When local rabbis faced difficult issues in applying Jewish law to specific circumstances, they often wrote to the most respected rabbis to seek guidance. These queries included the particulars of each matter, references to the applicable Talmudic passages involved, and the rabbi's own interpretation.

In turn, an answer would be forthcoming from the rabbi whose opinion had been sought. His response would include the basis for his conclusion and a reasoned argument to substantiate it. Over the years, these responsa *(Teshuvot)* were collected into printed volumes, providing even more material to be read and studied.

The tradition of writing responsa continues in contemporary times. A number of rabbis have even issued responsa on matters pertaining to modern technology. Consider the late Rabbi Moshe Feinstein, who wrote responsa on such topics as the permissibility of cosmetic surgery, how to make dishwashers kosher, and artificial insemination. No doubt the practice of issuing responsa will continue as Judaism faces even more complex issues, such as DNA cloning.

Writings of the Kabbalah

Although Jewish mysticism is discussed in more detail in Chapter 3, it's worth mentioning the writings of the Kabbalah again here. The primary written work in this area of Judaism is the *Zohar,* followed by many other works.

For example, in the first half of the twentieth century Rabbi Yehuda Ashlag, who emigrated to Israel from Poland, authored a commentary of the Zohar titled *Ha-Sulam* (the ladder). Subsequently, his eldest son, Rabbi Baruch Shalom Ashlag, wrote books elaborating on his father's work.

CHAPTER 6

Living in Accordance with the Law

Judaism is a religion that goes beyond a system of beliefs. It speaks to human conduct and enters into the very marrow of daily existence. There is not an aspect of human lives that it does not touch upon. Why the need for such extensive laws? What reason for so much promulgation of rules and regulations? This chapter considers these questions and explores the system of laws known in Judaism as the Halakhah.

The Role of Halakhah in Judaism

The word *halakhah* means "law," but it may be translated literally as "the path that one walks." Halakhah is Jewish law and accumulated jurisprudence. The word is derived from the Hebrew root of three letters, *heh-lamed-kaf,* which carries the meaning of travel or walking.

Judaism teaches that humans are dualistic creatures that have both a spiritual and a physical side. There is a constant tension and need to preserve a careful balance between them. While the physical aspect is important, and the need to maintain a healthy body and satisfy corporeal pleasures is recognized, more importance is attached to the ethereal element of human nature, which may be said to represent the soul. As you might recall, the physical body is the product of human parents. But the soul is the gift of God, and thus it should be the more cherished aspect of a human being.

FACTS

Sigmund Freud, a secular Jewish psychiatrist who lived in nineteenth-century Vienna, may have been inspired by the Halakhah and its role in Judaism in his own psychoanalytic theories. Freud divided the mind into the "id," which represents amoral drives and desires; the "superego," which corresponds to the conscience; and the "ego," the intermediary or referee that keeps the id and the superego in balance.

Judaism acknowledges that, left to their own drives and desires, people tend to stray from acting in harmony with the spiritual side of their constitution. God gave the Jews the Halakhah in order to keep the balance of the physical and spiritual aspects. Ever since, they have been working on interpreting and adapting it. From a very practical point of view, like all jurisprudence and rules of law, Halakhah keeps things in check.

The Spiritual Component of Halakhah

Unlike most codes of jurisprudence, Halakhah does not consist only of prohibitions. Quite the contrary, there are instructions and obligations requiring the performance of affirmative actions. Halakhah imposes a number of duties in the belief that they help add a dimension of spirituality to human lives.

In part, this reflects the fact that just as the *kohanim* (priests) in the Holy Temple diligently followed the requirements of Halakhah that pertained to maintaining the sanctity of the Temple, Judaism likewise teaches that every Jewish home is, in its own way, a "holy" temple *(mikdash me'at)* that must be hallowed. In fact, each individual is charged to do what he or she can to make the world more sacred.

This has been succinctly and repeatedly stated in the Torah: "So that you remember and do all My Commandments, and you will be holy to your God." (The requirements of Halakhah cannot be followed by rote, or they will lose their purpose. It is this type of perfunctory behavior against which Hasidism rails.)

Sometimes It's All in the Details

The Halakhah consists of *mitzvot* (commandments) from the Torah, laws enacted by rabbis, and established customs and traditions. If you follow the Orthodox view of Judaism, all are equally binding. However, the penalties provided for violating laws instituted by rabbis are less severe than those for violating the laws in the Torah.

QUESTIONS?

Can a person heed all of the Halakhah?
It is probably impossible to comply with all of the commandments and laws. Many are inapplicable, and each individual is not expected to fulfill what does not apply. For example, if you are not a farmer, you need not observe the commandments pertaining to farming.

Mitzvot—the Commandments

In its most limited sense, *mitzvot* are the commandments that appear in the Torah. The 613 *mitzvot* of the Torah are at the heart of the Halakhah and deal with all aspects of our lives. However, the word *mitzvah* may be defined either as a "commandment" in general or as "divine commandment." Moreover, it can also mean a "meritorious act" or "good deed." Interestingly, many Jews who are barely aware of this distinction frequently employ the second meaning of performing a meritorious act. To them, "mitzvah" has come to mean doing a "good deed."

Generally, *mitzvot* include all the laws and practices of Halakhah, including those issued by the rabbis and established customs. The first and foremost of all the *mitzvot* are the "ten statements."

The Ten Statements

The Ten Statements divulged by God to Moses at Mount Sinai and given to the Hebrews are, indeed, commandments. However, they are part of 613 commandments in the Torah—in fact, each of the 613 commandments fits into one of ten categories of commandments represented by the Ten Statements.

The "Ten Commandments" is a misnomer and does not exist anywhere in the Torah. In fact, the words used in the Torah, *Aseret Had'varim,* may be better translated as "Ten Statements" or "Ten Words." The word "commandments" appears in the King James Bible and reflects an incorrect translation of the Hebrew.

The Ten Statements appear twice in the Torah, at Exodus 20:2–14 and Deuteronomy 5:2–18. (There are a few minor discrepancies between the two.) The following list is taken from Exodus:

1. I am the Lord your God who brought you out of the land of Egypt, the house of bondage: You shall have no other gods beside Me.
2. You shall not make for yourself a sculptured image, or any likeness of what is in the heavens above, or on the earth below, or in the waters under the earth. You shall not bow down to them or serve them. For I the Lord your God am an impassioned God, visiting the guilt of the fathers upon the children, upon the third and upon the fourth

The Ten
Statements

Photo courtesy of © 2001 Brand X Pictures

generations of those who reject Me, but showing kindness to the thousandth generation of those who love Me and keep My commandments.

3. You shall not swear falsely by the name of the Lord your God; for the Lord will not clear one who swears falsely by His name.

4. Remember the Sabbath day and keep it holy. Six days you shall labor and do all your work, but the seventh day is a Sabbath of the Lord your God: you shall not do any work—you, your son or daughter, your male or female slave, or your cattle, or the stranger who is within your settlements. For in six days the Lord made heaven and earth and sea, and all that is in them, and He rested on the seventh day; therefore, the Lord blessed the Sabbath day and hallowed it.

5. Honor your father and mother, that you may long endure on the land which the Lord your God is giving you.

6. You shall not murder.

7. You shall not commit adultery.

8. You shall not steal.

9. You shall not bear false witness against your neighbor.

10. You shall not covet your neighbor's house: you shall not covet your neighbor's wife, or his male or female slave, or his ox or his ass, or anything that is your neighbor's.

How many English translations of the Hebrew Bible are there? Throughout much of Jewish history, the Jews studied Hebrew so that they could read the Bible in the original. Eventually, though, scholars translated the Bible into their respective native languages. An English version published by the Jewish Publication Society in 1962, and then revised in 1985, is the most widely used translation today.

The 613 Commandments

Because the 613 *mitzvot* emanate from God, these commandments cannot be changed or modified. They are, however, subject to interpretation, including the manner in which they are applied. Some of the *mitzvot* are obvious, while others are inferred and yet others are ascertained by Talmudic logic. And while there are 613 distinct *mitzvot,* a number of these overlap or are repetitive.

Remember that what makes Halakhah unique is that Jewish Law means more than prohibitions—it includes obligations as well. Hence, it should come as no surprise that of the 613 *mitzvot,* 365 are negative and 248 are positive. Consistent with all other aspects of Judaism, the intention in which the act is carried out is critical. The rabbis have often used the phrase *simcha shel mitzva* to emphasize that a mitzvah performed out of a sense of requirement is not as meaningful as one performed out of desire and with enjoyment.

ESSENTIALS

The number 613 is of consequence because it is the numeric value of the word "Torah." This is calculated as follows: *tav* = 400, *vav* = 6, *resh* = 200, *heh* = 5, plus 2 for the two *mitzvot* that precede the Torah text ("I am the Lord your God and you shall have no other gods before Me").

As was said earlier, no person is capable of observing all 613 *mitzvot.* In fact, most do not apply to any given individual. Some of these *mitzvot* are pertinent only to the land of Israel. Others concern the Temple and *kohanim,* while many *mitzvot* have to do with animal sacrifices and offerings.

While all of the 613 *mitzvot* will not be listed here, perusing the following categories will give you a good grasp of the extent to which these commandments pervade the Jewish life:

- God
- Torah
- Signs and symbols
- Prayer and blessings
- Love and brotherhood
- The poor and unfortunate
- Marriage, divorce, and family
- Sexual relations
- Times and seasons
- Dietary laws
- Business practices
- Employees, servants, and slaves
- Vows, oaths, and swearing
- Sabbatical and Jubilee years
- Court and judicial procedures
- Injuries and damages
- Property and property rights
- Criminal laws
- Punishment and restitution
- Prophecy
- Idolatry and idolatrous practices
- Agriculture and animal husbandry
- Clothing
- The firstborn
- *Kohanim* and Levites
- Tithes and taxes
- The Temple and sacred objects
- Sacrifices and offerings
- Ritual purity and impurity
- Lepers and leprosy
- The King
- Nazarites
- Wars

As you have seen, some of the *mitzvot* categories are no longer applicable to modern life. Jews no longer need to concern themselves with laws associated with animal sacrifice, dealing with lepers, or keeping slaves, for instance. However, many subjects are still quite relevant, even though at first glance you may think otherwise.

Halakhah Beyond the 613 *Mitzvot*

In addition to the commandments, rabbis assembled laws to help keep people from unintentionally violating a *mitzvah*. Any such law that is not a *mitzvah* but that still belongs to the Halakhah is known as a *gezeirah*. For instance, in order to keep the *mitzvah* of avoiding work on the Sabbath, you would obey the *gezeirah* that instructs not to touch any implement of work, such as a hammer.

Furthermore, Halakhah includes the type of law known as the *takkanah*. These laws are established by the rabbis and may vary from one community to another. Since Chanukah is a post-biblical holiday, the command to light candles during that time is a *takkanah*.

FACTS

It was a *gezeirah* that established the practice of adding a second day to the celebration of most holidays in the Diaspora. This way, Jews living outside Israel would not accidentally violate the command to celebrate the holiday because of some confusion with the calendar. Once uniform calendars became the norm, there was some thought of eliminating the added day, but the rabbis opted to continue the practice as a *minhag*.

Finally, a *minhag* is a custom that has been observed for so long and by so many that it became binding. Although all of these additional laws of *gezeirah, takkanah,* and *minhag* joined the Jewish tradition much later than the *mitzvot* of the Torah, they are now equally valid components of the Halakhah.

Speech and *Lashon Ha-Ra*

In October 2001, Peter Levin, an attorney and legal pundit, found himself in a bit of a dilemma. He was covering the trial of Rabbi Fred Neulander, who stood accused of hiring a "hit man" to murder his wife. It seems word reached Mr. Levin from several rabbis that his reporting on the case might create a situation of *lashon ha-ra* (forbidden speech or slander). Having decided several years earlier to become a more observant Jew, Mr. Levin carefully reflected on his predicament but ultimately opted to report on the case.

What the rabbis who cautioned Mr. Levin had in mind was their concern over the laws governing speech, specifically the laws proscribing gossip or utterances that would wrong another. Judaism recognizes the harm that speech can cause. Unlike many other transgressions against another person, where restitution of some sort can often be made, words that leave the lips of the speaker are like arrows released by a bow. They cannot be retrieved, nor their damage undone. Moreover, gossip and disparaging words may be inciting and result in violence.

Hence, there is no forgiveness for *lashon ha-ra* (disparaging speech), and it is expressly prohibited. It is no matter whether what one says is true or false, whether it is a secret or known by others, or whether it is derogatory. While there are several exceptions to this ban, such as providing testimony in a court of law or revealing information to protect someone from serious harm, the bottom line is that it is forbidden to gossip or carry tales or speak of others. Even listening to gossip violates this interdiction.

"Kosher" Sex

You are probably familiar with the fact that in the Bible, the verb "to know" is used to represent sexual relations. The use of this word, perhaps more than anything else, reflects Judaism's emphasis upon the unity in sexual intimacy of the heart and mind with the physical body. Although Judaism assigns libidinous desire to the realm of "evil" impulses that must be controlled, Judaism also recognizes the importance of sexuality, which may be a beautiful, meaningful, and even holy act. Hence, the *mitzvot* that deal with sex are both positive and negative.

There are two major objectives behind Halakhah concerning sex. First, as alluded to above, the sexual act is seen as an opportunity to achieve spiritual unity and create a "holy" encounter. It can add a deeper dimension to the marital relationship. The other main objective is to procreate and observe God's mandate to "be fruitful and multiply." Therefore, any sexual act that results in the destruction of semen, such as ejaculation outside the vagina, is forbidden.

This law may explain why sexual acts between men are forbidden, but an interdiction on sexual relations between women is absent (though this does not mean that Judaism condones lesbianism). It may also account for why homosexual desires do not violate Halakhah. It is only the sexual act itself that is prohibited. Masturbation is likewise enjoined, for the obvious reason that it allows for the "spilling of seed."

Given the value placed upon human life and the *mitzvah* to procreate, birth control and abortion are acceptable only in limited circumstances.

Generally, both are permitted when the mother's life is in jeopardy. With advances in methods of contraception, there has been more liberalization in the area of birth control. While a condom is not allowed because it destroys the "seed" (semen), the pill is permissible. This is a perfect example of how *mitzvot* must continually be interpreted when new situations and conditions arise.

ALERT

A man is required to satisfy his wife by having sex with her regularly and ensuring that it is pleasing. In fact, the Talmud specifies the frequency of this obligation and discusses the quality of sex. While men have these responsibilities, women do not, although a woman may not withhold sex from her husband on a whim.

The Laws of *Niddah*

A lesser-known area regarding the *mitzvot* that govern sex has to do with the law of *niddah* (separation). According to this law, men may not have sexual relations when their wives are menstruating and must further wait a minimum of seven days after there is no sign of bleeding. As soon as possible after the seventh "clean day," the woman is to immerse herself in a *mikvah* (a ritual pool). Thereafter, sexual relations should be resumed.

Because of this law, a husband and wife may not have sexual relations for at least twelve days out of each month. It has been suggested that the law of *niddah* improves the quality of sex, by limiting the time in which husband and wife may engage in intimate relations. Furthermore, a period of abstinence each month may increase male fertility.

FACTS

A *mikvah* serves to purify and has several functions. A Jewish bride immerses herself in the *mikvah* before her wedding. Women immerse themselves after menstruation and giving birth. The Orthodox (and sometimes other Jews) use the *mikvah* as part of the conversion process for men and women seeking to become Jews. The rules and regulations governing the *mikvah* are detailed, and a *mikvah* can usually be found in more observant Jewish communities.

Performing Good Deeds (Tzedakah)

Photo courtesy of Joshua Marowitz and Joshua and Ali Hurwitz

The *pushke* or *tzedakah* box, a repository for charity money collected in the home

If you recall, 248 out of 613 *mitzvot* involve positive action. That's what *tzedakah* (charity) is all about, the performing of good deeds. To be specific, "charity" is actually a misnomer; in fact, there is no Hebrew word for "charity." *Tzedakah* comes from the root *tzedek* (righteous). The idea behind *tzedakah* involves the obligation to establish justice by being righteous, compassionate, and helpful to others.

Practicing *tzedakah* is not an option. It's an obligation.

Maimonides organized the fulfilling of *tzedakah* into various degrees of giving, beginning with the least meritorious:

- Giving begrudgingly
- Giving less than you should, but giving it cheerfully
- Giving after being asked
- Giving before being asked
- Giving when you do not know the recipient's identity, but the recipient knows your identity
- Giving when you know the recipient's identity, but the recipient does not know your identity
- Giving when neither party knows the other's identity
- Enabling the recipient to become self-reliant

The Laws of *Kashrut*

Kashrut are dietary laws that specifically set forth the foods that Jews are permitted to eat and how these foods must be prepared. The word *kashrut* means "fit," "proper," or "appropriate," and this group of laws contains a fair amount of *mitzvot* on the proper way of eating.

In times past, eating and drinking carried grave religious obligations. Strict adherence to dietary laws reinforced the identity of the Jews as being a holy and chosen people. Further, some have claimed that the Jewish dietary laws afforded beneficial health effects, although this became less of a factor with the advent of refrigeration. Adhering to the laws of *kashrut* calls for greater attention and respect of food, and maintaining a kosher kitchen ensures that a home remains open to observant Jews.

ESSENTIALS

People who are *glatt kosher* may not consume animals with lung adhesions (each slaughtered animal's lungs must be inspected by the butcher, who establishes whether it is *glatt kosher*). In fact, the word *glatt* means "smooth" or "free of adhesions." The practice of *glatt kosher* is based on an interpretation of the *kashrut* commandment in the Torah. However, not all observant Jews practice *glatt kosher.*

However, the primary reason for keeping kosher is because God commanded their fulfillment as *mitzvot.* In fact, the laws of *kashrut* belong to a category of *mitzvot* known as *chukkim,* laws that don't have any logical reasons behind them. Although certain branches of Judaism do not require their members to adhere to *kashrut,* and others are less demanding in its application, keeping kosher is nevertheless a fundamental component of Halakhah.

What Is Treyf?

Treyf is any food or thing that is not kosher. This may include foods that are prohibited for consumption in general as well as foods prepared incorrectly. The Torah specifies which animals cannot be consumed. Animals that do not have cloven hooves and do not chew their cud may not be eaten—hence, no pork. As to creatures that inhabit the waters, observant Jews are restricted to fish that have both fins and scales—so shellfish are forbidden. Insects, rodents, reptiles, and amphibians are strictly off limits. In any event, why would you want to eat insects and rodents? Products derived from *treyf* animals are likewise not permitted—this applies to milk, eggs, fat, and organs.

It's not enough to eat "kosher-style" foods in order to keep kosher. Often, restaurants and food markets may advertise "kosher-style" products, but such products are not necessarily kosher. Traditional Jewish foods such as bagels, blintzes, and even *matzah* (unleavened bread eaten at Passover) and grape wine may not be kosher if they are not prepared in strict accordance with *kashrut*.

Kosher Slaughtering and Preparation

Although Judaism does not require vegetarianism, the method in which animals are slaughtered and primed is critical. Animals may be slain for food, skins, and clothing only when there is a genuine need. Cruelty toward animals and hunting for sport are strictly forbidden. This may explain why you probably don't know many Jewish hunters!

Animals must be slaughtered in the most humane way possible, and there are specific *mitzvot* that govern animal slaughter. The ritual slaughterer, known as a *shochet,* carries out this act with a swift stroke of the blade across the throat of the animal. Animals who have not been slaughtered properly are deemed *treyf* and may not be consumed.

A *shochet* receives his authority directly from rabbis and is subject to their supervision. *Shochet* must be fully conversant with the rules governing *kashrut*. They must be physically healthy, mentally capable, and of good character and repute. Before acting on his own, a *shochet* serves an apprenticeship.

According to the Torah, the essence of life is in the blood. To consume the blood of an animal is to consume its life, an act strictly prohibited by Jewish law. Following the slaughter, animals must be drained of blood. All residual blood is drained from the meat during food preparation, either by broiling, soaking, or salting.

Meat and Dairy

Probably one of the better-known aspects of *kashrut* is the separation of meat and dairy products. The basis for this is found in the Torah: "You shall not boil a kid in its mother's milk," a statement that appears in the Torah three times.

The separation includes not only the foods themselves but also the utensils involved in cooking, the plates and flatware used to serve and eat the food, and the towels and dishwashers employed in cleaning up. Further, you must be cognizant of your own digestive system and wait at least several hours before moving from *fleishig* (meat) to *milchig* (dairy) in order to avoid mixing the two inside you!

CHAPTER 7

The Place of Prayer in Judaism

Prayers are an important part of Judaism. They range from daily private prayers, blessings, and recitations, to public prayers that are part of the liturgy recited in the synagogue. This chapter will explore the special place that prayer occupies in Judaism, as well as where and how Jews pray.

The Dynamic of Prayer

In Judaism, prayer is more than a matter of self-assessment that you can accomplish by setting aside some quiet time to contemplate, taking a solitary walk in the woods, or, as many people have done, engaging in meditation (practiced over the centuries by some Jews, particularly those engaged in the mystical element of Judaism). Judaism expects more than just reflection. It demands that the praying person involve the whole of one's being in prayer. The Talmud defines prayer as *avodat halev,* the "service of the heart," because prayer should express the deepest feelings and longing of the soul. In furtherance of this, the more observant Jews use the entire body in the act of praying. This practice is known as *shuckling* (swaying).

FACTS

The Hebrew word for "prayer" is *tefilah.* This word is derived from the verb *lehitpalel* (to judge oneself), which reflects the introspective aspect of prayer in Judaism. Eastern European Jews also use the word *daven* (pray), which is derived from the English word "divine"; this word choice indicates that prayer is directed toward God.

In Judaism, prayer is to be neither taken for granted nor performed perfunctorily. Words should not be recited by rote. What you say when praying is not as important as how you say it. The word that best describes the nature of Jewish prayer is *kavanah* (intent).

Kavanah

Consider this Hasidic tale that illustrates *kavanah* better than any scholarly elucidation on the subject. On the day after Yom Kippur, the Ba'al Shem Tov ordered his driver to take him to an inn in the forest. As soon as he entered, the owner begged to confess to the Ba'al Shem Tov how on Yom Kippur, while having every intention to go to *shul* (synagogue), he simply could not get away from his establishment since one customer after another continued to arrive. When he realized that it was too late to go to services, he decided to pray by himself. Not having learned Hebrew, all the poor innkeeper could do was recite the Hebrew alphabet and after doing this, he added, "Here, God, here are your holy letters, you put them into the right words. . . ."

The Ba'al Shem Tov put his arms around the man and said, "It was revealed to me in a vision that on this Yom Kippur your prayers had opened the gates of heaven, and I came to find out how to do it."

While the innkeeper was ignorant of the liturgy for Yom Kippur and was not even proficient in Hebrew, the Ba'al Shem Tov instantly saw how special the innkeeper's prayers had been because the man was filled with *kavanah*. What mattered was his intention—without *kavanah*, reciting all the prayers in the *Siddur* (prayer book) would be pointless.

The Origins of Prayer

Religious observances took place at the Temple in Jerusalem prior to its second destruction two millennia ago. Many of these rituals involved sacrifices. When the First Temple was destroyed and the Babylonian Exile occurred in the sixth century B.C.E., prayer served as a substitute for sacrifice to exiled Jews, though some Jews may have practiced prayer even before that time.

Without doubt, the oldest daily prayer in Judaism is the *Shema*. The *Shema* is recited in the morning and at night, as commanded in its first paragraph, "When you recline [retire] and when you arise." Soon after the Babylonian Exile, Judaism saw the introduction of another central prayer, the *Shemoneh Esrei* (eighteen), a multifaceted prayer comprised of nineteen benedictions (eighteen original ones plus an additional benediction that was added later on).

Where Jews Pray

The most important thing to remember about prayer in Judaism is that a Jew can pray anywhere. This is beautifully expressed in *Midrash Tehillim:* "When you pray, pray in the synagogue of your city; if you are unable to pray in the synagogue, pray in your field; if you are unable to pray in your field, pray in your home; if you are unable to pray in your home, pray on your couch; and if you are unable to pray on your couch, meditate in your heart."

Beth Sholom
Congregation
(Elkins Park,
PA), designed
by Frank Lloyd
Wright

Photo courtesy of Joshua Marowitz

However, as we shall see, Judaism prefers that prayer be conducted in an assemblage. Special places dedicated for prayer are generally called synagogues. The word "synagogue" is a Greek translation of the Hebrew *beit k'nesset* (place of assembly), and related to the word "synod."

Origin of the Synagogue

The origin of the synagogue is not clear. There are those who believe synagogues were in place during the time of the First Temple, while others maintain that synagogues grew out of devotional services that accompanied the daily sacrifices in the Second Temple. Some also hold the opinion that the synagogue is a product of Jews in exile in Greek-influenced lands.

However, most scholars trace the beginnings of the synagogue to the Babylonian Exile in the sixth century B.C.E. By the time the Second Temple fell (70 C.E.), there seems throughout the Roman world to have been a synagogue present wherever Jews dwelt. It is estimated that as many as 480 synagogues were in existence in Jerusalem around that time.

ESSENTIALS

While the Conservative movement usually uses the word "synagogue," Reform Jews often employ the word "temple," referring to the Temple in Jerusalem. The Ashkenazic Orthodox commonly use *shul,* a Yiddish word derived from the German word for "school," since the *shul* is a place of learning as much as a place of prayer.

Functions of a Synagogue

A synagogue can serve several purposes. It is best known as *beit ha-tefillah,* a house of prayer. Since Jews are encouraged to pray in groups and certain prayers require the presence of a *minyan* (ten men), there must be a physical facility to accommodate the gathering.

However, synagogues have other functions as well. The synagogue acts as a *beit midrash* (house of study). In addition to preparation for a bar or bat mitzvah, a synagogue provides opportunities to continue the study of Judaism. A synagogue may also offer social services to the community and sponsor social events.

Contemporary synagogues vary in many ways: size, organizational structure, the extent to which they conduct nonreligious activities, and which values they reflect. However, because the synagogue remains first and foremost the house of prayer, most synagogues are similar in their physical layout.

Configuration of a Synagogue

The section of the synagogue where prayer services are held is often called the sanctuary. Smaller *shuls* have no other sections, but many synagogues do have other elements, such as study rooms, banquet halls, or areas for children.

In Orthodox synagogues, the sanctuary is divided, with separate places for men and women. The women may occupy an upper floor, or the side or rear of the first floor, in which case they are separated by a *mechitzah* (wall or curtain).

Since Jews must face in the direction of Jerusalem when praying, synagogues in the United States and Europe are constructed with the front facing the East. On the eastern wall is set the *Aron Kodesh* (Holy Ark), in which the Torah scrolls are stored behind an inner curtain called a *parokhet*. (For more on the Holy Ark and other ritual objects, see Chapter 8.)

The Synagogue's Cast of Characters

Judaism accepts both public and private prayer, and there is no need for guidance or help in worshipping. However, traditional roles for synagogue functionaries have gradually evolved. To understand how synagogue services work, it will be helpful for you to learn more about these roles.

The precursors to those who officiate at the religious services are the *kohanim*, descendants of Aaron who were enjoined by God to perform certain sacred duties in connection with the services in the Temple. The services, described in detail in the Torah, had to do with animal sacrifices and purity ceremonies. The role of this priestly class became largely irrelevant after the Temple's destruction.

FACTS

For centuries, there has been very little to distinguish the *kohanim* from the levites. However, some distinctions remain in religious practices. For example, the first *aliyah* (recital of a blessing over the Torah reading) is given to a *kohein* on *Shabbat*. The second *aliyah* is assigned to a levite. This reflects the *kohanim*'s special status as the priestly class.

The levites, from the tribe of Levi, were another caste of Jews with special responsibilities related to service in the Temple. However, their duties were less illustrious than those of the *kohanim*. Naturally, their jobs also ceased to exist after the Temple was destroyed.

With the Temple in ruins and Jews scattered all over the globe, the thing that probably held the Jews together was their knowledge of Torah. Learning became the highest priority, and rabbis (teachers) became the leaders of the community.

The Rabbi

The word "rabbi" comes to us from the Hebrew word *rabi,* which means "my teacher." A rabbi is not a priest. Nor is a rabbi an intermediary between a person and God. A rabbi need not be a *kohein,* since his position has nothing whatsoever to do with the tasks performed by the priests in the days of the Temple. A rabbi has no more authority to discharge Jewish rituals than any other Jew. Nor is a rabbi needed to lead prayer services—anyone can do this. As a result, there is a true democratic form of worship in services.

How does one become a rabbi? The answer is much different today than it was thousands of years ago. According to tradition, Joshua became a rabbi when Moses laid his hands on Joshua's head and "ordained" him. The Hebrew term for ordination is *semicha* (to lean upon). Originally, in order to become a rabbi, a man had to study with a rabbi who had been ordained through the *semicha* process. Once the studies were completed, the *semicha* procedure would be consummated with the setting of hands upon the head. Through this tradition, all rabbis had a direct link to Moses.

SSENTIALS

The *semicha* process was generally restricted to the land of Israel. This is why, in general, Talmudic sages who lived in Israel were called *rabbi* while those living in Babylon were called *rav.*

The process of *semicha* had largely come to an end by the year 200 C.E., after the destruction of the Second Temple in 70 C.E. and the subsequent dispersion of the Jewish people. In the centuries that followed, there was no set formula for becoming a rabbi. Rabbis generally attained their status by studying Halakhah and tradition. A rabbi had to be able to answer questions that were posed by members of the community. While a rabbi is a respected figure in Judaism who wields a degree of authority, his authority is derived from his position as a person of knowledge and not out of any special relationship to God. When a rabbi leads a prayer service—as rabbis generally do—they are at the forefront because this is a place they earned through hard work and study, not because of hierarchical status.

ALERT

Do not confuse the Yiddish words *rebbe* and *reb.* In a Hasidic community, a *rebbe* is a spiritual master and guide, a position often determined by lineage. *Reb,* however, is a general term of respect, similar to the English term "Mr."

Today, you can become a rabbi by attending a yeshiva or seminary. After graduation, the rabbi is ordained, usually through one of the branches of Judaism. (This is why Reconstructionism did not truly become a movement until the late 1960s, when it established an institution to train its own rabbis.) However, it is still possible to become a rabbi by being ordained by another rabbi (though this is rarely performed). In Israel, it is not uncommon to be ordained by both the Chief Rabbinate and an individual rabbi. (The latter practice is called a "private" *semicha.*)

Although the prayer service is not required to have a leader, rabbis usually perform this role. Since most prayers are frequently chanted (sung), the obvious question becomes, "What happens if the rabbi can't carry a tune?" After all, being learned in Torah does not necessarily correlate to knowing how to sing. Often, singing the prayers is a job designated for another person—the cantor.

The Cantor

The cantor *(chazzen)* leads the congregation in the chanting of prayer. Generally, though this practice can vary, the cantor sings the opening words of a prayer, the congregation joins in, and then the cantor sings the final verse. The cantor plays a pivotal role in the service because his melodies should inspire and assist the congregants in mustering *kavanah* for prayer.

Nothing in Judaism obligates a congregation to have a cantor, nor are there specific qualifications for the position. Typically, any person with good moral character, an ability to sing, and a knowledge of the prayers and tunes could serve as a *chazzen*. Unlike the rabbi, who assumes his position through scholarship and erudition, the *chazzen* gets his job simply through his ability to sing.

In modern times, cantors are trained professionals. They may have been ordained as clergy, or they may have earned university degrees and/or teaching certificates. Some Reform, Conservative, and Reconstructionist synagogues have opened the post of the cantor to women.

Aside from leading the congregation in the prayers, the cantor may prepare young people to chant the *Haftorah* (weekly Torah portion) for their bar or bat mitzvah. While the cantor's status as religious leader and educator has become prominent in most synagogues, some smaller congregations cannot afford to hire a full- or even part-time professional. Sometimes a cantorial student is hired, but if this is not feasible, then either the rabbi or a *gabbai* (lay person who volunteers to fulfill duties in the religious service) assumes the responsibility.

The Jewish Liturgy

Liturgy is a form of public worship. In Judaism, the liturgy goes back to the days of the Temple. Even after the destruction of the Second Temple, group prayer was considered essential to Judaism, which is why the Jews recite most prayers in the first-person plural, "we," and not the singular "I." If circumstances do not permit otherwise, Judaism encourages a person to pray alone in addition to the customary blessings an individual can make throughout the day. However, in order to conduct a formal public service, a *minyan* is needed.

The prerequisite of a *minyan* is satisfied with the presence of ten adults, all thirteen years of age or older. Orthodox Judaism requires ten men, while Reform and Reconstructionist synagogues allow the number to include women. Conservative congregations vary over their respective gender policies concerning a *minyan*.

The word *minyan* is derived from the Hebrew word for "to count" or "to number." The concept of a *minyan* has ancient roots. One *midrash* ties the custom to the time Moses dispatched twelve spies into the Promised Land, ten of whom provided a pessimistic report. In the Bible, these ten men are referred to as "an evil congregation." Therefore, the rabbis deduced, ten people constitute a congregation.

Hebrew Is the Language for Prayer

Although the Talmud clearly states that one can pray in any language, Hebrew has traditionally been the language for prayer in Judaism. In the past, this tradition was a point of contention, and one of the first changes the Reform movement made was to pray in the vernacular. However, in recent years Hebrew has begun taking a more prominent position in Reform prayer books. As for the Orthodox, Hebrew remains the exclusive language for prayer. The Conservative and Reconstructionist liturgies rely on Hebrew to a large extent.

The use of the vernacular in prayer goes back to the time of the Talmud. In fact, the *Kaddish* (one of the most solemn and ancient prayers in Judaism) is not in Hebrew at all! The *Kaddish* is written in Aramaic, the language used by the Jews at the time the prayer was formulated.

There are several sound reasons why Hebrew should be your language of choice for prayer, even if you do not understand a single word of it. First of all, you will generally get an English translation alongside the Hebrew text, so there will be no problem in your understanding the prayer. And don't worry about the literal translation for each word—it really doesn't matter. Hebrew is an ancient language full of subtleties and nuances, so a word-for-word translation won't necessarily do the prayer justice anyway.

Just knowing you are praying in the same language used by Jews thousands of years ago—the same language in which the covenant with God was formed—is bound to instill strong emotions and raise your level of *kavanah*. But one of the most important justifications for the use of Hebrew in the prayer service is unity. With Jews dispersed to the four corners of the Earth, this universal language for prayer has helped preserve Jewish identity. Having the prayers in Hebrew allows any Jew to join any congregation anywhere in the world and be able to pray with fellow Jews.

Prayers

Prayer helps form the foundation of Judaism. The origin of the liturgical prayers spoken in synagogues is attributed to the "Men of the Great Assembly." These are the prophets, sages, scribes, and teachers who, in the centuries after the return from Babylon, continued the work of Ezra and his followers.

Observant Jews pray three times a day in formal worship, and a slew of blessings and prayers can be said individually. The daily prayers follow a basic pattern, with some variation on *Shabbat* and holidays (and, of course, among the different branches of Judaism).

Shacharit (the morning service) is composed of the following prayers:

- Morning blessings
- *Pesukei D'Zimra* (verses of praise)
- *Shema* and its blessings
- *Shemoneh Esrei,* also known as the *Amidah*

- *Musaf* (added on *Shabbat* and during holidays)
- *Hallel* (said only on special days)
- Torah reading (on Mondays, Thursdays, *Shabbat,* and holidays)
- *Ashrei, Aleinu,* and other closing prayers, psalms, and hymns (not on *Shabbat* and holidays)

The *Mincha* is the afternoon service, which consists of the *Ashrei, Shemoneh Esrei,* and *Aleinu.* In the evening, the congregation conducts the *Ma'ariv* service. During this time, it recites the *Shema,* followed by the *Shemoneh Esrei* and the *Aleinu.*

ALERT

One of the most well-known prayers is the *Kaddish,* which is recited for a period of time after the death of a parent. However, that is not the only purpose of the *Kaddish.* In fact, it appears throughout the *Siddur* (prayer book), separating each portion of the service.

Three times each week (Monday, Thursday, and *Shabbat*) and on holidays, a portion, known as a *parshah,* is read from the Torah. On *Shabbat,* the *Haftorah* (sometimes *Haftarah,* "concluding portion"), which consists of a passage from the prophets, follows the weekly *parshah* (Torah portion). There is much ceremony connected with the reading of the Torah as it is removed from the Ark, paraded around the sanctuary, and then laid to rest on the *bimah* (pedestal, similar to an altar), where it is read.

Blessings

Remember how God chose the Jews to be a holy people? This honor came with the responsibility of making the world a holy place. What better way to demonstrate an appreciation for the world and all therein than to bless each thing and every occasion!

The word *berakhah* (blessing) comes from the Hebrew root *bet-resh-kaf,* from which the word *berech* (knee) is derived. The connection between a blessing and a knee has to do with the practice in prayer services of bending the knee and bowing when reciting a *berakhah*, a gesture that demonstrates respect.

In addition to the *birkhot* (blessings) that are contained in formal prayer services, there are blessings that are appropriate for almost every type of daily occurrence, beginning with waking in the morning and ending with going to sleep at night. *Birkhot* generally fall into one of three categories: those said before enjoying a material pleasure, such as eating or drinking (*birkhot hanehenin*); those recited before performing a *mitzvah* such as lighting candles (*birkhot ha-mitzvot*); and those said at special times and events such as seeing a rainbow or hearing thunder (*birkhot hoda'ah*).

By acquainting yourself with the numerous *birkhot* and reciting them when appropriate, you can go through each and every day adding a dimension of spirituality to your life and the world in which you live.

FACTS

All *birkhot* begin with the phrase *"barukh atah adonai, elokaynu melekh ha-olam,"* which means, "Blessed art Thou Lord, our God, King of the Universe." However, making a blessing does not mean you are blessing God. In fact, by saying a *berakhah*, you are acknowledging the wonder of God and the world God created.

Becoming a *Mavin* at the Prayer Service

You might be a Jew who would like to participate in the prayer services, but you feel uncomfortable because you are not familiar with how to conduct yourself in the service. A review of the protocol of the service will bolster your confidence. If you are not Jewish and find yourself in a synagogue service, being able to follow along and knowing the basic protocol will at least make you comfortable and hopefully enhance the service for you.

Mavin is the Yiddish word for "expert" or "knowledgeable person." While the material that follows may not make you a *mavin* at the prayer service, it should help you feel at home—which is exactly how you should feel in a Jewish house of worship!

The *Siddur*

The word *siddur* means "order" or "arrangement," and the *Siddur* is a prayer book that includes daily prayers, the liturgy of the *Shabbat* service, and special prayers for various holidays. The *Siddur* is based on a collection of prayers compiled centuries ago in an academy in Babylon. Naturally, there have been additions and amendments since then, as well as differing styles among various communities and branches of Judaism.

Since this single volume contains the prayers for all the daily services, *Shabbat,* and some festivals, make sure you know which service you are attending so you can get to the right section. Unfortunately, the sections do not always appear in the exact order in which they are recited, and you may find yourself flipping back and forth between the pages. Normally, the prayer leader will guide the congregants, but this is not always the case, particularly with the Orthodox. If you get lost, don't be afraid to ask somebody to help you find your place in the *Siddur*. After all, you're offering that person an opportunity to perform a *mitzvah*!

Some Points of Prayer Etiquette

During prayer service, you will generally be required to make three basic responses. There is the customary *amen* (translated from Hebrew

Tallit, a prayer shawl worn during prayer services

Photo courtesy of Joshua Marowitz

as "so be it"). *Amen* is an affirmation, and it should be said with intensity. Another common response takes place when someone says, *"barukh atah adonai"* ("blessed is the Lord"), and others then rejoin, *"barukh hu u'varukh shemo"* ("blessed is He and blessed is His Name"). Finally, whenever someone recites, *"barukhu et adonai ha-m'vorakh"* ("bless the Lord, the Blessed One"), the congregation responds, *"barukh adonai ha-m'vorakh l'olam va-ed"* ("blessed is the Lord, the Blessed One, forever and ever").

There's a good deal of standing during the service, so when you see the congregation rising, it's best to follow their lead. Generally, people will rise when the Ark is open, when the Torah is being carried around the room, during the *Shemoneh Esrei,* and while the *Aleinu* is recited. In any event, in most congregations the rabbi will tell you when to rise and when to sit. In those very observant congregations where this may not happen, just follow the people on either side of you!

QUESTIONS?

Do you know how to bow properly?
First, you bend the knees, then bend forward while straightening the knees, then return to the standing position. It's something like diving into a pool of water, except your arms don't move since you're holding the *Siddur*. There are specific times during the service when you are expected to bow, so don't get carried away.

Whenever there is a Torah reading, the Torah is paraded about, giving the congregants an opportunity to kiss this holy scroll. When the Torah passes, you can touch the cover with your hand, *Siddur,* or *tallit* (prayer shawl), and then kiss your hand or the object that had just touched the Torah. This action will demonstrate your reverence for the Torah, the holiest object in Judaism.

CHAPTER 8

Judaica: Religious Objects and Attire

Idolatry in any form is anathema to Judaism. However, this is not to say that Judaism is without its very own special objects, apparel, and symbols, which you will find in the synagogue as well as in Jewish homes. Many of these objects and symbols were created in order to observe *mitzvot*, while others are derived from custom and tradition.

The Torah Scrolls

The Torah scrolls, which comprise the Five Books of Moses, are kept in a cabinet known as the Holy Ark. A specially trained scribe known as a *sofer* handwrites the scrolls using a special method of handwriting with "crowns" (stylistic embellishments that look like crow's feet over the upper points of the letters). The text of the Torah includes neither vowels nor musical notes. Those who would like to read the Torah during the services must therefore become skilled in reading the script as well as knowing the appropriate chant melodies.

The scrolls themselves are parchments, prepared from the skin of a kosher animal. You will never have the opportunity to touch this parchment with your hand—if you are reading from the Torah scrolls, you must follow the text with a silver pointer called a *yad* (hand), which makes sense because the *yad* is in the shape of a hand with a pointing index finger.

SSENTIALS

Special ornaments adorning the Torah scrolls must be removed before the Torah scrolls can be read. This process of "undressing" the Torah involves removing the crowns, the *yad,* the breastplate, and the mantle. Once the Torah reading is complete and the Torah scrolls can be returned to the Ark, the Torah is "dressed" by replacing these accessories.

The Torah scrolls are read from a raised platform, known as the *bimah,* which is located in the center or at the front of the sanctuary. In Sephardic synagogues, the *bimah* is called the *teyvah* and the Holy Ark is known as the *heichal.* Once the reading is complete and the Torah has been dressed, it is returned to the Ark where other sacred objects are stored.

The Eternal Lamp and the Menorah

Just above and in front of the Ark you will find the *ner tamid* (eternal lamp). In Exodus 27:20–21, God ordained that a burning light be maintained at all times outside the curtain that conceals the Ark of the Covenant.

Because there is no similar *mitzvah* to keep a menorah, it is not always present in synagogues. The word "menorah" comes from the Hebrew word for "candelabrum." It first appears in Exodus 25 (and later in Exodus 37) in a detailed description of a seven-branched gold candelabrum fashioned by artisan Bezalel for the tabernacle in the wilderness, where the Jews who wandered in the desert prayed to God. Much later, long after the Jews entered the Promised Land, they built the Temple in Jerusalem, and priests placed the Temple Menorah there.

The modern menorahs you find in synagogues symbolize that original menorah in the Temple, but they cannot be exact replicas of the Temple Menorah (for reasons of deference). Consequently, synagogue menorahs frequently have six or eight branches (instead of seven) or, at the very least, a different design than that of the Temple Menorah.

Special Clothing for Prayer Services

There are no *mitzvot* directing you how to attire yourself for attendance at synagogue. Obviously, you should dress modestly, particularly if you attend an Orthodox synagogue—so exercise your common sense and good taste. However, commandments do exist about specific articles of clothing, like the *tefillin* and *kippot* (skullcaps), which should be worn in synagogue during prayer services.

Tefillin

Putting on *tefillin* is a *mitzvah* that appears in four different places in the written Torah, which commands: "And you shall bind them as a sign on your hand, and they shall be as frontlets between your eyes." Jews fulfill this commandment by "laying" *tefillin*. *Tefillin* consist of two cases with small pieces of parchment that contain the four portions in the Torah (Exodus 13:1–10 and 11–16; Deuteronomy 6:4–9 and 11:13–21) in which the Jews receive the commandment to wear *tefillin*. During prayer, these cases are bound on the arm and head with special leather straps.

The importance of *tefillin* in prayer services is manifested by the word itself, which is derived from the Hebrew word *tefillah* (prayer). However,

Tefillin

Photo courtesy of Joshua Marowitz

observant Jews wear *tefillin* only for morning prayer services that do not fall on the Sabbath and during major holidays like Yom Kippur.

Why not lay *tefillin* on the Sabbath? Doesn't it seem to make sense, given that *Shabbat* is such a holy day? The procedure of laying *tefillin* is so intricate that it requires a great amount of concentration. As a Jew places *tefillin* on his head, arm, and hand, his mundane preoccupations and everyday concerns dissipate, and he begins to pray with a clear head. However, this step is entirely unnecessary on *Shabbat,* when his head should already be cleared from distractions of everyday life.

ALERT

Sometimes *tefillin* is translated as "phylacteries," a word that derives from the Greek for "protection" or "fortress." However, you should generally refrain from using this term. Many Jews find it offensive because this title assumes that *tefillin* are nothing more than amulets to ward off evil spirits.

How do you go about putting on *tefillin*? You can easily find books and Web sites that provide detailed instructions with diagrams that explain the method of laying *tefillin.* It's easy enough as long as you are good at following directions. However, the best way to learn is to go to a synagogue during a weekday morning service and ask someone to teach you. You will have no problem finding an eager instructor, particularly at Orthodox *shuls,* where all men know how to do this.

Kippah or Yarmulke

A *kippah* (Hebrew) or *yarmulke* (Yiddish) is a skullcap worn by Jews in the synagogue. There are no *mitzvot* for wearing a *kippah,* but it has become a distinctly Jewish tradition. Many Jewish men, particularly the Orthodox, wear *kippah* at all times as a reminder that they are always before God and as a sign of respect to Him.

FACTS

The word *yarmulke* comes from the Tartar (via Polish). However, some rabbis believe this word is actually derived from the Aramaic *yerai malka*, "respect for the Sovereign." The word *kippah* comes from the Hebrew for "head covering."

Wearing a *kippah* during prayer is an ancient Jewish practice. During the early Middle Ages, rabbis began to instruct Jewish men not to go about bareheaded. The Reform Jews eliminated this custom entirely but later reinstated the practice of wearing *kippot* in the temple.

Women are not required to wear a *kippah*, but some congregations require married women to cover their heads. In such instances, a piece of lace is generally provided, or a woman may don a *kippah*.

Tallit and Tzitzit

Tallit is the Hebrew word for "prayer shawl." The biblical basis for wearing a *tallit* is found in Numbers 15:37–41, where God instructs Moses to tell the Children of Israel to make *tzitzit* (tassels) on each corner of the *tallit* and on the corners of their clothing. The reason for this *mitzvah* is that *tzitzit* remind the devout of God's commandments.

FACTS

The *tzitzit* are highly symbolic and are made in accordance with very specific configurations. The kabbalists engaged in all sorts of esoteric practices with the number of knots, double knots, and windings of the *tzitzit*. They counted thirty-nine windings in each fringe and derived an identical numerical value with the phrase *adonai echad* ("the Lord is one," the end of the *Shema* prayer).

The *tallit* is worn during prayer in the synagogue and at home. Wearing a *tallit* during prayer is a *mitzvah* commanded to Jewish men.

Women need not wear a *tallit,* although some congregations permit or even recommend this practice.

Traditional Dress Code

Many customs and traditions are associated with the way observant Jewish men and women dress. For example, a man must not dress as a woman nor may a woman dress as a man. Another *mitzvah,* known as *shatnez,* prohibits combining wool and linen in a piece of clothing.

Judaic Decoration

Although Jews are not commanded to "advertise" their Jewishness (except, perhaps, by wearing a *kippah* or *tzitzit*), some Jews like to demonstrate their beliefs or heritage by adorning themselves with certain symbolic objects.

The *magen david* (Star of David)

Photo courtesy of Joshua Marowitz

The most popular symbol of Judaism is the *magen david* (the six-pointed Star of David), though there exists no proof whatsoever to substantiate the fact that the *magen david* has anything to do with King David. Indeed, it is very unlikely that the *magen david* dates back all the way to biblical times.

No one can say with any certainty just when the *magen david* first appeared. By the seventeenth century, it had become a popular symbol for adorning synagogues. When the Zionist movement adopted the *magen david* as its emblem at the end of the nineteenth century, it became the universal symbol to represent Judaism and the Jewish people. Today, it is part of the flag of the modern state of Israel.

Another symbol that appears on necklaces and other jewelry is the *chai.* The *chai* consists of the two Hebrew letters, *chet* and *yud,* which make up the word for "life" or "living." The *chai's* significance has to do with the value Judaism places upon life.

The *chai* (made up of letters *chet* and *yud*)

Photo courtesy of © 2001 Brand X Pictures

A less likely choice in terms of jewelry that represents Judaism, but one that is usually found in Jewish gift shops, is the *hamesh* (or *hamsa*), an inverted hand with the thumb and pinkie pointed outward. The *hamesh* hand is also found in Arab cultures and may originally have become popular as an amulet.

The Mezuzah

Affixing a *mezuzah* on the doorpost is much more than a tradition. Indeed, this practice is mandated by the commandment found in Deuteronomy 6:4–9 (the Shema): "And thou shalt write them upon the doorposts of thy house and upon thy gates." This passage, along with a portion from Deuteronomy 11:13–21, is inscribed on a tiny scroll (the *klaf*) housed in a small case. The container is usually wooden, ceramic, or metal, and contains the letter *shin* (the first letter of *El Shaddai,* "God Almighty").

The *mezuzah*

Photo courtesy of Joshua Marowitz

Implicit in the act of affixing a *mezuzah* to the doorpost is the sentiment that the spirit of Godliness will permeate the home and all who reside therein. Furthermore, the words in the *mezuzah* resonate with the central precepts of Judaism—the unity of God, the love of God, the importance of tradition, and the transmittal of these values to one's children. Following precepts in the Talmud, some Jewish families affix a *mezuzah* to the doorpost of each room (except the bathroom and kitchen). When leaving or entering the house, many Jews will touch the *mezuzah* and then kiss the fingers that touched it.

QUESTIONS?

Do people remove the *mezuzot* when they move?
Since a *mezuzah* must be treated with reverence, you should take it with you. However, if you know that a Jewish family is moving in and that it will be treated with respect, you should leave it attached.

Religious Objects in the Jewish Home

What you find in a Jewish home depends, of course, upon how observant the family is as well as on what branch of Judaism they follow. The following list includes some common religious objects you might encounter:

- Chanukah menorah. These menorahs have nine branches and are used in celebrations of Chanukah (see Chapter 12).
- *Shabbat* candles. Families who observe the *Shabbat* light candles just before *Shabbat* commences (see Chapter 9).
- *Kiddush* cup. A wine glass or chalice used for reciting the *Kiddush* (a prayer that sanctifies the *Shabbat* or a particular holiday).
- Spice box. This object is used in the ceremony of the *Havdalah*, which marks the end of *Shabbat* (see Chapter 9).
- *Challah* cover. A cloth used to cover *challah* (special *Shabbat* bread) and other types of food, especially during holiday dinners.

Many Ashkenazic Jewish homes also have a *pushke,* a container used for collecting money in observance of the *mitzvah* of giving to charities and helping the less fortunate. Members of the family put their spare change or whatever money they can afford into the *pushke.*

Naturally, there are many articles that can contribute to a Jewish environment in your home. You can have a Bible and a *Siddur* (prayer book); books about Judaism and Jewish history, philosophy, and culture; even Jewish art and music.

CHAPTER 9

The Sabbath

Shabbat is the most important day of the week. In fact, the Jewish tradition considers *Shabbat* more sacred than Yom Kippur (the Day of Atonement). The Jews received the commandment to observe *Shabbat* in the Ten Statements, which admonishes: "Remember the sabbath day and keep it holy." This charge, a sign of the covenant between God and the Jewish people, carries with it both a blessing and a responsibility.

What *Shabbat* Means to Judaism

The word *Shabbat* comes from the Hebrew root *shin-bet-tav*, which carries the meaning of "to rest" or "cessation of labor." *Shabbat* is also sometimes referred to as "the Queen of the week" or "the Bride," in part because mystics believed the *Shechinah* ("God's Presence," a feminine word) descends each Friday night as the sun sets.

FACTS

In Judaism, the day does not begin in the middle of the night or with the sunrise, but in the evening, at sunset. Hence, *Shabbat* begins exactly eighteen minutes before sunset and ends on Saturday night, after three stars appear in the night sky (approximately forty minutes after sunset).

On the Sabbath, the seventh day of the week, Jews rest and turn their minds toward prayer and toward the home. Observant Jewish families gather at home to welcome the *Shabbat* as well as to end it the following evening. This day is central to both Judaism and the Jewish people. According to Achad Ha-Am, a Jewish writer, "More than Israel has kept the Sabbath, the Sabbath has kept Israel."

Remember and Observe

God commanded the Jews to "remember" and "to observe" *Shabbat* (Exodus 20:8 and Deuteronomy 5:12), a two-fold injunction. Halakhah and all of the *mitzvot* having to do with *Shabbat* are designed to serve this purpose.

A very important caveat is in order. Not all Jews remember and observe *Shabbat* in the same fashion. Naturally, the Orthodox assiduously follow Halakhah concerning *Shabbat* because the Sabbath occupies such a paramount position in Judaism and because it is also the holiest day on the calendar. To a large extent, much of what follows will be in the Orthodox tradition. However, the different branches of Judaism, all of which observe the Sabbath and encourage their members to do likewise, do not abide by all the interdictions. Some have even added their own unique customs.

Interdictions

As with all Jewish law, there are both prohibitions and affirmative obligations associated with *Shabbat*. The prohibitions are called the *melachah*. This term can be loosely translated to mean "work," but a more precise definition would be work that is creative or that exercises dominion over the environment. *Melachah* does not include any expenditure of energy or physical labor.

For example, flipping a light switch does not require much energy or effort, but because it is a creative act it is therefore prohibited during *Shabbat*. Walking up a flight of stairs, on the other hand, is permitted. Although it does require an expenditure of energy, it is not a creative act and does not exercise control over the environment.

There are two underlying explanations regarding the prohibition of turning on a light. The first reason has to do with the interdiction against cooking that involves heating metal. Secondly, one is forbidden to build on *Shabbat* and turning on a light switch completes (or builds) a circuit.

Working within the definition of what is prohibited on *Shabbat*, the rabbis have established thirty-nine categories of forbidden acts, which they set forth in the *Mishna*. Some of these categories are the following:

- Plowing
- Baking
- Slaughtering
- Writing ("creating" words)
- Building
- Kindling a fire
- Hitting with a hammer
- Weaving
- Tying
- Taking an object from the private domain into the public or transporting an object in the public domain for over seven feet

In addition to these enjoined activities, Jews observing *Shabbat* cannot come into contact with any instrument that could be employed for a prohibited purpose. So, for example, you should not even hold an unlit match that could be used to kindle a fire or pick up a pen that could be used to write.

QUESTIONS?

Why can't I drive a car on *Shabbat*?
Since the automobile operates by means of an internal-combustion engine necessitating the burning of gasoline, driving would violate the interdiction against kindling a fire. Second, given the distances normally traveled by car, the prohibition of transporting an object in the public domain would likely be violated.

On *Shabbat*, you can't turn on a television set (though you could turn it on before *Shabbat* and let it stay on). You can't hop in the car and go out for dinner or to see a movie; you can't even make yourself a freshly brewed cup of coffee to start the morning off! These restrictions are not meant to punish: The intent is to remove you from the mundane life. The activities in which you are expected to engage will fill the time for you and your family in an exceptional way.

Nontraditional *Shabbat* Observances

Don't be surprised to see a Jewish family that drives to a Friday night *Shabbat* service at their Reform Temple and then goes about their business on Saturday morning. Nor should you take umbrage at families who leave a Conservative synagogue following Saturday morning services and go out to a restaurant for lunch. Nor is there anything unusual with a family hiking in the woods, taking in the beauty of nature, or talking amongst themselves on an early Saturday afternoon. The important thing to note is not the differences among Jews and how they choose to observe *Shabbat* but rather the fact that *Shabbat* is held in such high esteem by all branches of Judaism.

Preparing for *Shabbat*

In preparation for *Shabbat,* the most important step to take is to prepare to receive the Divine Presence and welcome the Sabbath Queen. In other words, you need to put yourself in a "*Shabbat* state of mind." Remove all thoughts of work and everyday concerns. Look ahead toward a time of rest, study, and worship, and a time for togetherness with family, friends, and your community.

Other more practical steps include cleaning the house, setting the *Shabbat* dinner table and preparing the *Shabbat* meal, bathing, and dressing up for the occasion. These practical and spiritual preparations begin on Friday afternoon, before the holiday commences.

Greeting the *Shabbat* Queen

As the *Shabbat* begins, the mother of the family will traditionally light two candles, which represent the *mitzvot* to "remember" and "observe."

Shabbat candlesticks

Photo courtesy of © 2001 Joshua Marowitz

(Some families follow a slightly different tradition and light a candle for every person present at the table.) The candles may be of any color, but they are usually white. Unlike other blessings that take place before the act, the woman of the house first lights the candles (at least eighteen minutes before sunset) and then makes the blessing—to do otherwise would require striking a match on the Sabbath. Then, the man of the house recites the *Kiddush* over the wine.

If there is no woman of the house, it is perfectly acceptable for the man of the house to light the candles. Similarly, if there is no man to say the *Kiddush*, a woman may do this.

The family can then greet each other with the words *shabbat shalom!* (in Hebrew) or *gut shabbes!* (in Yiddish), for the Sabbath has begun. At this time, some families attend a brief *Shabbat* service *(kabbalat shabbat)* and then return home for dinner.

The *Shabbat* Dinner

The *Shabbat* dinner is an event where you can use your imagination to create the ambiance befitting the special occasion. On this day, you should use your best china and silverware; people often add a vase filled with fresh flowers and a white tablecloth. In addition to these decorative

The *Kiddush* cup

Photo courtesy of Joshua Marowitz

steps, the *Shabbat* dinner table requires a *Kiddush* cup, wine or grape juice, two *challahs* (special *Shabbat* bread loaves) with white covers, and candles.

Just before dinner, people wash their hands, and make a blessing over the *challah* (this blessing is known as the *motzi*). Another beautiful custom that may take place at the *Shabbat* dinner table is the parents blessing their children.

It is also customary to sprinkle salt over the *challah* or to dip the *challah* in salt. One explanation for this custom is that salt was a valuable commodity in Roman times and available only to a free people. Another reason has to do with the fact that ever since the destruction of the Temple, the home has become a small sanctuary with a table and altar. Given that sacrifices were offered with salt, sprinkling salt on the *challah* is a link to the times of Temple Judaism.

The only requirements for the Sabbath meal are bread and wine. Of course, the food is subject to the laws of *kashrut* and may not be cooked once the *Shabbat* begins. Traditional foods at the Ashkenazic *Shabbat* table are gefilte fish, chopped liver, chicken soup with *matzah* balls or noodles, roast chicken or brisket of beef, and noodle or potato *kugel.* Among Sephardic Jews, customary meals may consist of fish, eggplant salad, lamb roast, stuffed grape leaves, and white rice.

During dinner, conversation is open to any subject, but it is a time for the family to move beyond the perfunctory small talk that exemplifies a typical evening meal. During or after the meal, some families will sing Sabbath songs. At the meal's conclusion, the *birkat ha-mazon* (the grace after meals) is recited.

It is customary to invite a stranger, traveler, or poor person to be a guest at a *Shabbat* dinner. Another common practice is to set aside a sum of money for charity before the lighting of the Sabbath candles and the welcoming of *Shabbat.*

It is customary to eat three meals during the Sabbath. *Sholosh seudot* or *seudah shelishit* (the third meal) generally takes place in the late afternoon. While there is no *Kiddush,* hands must be washed and the *motzi* blessing recited over two loaves of *challah.* Since it is understandable that the family may not be terribly hungry at this time, a light meal is typically served.

Attending the Sabbath Services

While individual prayers and family ceremonies are important in Judaism, the community prayer is indispensable. Although much of the Sabbath is celebrated among family and friends, the opportunity to do so with your "extended family," so to speak, should not be missed. The synagogue affords an excellent setting for the Jewish community to gather together to welcome *Shabbat* and to reaffirm the covenant with God and with one another.

On the eve of *Shabbat,* the *kabbalat shabbat* service welcomes the Sabbath. It is followed by the Sabbath evening or *ma'ariv* service with additional prayers. In some synagogues, particularly those that practice Reform Judaism, the main Sabbath service may be held on Friday night. Following services, most Reform and Conservative congregations have an *oneg shabbat* (joy of the Sabbath), where refreshments are available and the congregation has the opportunity to socialize.

On Saturday, Sabbath observances continue with the morning service, which has three parts: *shacharit* (morning service), the Torah reading, and *musaf* (additional *Shabbat* prayer service). Again, following this service there is a *Kiddush* where wine and perhaps cakes and cookies are served. At this time, the family can return home to enjoy the rest of *Shabbat*.

Other Sabbath Activities

In addition to attending synagogue services on *Shabbat,* there are other activities you get involved in to bring a special dimension to this festive day. The main activities conducted during *Shabbat* revolve around praying, reading, and studying. Naturally, the congregation performs a public reading of the Torah during the Saturday morning services, but readings from the Talmud and religious discussions may follow later on that day, whether at the synagogue or at home.

FACTS

In the six Sabbaths between Passover and *Shavuot,* fathers and grandfathers traditionally engage their children in discussions of the *pirkei avot* (Wisdom of the Fathers) or portions of the Mishna.

But things need not always be so serious. Some people play games, such as chess or checkers, take family walks, or engage in other leisure activities. The point is for people to try and remove themselves from the ordinary and enter the holiness of *Shabbat*.

Separating from *Shabbat*

Shabbat ends at nightfall when three stars appear in the night sky, usually about forty minutes after sunset. At this time, the family performs the *Havdalah* (separation) ceremony.

During *Havdalah,* blessings are made over the wine, a specially woven or braided multiwick *havdalah* candle, and a box called a *bsamim,* which contains sweet-smelling spices. Each of these objects represents something.

- The wine cup is filled to the brim, expressing hope that the upcoming week will be filled with divine blessings.
- Blazing like a torch, the *havdalah* candle's flame signifies light and guidance through life.
- The spices remind the devout to make an effort to bring some of the sweetness of *Shabbat* into the coming week.

It is a wonderful idea to include children in this ceremony by having them hold the candle and the spice box. At this time, the family recites the final blessing regarding the division between the consecrated and the worldly, which reflects how the Sabbath is distinct from the other days of the week.

Judaism is unique in that its holiest day also occurs the most frequently, once every seven days. But there are other holy days and festivals on the calendar that afford a variety of opportunities to fulfill your life as well. The only other occasions that are considered nearly as consecrated as *Shabbat* are the Days of Awe, which include Rosh Hashanah and Yom Kippur.

CHAPTER 10
Rosh Hashanah and Yom Kippur

The annual cycle of Jewish holidays (outlined in Chapters 10 to 15) begins with the Days of Awe, a ten-day period that generally falls sometime in September or October. The Days of Awe begin with the celebration of Rosh Hashanah (the Jewish New Year) and end with Yom Kippur (the Day of Atonement), the most solemn and introspective day of the year.

Days of Awe

According to the Jewish tradition, every person has within him or her the capacity to do good and evil. Every day, each person faces choices between right and wrong. Judaism recognizes that people are not perfect and that they make mistakes. These mistakes may be corrected through a process known as *teshuvah* (turning or returning to God), which begins with an intense examination of one's actions and the desire and intent to strive toward being a better person.

ESSENTIALS

In the Jewish calendar, the Days of Awe are the time of the year when you can make a concerted effort to engage in *teshuvah*. In fact, this ten-day period is known as *Yamim Noraim* (Days of Repentance).

During the Days of Awe, Jews seek forgiveness for their sins, but individually they also make an effort to become better people. They are expected to seek reconciliation with other people and request forgiveness for any sins committed against them. God will only forgive sins committed against Him. If you act unjustly toward another person, you must seek that person's forgiveness.

According to tradition, God has a heavenly ledger known as *Sefer Ha-Chayyim* (The Book of Life). During the Days of Repentance, He writes down the names of those who will have a good life and those who will not, those who will live and those who will die in the ensuing year. He opens the Book of Life on Rosh Hashanah and closes it at the conclusion of Yom Kippur. Your actions during this period can alter the initial determination. Hence, in addition to *tefilah* (prayer) and performing acts of *tzedakah* (good deeds and charity), the process of *teshuvah* is very important in trying to affect your life's course over the next year.

In addition to Rosh Hashanah and Yom Kippur, other special days take place during the Days of Awe. On the third day, observant Jews participate in a minor fast known as *Tzom Gedaliah*. This fast marks the assassination of the last governor of Judea after the destruction of the First Temple. The Sabbath that occurs during the Ten Days of Repentance is known as *Shabbat Shuvah,* the Sabbath of Return. A special *Haftorah* is read, and a rather lengthy sermon about repentance is often given from the Books of the Prophets, Hosea, Micah, and Joel.

Rosh Hashanah

Rosh Hashanah (head of the year) is commonly known as the Jewish New Year. This Jewish holiday, which kicks off the Days of Awe period, commemorates the creation of the world. Most Reform Jews and Jews living in Israel celebrate Rosh Hashanah for one day, but the other branches of Judaism observe Rosh Hashanah for two days.

FACTS

Rosh Hashanah begins a new calendar year, but there are three other "new year" celebrations: *Nisan,* the month in which Passover occurs, begins the counting of the calendar months and counting the reign of kings; *Elul,* the month preceding Rosh Hashanah, is the symbolic new year for tithing animals, a form of charity; and *Tu B' Shevat,* the fifteenth day of *Shevat,* is the new year for trees.

The History of Rosh Hashanah

In the Torah, there are two distinct commandments to observe Rosh Hashanah. In Leviticus 23:24–25, it is written that on the first day of the

The *shofar*

Photo courtesy of Joshua Marowitz

seventh month, there "shall be a solemn rest unto you, a memorial proclaimed with the blast of horns, a holy convocation. . . ."

Later, in Numbers 29:1, it is proclaimed that this day shall be a "holy day," a day when Jews should not work, and a day when "the shofar is trumpeted." In fact, the Torah only refers to Rosh Hashanah as *Yom Teruah* (the day of the sounding of the *shofar*) or *Yom Ha-Zikaron* (the day of remembrance). *Yom Ha-Zikaron* is a reference to Abraham's willingness to sacrifice his only son, Isaac, in demonstration of his unswerving obedience to God.

The phrase "Rosh Hashanah" emerged much later, sometime during the Talmudic times (the first five centuries C.E.). However, the holiday itself was well established by the fourth century B.C.E., after the Babylonian exile when some Jews had returned to Jerusalem to construct the Second Temple.

Preparations for Rosh Hashanah

Given the importance of this period, preparations for the Days of Awe begin in the preceding month of Elul, when it is customary to blow the *shofar* during weekly services in synagogue.

QUESTIONS?

What is a *shofar*?
A *shofar* is a trumpet made of a ram's horn. In biblical times, blowing the *shofar* heralded important events such as holidays, the new moon, or preparation for war. It is also symbolic of Abraham's aborted sacrifice of Isaac, when a ram was offered in Isaac's stead. Today, its plaintive and evoking tone is designed to stir the heart of every Jew to repentance and toward a closer relationship with God.

It is considered a great honor to blow the *shofar,* which is no ordinary ram's horn. A special cleaning process is conducted where the ram's horn is treated and hollowed to produce three basic sounds: *teki'yah*, a single blast; *teru'ah*, a series of three short blasts; and *shevarim*, a series of nine short staccato blasts.

As the month of Elul draws to an end, there is a special *Selichot* (forgiveness) service on the Saturday night before Rosh Hashanah, when the congregation recites a series of important prayers. Around midnight, the congregation reviews the thirteen attributes of God, a ceremony that helps to prepare everyone for the approaching holy days.

During this season of the new year, it is customary to send *Shanah Tovah* (good year) cards to friends and family. You might want to get them in the mail before the holiday begins. You should also make sure that you have on hand the items and food you will need when Rosh Hashanah arrives, including the following items:

- Holiday candlesticks and candles
- Wine and decanter
- Wine cups for everyone
- Two round *challahs*
- *Challah* cover
- Holiday bread knife
- Cut or sliced apples
- Jar or dish of honey
- Flowers

Home Ceremonies and Activities

Since Rosh Hashanah is a holiday, it is customary to follow the Torah principle of *Hiddur Mitzvah,* which requires taking additional time and effort to make the ritual more beautiful and exceptional. That's why the list of things you need is similar to what you would use for the *Shabbat* dinner—including your best dishes, glassware, and fine linen. Fresh flowers are always appropriate.

FACTS

One reason the *challah* on Rosh Hashanah is round is to symbolize a crown and remind the Jewish people of the sovereignty of God. Another explanation is that the round *challah* represents the circle of life and the hope that life will continue for eternity.

Just as on *Shabbat* and other holidays, Rosh Hashanah is welcomed by the lighting of two candles, for which the mother recites two special blessings. Then, the father says the *Kiddush* and a special blessing over the wine or grape juice. The *motzi* is made over two loaves of *challah,* which are made round especially for Rosh Hashanah.

The Rosh Hashanah Dinner

Although there are no special menus designated for the Rosh Hashanah dinner, traditional meals are similar to *Shabbat* dinners and include apples and honey. Dipping apples in honey is symbolic of having a sweet new year. Honey is also spread over bread or included in recipes such as honey cakes or *tzimmes*, a sweet stew consisting of carrots, cinnamon, yams, and prunes. There is also a custom to make a brief prayer and to eat a number of symbolic foods such as carrots, leeks or cabbage, beets, dates, gourds, pomegranates, and fish.

Other Customs

Rosh Hashanah is a day of rest, and much of the time is spent in a synagogue. A popular activity undertaken during the afternoon of the first day of Rosh Hashanah is *Tashlikh* (casting off). The ritual involves walking to a body of water, reciting designated prayers, and then emptying one's pockets or tossing bread crumbs into the water, a ceremony that symbolizes casting-off sins. Should the first day of Rosh Hashanah occur on *Shabbat, Tashlikh* is postponed to the next day. As always, *Shabbat* takes precedence over any other day of the year.

FACTS

Whenever you greet a Jew during the Days of Awe, it is appropriate for you to wish them a good year. To do this you can simply say, *L'shanah tovah!* (For a good year!) Or, you can use the more formal version, *L'shanah tovah tikatevu v'taihatemu!* (May you be inscribed and sealed for a good year!)

Many people visit the graves of their loved ones during this season. While people probably have other reasons for carrying on this custom today, it likely originated with the belief that the thoughts or prayers of the deceased can intercede in heaven on behalf of the living.

Obviously, such assistance would be particularly welcome during the Days of Awe.

Synagogue Services and Liturgy

Unlike most of the holidays and festivals of the Jewish calendar, Rosh Hashanah and Yom Kippur are primarily observed in the synagogue rather than the home. The *shofar* is sounded for a total of 100 notes on each day; the extended final blast is called *teki'yah gedolah*. During these days, some married men, especially the Orthodox, put on a *kittel*, a white ankle-length robe worn over clothes to signify purity.

Three central prayers dominate the Rosh Hashanah services: *Avinu Malkeinu, Unetaneh Tokef,* and the *Musaf Amidah.* It is during the *Musaf Amidah* that the *shofar* is sounded. These prayers begin somewhat earlier in the morning and last into the early part of the afternoon. In addition to these prayers, the congregation reads a portion of the Torah. On the first day, one of the readings has to do with the birth of Isaac. On the second day, the Torah portion recounts Isaac's halted sacrifice.

Yom Kippur

Yom Kippur, the last of the Days of Awe, is observed on the tenth of *Tishri*. While *Shabbat* is the holiest of days, it is only human nature to regard Yom Kippur, which occurs only once a year as opposed to once a week, as something very special and out of the ordinary. This is why you will see some Jews, who never attend a *Shabbat* service during the rest of the year, go to synagogue on Yom Kippur.

Yom Kippur is the "Day of Atonement." It is a day to atone for the sins of the prior year. Yom Kippur is sometimes referred to as the "Sabbath of Sabbaths" and has been an integral part of Judaism for thousands of years.

Prohibitions on Yom Kippur

Almost everyone, even non-Jews, knows that Yom Kippur is a day when Jews are forbidden to eat and drink. In fact, fasting is only one of five prohibitions that must be obeyed. Following the rules governing fasting is very simple. You don't eat and you don't drink! The fast commences before sunset on the evening of Yom Kippur and ends after nightfall the next day.

There is no need to have a reason to fast. It is a *mitzvah* from God that appears in the Torah. However, many Jews need explanations to justify the practices of Judaism, and many rationales have been offered in this regard. For one, refraining from consuming food or liquid is a concrete expression of the gravity of the day. It helps each person attain the state of mind required to focus on the spiritual. Furthermore, fasting manifests a form of self-mastery over bodily needs. Another more socially conscious justification states that by fasting, people can identify more readily with the poor and the hungry. Any of these reasons, or any one that is important and meaningful to you, will do. The point is that fasting is fundamental to the observance of Yom Kippur.

Jews need to observe the *mitzvah* to fast as long as it does not pose a physical threat. Children under the age of nine and women in childbirth (that is, from the time the labor commences to three days following the birth) are absolutely not permitted to fast. Older children, not yet bar or bat mitzvah, and women from the third to the seventh day after childbirth, are permitted to fast, but should resume eating or drinking if they feel the need.

In addition to fasting, the following prohibitions apply to observing Yom Kippur:

- No washing or bathing
- No using creams and oils (a prohibition that extends to deodorants and cosmetics)
- No sexual relations
- No wearing leather shoes

One reason for not wearing leather shoes is the incongruity of deriving a benefit from the slaying of one of God's creatures while praying and beseeching God for a long life. This proscription might explain why it's not uncommon to see men wearing formal suits and canvas sneakers on Yom Kippur.

The History of Yom Kippur

The first Yom Kippur occurred at the time Moses received the Ten Statements at Mount Sinai. Returning to the base of the mountain, and upon seeing the Israelites worshiping a golden calf, Moses destroyed the original Ten Statements. Later, when Moses ascended Mount Sinai for the second time, the Israelites fasted from sunrise to sunset, praying for forgiveness. On the tenth day of Tishri, Moses returned with the second set of the Ten Statements and, having found that the Hebrews were truly repentant, announced that God had forgiven them.

Thus, in Leviticus 16:29–31, it is written that every year on the tenth day of Tishri "you must fast and do no work. . . . This is because on this day you shall have all your sins atoned. . . . It is a Sabbath of Sabbaths to you. . . . This is a law for all time."

It doesn't get any clearer than this. For thousands of years, Jews have refrained from work, have fasted, have prayed, and have done everything in their power to fulfill the obligation to honor this "Sabbath of Sabbaths."

Observances Throughout History

Over the centuries, Jews have been observing Yom Kippur in different ways. For example, in biblical times the high priest sacrificed animals as an offering to seek forgiveness for sins. Later, the high priest of the Temple atoned ritually for the sins of the Israelites by symbolically placing them on two goats—one to be sacrificed and the other sent to its death in the wilderness. It is said that this is the origin for the word "scapegoat."

Another ancient practice is the custom of *Kapparot* (atonements), which takes place on the afternoon before Yom Kippur. A live chicken is swung around one's head while a special prayer is recited. The chicken is then slaughtered and given to the poor, or a donation is made to a charity. Though not common, this practice is still performed by very observant Jews and many Sephardim (both religious and secular) living in Israel.

Today, forgiveness from God is sought through prayers of penitence and by fasting. In addition, people pursue other activities, mostly of an introspective nature, to help them accomplish *teshuvah* and lead a better life.

Preparations for Yom Kippur

On the day before Yom Kippur, the Jews recite the *viddui* (confessional) during afternoon prayers. It is customary for men to wear white at this time and during all Yom Kippur services.

Preparations are also made for the final meal before the twenty-five-hour fast, the *Seudah Ha-Mafseket*. While there are no absolute requirements concerning what you should eat or drink at this time, the meal is traditionally very similar to what is served on *Shabbat* (except that *Kiddush* is not recited).

Families traditionally light candles that will burn throughout Yom Kippur. Unlike *Shabbat* and other holidays, you should not light the candles before you eat the prefast meal. Lighting the candles symbolizes the beginning of Yom Kippur, and eating dinner after lighting the candles would violate the *mitzvah* to fast.

From a practical standpoint, it is not a bad idea to minimize the intake of salt or anything spicy that would make you thirsty the next day and to be sure to drink a good deal of water. If not for yourself, then in consideration of others, don't forget to brush your teeth!

Synagogue Services and Liturgy

The liturgy for Rosh Hashanah and particularly Yom Kippur is so extensive that a special prayer book, known as the *machzor,* exists specifically for these services. The Yom Kippur services begin in the evening, with a special pre-*Ma'ariv* service called the *Kol Nidre,* named for the prayer with which it begins. The *Kol Nidre* (all vows) prayer is chanted with a haunting melody that is likely to stir the soul of even the staunchest stoic.

The prayer itself, which is a legal formula, was written in Aramaic and renders null and void all promises that are made to God but will not be kept in the ensuing year. (However, the *Kol Nidre* does not apply to promises made to other persons.) *Kol Nidre* is also considered to be a declaration by worshipers that they should not be held liable for oaths made either in anger or under duress.

FACTS

The mood of Yom Kippur is enhanced by the prevalence of white. More observant men often wear a *kittel,* a white ankle-length robe, over their clothes. The rabbi and cantor wear white robes. The Torah scrolls are dressed in white, and the table on which the Torah is read is covered in white. Even the *parokhet* (curtains) are white.

Following the *Kol Nidre* service is the customary *Ma'ariv* evening service with a special *Amidah* confessional. The *Ma'ariv* is chanted in a melody reserved for Yom Kippur. After *Ma'ariv,* it is time to go home and prepare for the full day of prayers (without nourishment!) that lies ahead.

The *Shacharit* (morning service) is similar to most morning services held on festivals, except that extra poems are recited and the *Shacharit Amidah* includes a confessional. The congregation reads a portion of the Torah and then a *Haftorah* from Isaiah (57:14–58:14), a passage critical of those who fast without having a true understanding of the day. A special memorial prayer, called *Yizkor,* is recited for those who have lost their relatives, particularly their parents.

Then the congregation goes on to the lengthy *Musaf* service. The two high points of the *Musaf* are the *Avodah* and the *Eleh Ezkerah*. In contrast to the length of the *Musaf,* the traditional afternoon service, the *Mincha,* is the shortest on this holy day. As you can see, you can spend the entire day in synagogue, although most congregations take a break after the *Musaf* to allow families to go home and rest.

SSENTIALS

It's interesting to note that in the Yom Kippur liturgy, all sins are confessed in the plural, using "we" and "us." This is because Judaism sees the individual in terms of a greater group and holds the belief that each person should assume responsibility for the entire community.

Neilah concludes the Yom Kippur service. During the entire service, which lasts about an hour, the Ark is kept open and the congregation must remain standing—not an easy thing to do, given that you are now just about at the end of the fast. The Hebrew word *neilah* means "locked," and symbolizes the closing of the gates of heaven. *Neilah* ends with a very long blast from the *shofar*. With Yom Kippur now concluded, families hasten home for the break-the-fast meal.

CHAPTER 11

Sukkot, Shemini Atzeret, and Simchat Torah

The seven-day festival of Sukkot occurs just five days after Yom Kippur. It is followed by Shemini Atzeret and Simchat Torah. These holidays are a joyous time of celebration that include activities and observances to be carried out in a jubilant spirit, even though these are holidays laden with history and meaning.

Sukkot—the Feast of Tabernacles

The word *sukkot* is Hebrew for "booths," and Sukkot is known as the Festival of Booths or the Feast of Tabernacles. In biblical times, Sukkot was considered the most important festival and was simply referred to as *ha-chag* (the festival). Sukkot, along with Passover and Shavu'ot, are the three pilgrimage festivals known as *shalosh regalim* commanded in the Bible. During each of these festivals, the Israelites made pilgrimages to the Temple in Jerusalem. But the holiday of Sukkot has deeper origins, reaching back even beyond the days of the Temple.

ALERT

It cannot be emphasized enough that you should have a good time during Sukkot. In fact, this festival is sometimes referred to as *Zeman Simkhateinu,* or the Season of Our Rejoicing.

History of Sukkot

Sukkot has its historical roots in the time the Israelites wandered in the wilderness for forty years as punishment for refusing to enter the Promised Land after the spies delivered a deceitful report claiming the inhabitants were too fierce to be overcome. (Appropriately enough, the forty years in the desert correspond to the forty days the spies spent in Canaan.)

To help ensure that the Israelites could survive in the desert, God created "clouds of glory" around the Israelites to protect them from the harsh elements. During this period, the Israelites lived in temporary dwellings, or booths, that are represented today by the *sukkah* (singular of *sukkot,* a booth or a tent). So that the Jews would never forget this part of their history, God commanded in Leviticus 23:42–43: "You shall live in booths seven days in order that future generations may know that I made the Israelite people live in booths when I brought them out of the land of Egypt."

Historically, Sukkot is also a harvest festival, sometimes referred to as *Chag Ha-Asif* (the Festival of the Ingathering). This holiday marked the end of the harvest, when farmers completed their work and traveled to the Temple in Jerusalem with their families to celebrate and offer their gratitude for a good harvest. During this time, they resided in booths.

Meaning of Sukkot

Sukkot is subject to *mitzvot* from God that appear in the Torah. In Exodus 23:16, Torah teaches the Israelites to celebrate the festival of ingathering when they "gather in" the results of their labors. In Deuteronomy 16:13, God instructs the Israelites to celebrate the Feast of Booths for seven days after the harvest.

Furthermore, this holiday reminds the Jews of those days of wandering in the desert and how God protected them with the "clouds of glory" that enveloped the Israelites from above, below, and all around—just as the *sukkah* surrounds you when you enter it. Spending time in a *sukkah* can serve as a reminder to all Jews that everything they have, including the shelter they live in, ultimately comes from God.

Customs and Observances

As you already know, the central custom and *mitzvah* of Sukkot is to dwell in a *sukkah,* a booth or temporary structure. In constructing a *sukkah,* the Jews must follow specific requirements. However, there are exemptions to this duty. For example, if sitting inside the *sukkah* causes physical discomfort—if, for instance, it's raining heavily or you are under attack by killer bees—you do not have to remain in the *sukkah.*

Many Jews invite guests to their *sukkah,* to fulfill the *mitzvah* of hospitality (*hachnasat orechim*). In accordance with another custom, called *Ushpizin,* seven symbolic biblical guests are invited to the *sukkah* each day. These guests are Abraham, Isaac, Jacob, Joseph, Moses, Aaron, and David. Recently, some Jews have begun extending this invitation to female biblical figures—Sarah, Rachel, Rebecca, Leah, Miriam, Abigail, and Esther.

The *mitzvot* of Sukkot also require that meals be eaten inside the *sukkah;* today, this is its primary function. There is a special obligation to eat in the *sukkah* on the first night of the holiday, even if it is raining. Again, the elderly and sick, as well as mothers with small children are not required to eat meals in the *sukkah*.

FACTS

Almost all foods may be eaten inside or outside the *sukkah* during this festival. However, the following foods may only be eaten inside the *sukkah*: any product made of wheat, oat, spelt, barley, or rye, and any grape or wine product.

Another exception specifies that a bride and groom are exempt from dwelling in a *sukkah*, and that if you are traveling, you are not required to locate a *sukkah* in which to have your meals.

Before eating any food in the *sukkah*, a blessing for the holiday must be made. It is customary to visit friends and go from *sukkah* to *sukkah* and to make *Kiddush* if partaking of a festival meal. There is also a blessing to be made before sitting in the *sukkah*. And like *Shabbat*, each time you eat a meal you say a blessing for washing the hands, the *motzi* over the bread, and a special blessing when eating food made from the five grains or when drinking wine. As with all holidays, Sukkot is welcomed with the lighting of candles on the night it begins.

Building a *Sukkah*

The *sukkah* must be at least three feet high and at least twenty-six inches in length and in width. The walls cannot exceed thirty feet in height (although some sources specify that they may be as tall as forty feet). You can construct the *sukkah* from cinder blocks, lumber, canvas or nylon sheeting attached to a frame of wood, metal piping, or any other suitable material.

The rules governing the *sekhakh* (covering) are very explicit; following these rules will ensure that the *sukkah* is "kosher." Because the *sukkah* is meant to be a booth, the *sekhakh* must be temporary, and the material allowed for its construction is limited. Only organic material grown from the ground that is no longer attached to the ground can be used for the *sekhakh.* Hence, wood of all kinds such as leafy branches and evergreens are usually acceptable, while metal, plastic, and glass may not be used.

The *sekhakh* must be spaced evenly, with gaps no wider than eleven and a half inches, so that the covering is ample enough to provide shade. Furthermore, the boards or beams used should be no wider than sixteen inches, so that people inside can still see the stars at night.

If it rains, do not add more material to fill in the gaps on the *sekhakh*! Otherwise, your *sukkah* will no longer be kosher. And a light rain is no excuse. In the event of inclement weather, the obligation to spend time in the *sukkah* remains, unless it is raining heavily.

Interior Decorating

When the *sukkah* is complete, it may be decorated, and here you have greater flexibility. The Talmud includes a number of suggestions for decorating a *sukkah:* hanging carpets and tapestries, nuts and almonds, peaches and grape branches, and wreaths made from ears of corn. More contemporary decorations are fruits, Indian corn, pictures of Jerusalem and other Jewish symbols or works of art (especially those made by your own family), and New Year's greeting cards.

An Alternative *Sukkah*

Perhaps constructing a traditional *sukkah* does not seem like a good idea, or maybe you live in an apartment with no back yard. In such cases, you have other options available to you (although these options do not fulfill the *mitzvah* to construct and dwell in a *sukkah*).

You can designate an area of your home as a symbolic *sukkah* and spend time decorating and then dwelling in this space. Or, you can establish a holiday table where you can place a miniature *sukkah* as a centerpiece and add other adornments. Most Jews have access to a communal *sukkah* that they can use to fulfill this special *mitzvah*.

Synagogue Services on Sukkot

While Sukkot is best known for what goes on outside the synagogue (namely, in the *sukkah*), the services and liturgy of Sukkot are also significant—and distinctive as well.

During Sukkot, the congregation follows each morning's *Amidah* with *Hallel* (psalms of praise). Also recited during the morning services are *Hoshanot,* which are hymns that ask God for forgiveness. These hymns are known as *Hoshanot* because they all begin with the Hebrew word *hoshanu* (save us).

ESSENTIALS

Hoshanot are chanted while parading in a procession (except on *Shabbat,* when the congregants recite the *hoshanot* while standing beside their seats) and serve as a reminder of similar processions that occurred during the time of the Temple. All *Hoshanot* but one were composed by Rabbi Elazar Hakallir during the Middle Ages.

Another custom practiced on Sukkot is the reading of the biblical Book of Ecclesiastes *(Kohelet).*

The Four Species

The Four Species *(arba minim)* has to do with one of the *mitzvot* associated with Sukkot. In Leviticus 23:40, it is written that God commanded that on the first day of the festival, "you shall take the product of goodly trees, branches of palm trees, boughs of leafy trees, and willows of the brook, and you will rejoice before the Lord your God seven days."

The Four Species include an *etrog* (a member of the citrus family native to Israel that resembles a lemon), a *lulav* (a dried palm branch), *aravot* (two willow branches), and *hadasim* (three myrtle branches). The *lulav, aravot,* and *hadasim* are bound together in a specific manner and referred to collectively as the *lulav.*

The *lulav* and *etrog* come into use twice during the service. During the *Hallel* prayer, members of the congregation shake and wave the Four Species. During the *Hoshanot* processions, conducted every day of

Sukkot (except *Shabbat*), people hold the *lulav* and *etrog* in hand, shaking and waving them in all directions, actions that symbolize God's omnipresence.

On the seventh day of Sukkot, the procession makes seven circuits around the *bimah* (the pedestal where the Torah scroll is placed during Torah readings). Therefore, this last day of Sukkot is known as *Hoshanah Rabbah* (the Great *Hoshanah*).

According to the Jewish tradition, the Four Species may symbolize four types of Jews. The *etrog* has taste and smell, and stands for those who possess knowledge and good deeds; the *lulav* has taste but no smell, representing knowledge but not good deeds; the myrtle, having smell but no taste, portrays those who have good deeds but no knowledge; the willow has neither taste nor smell and represents those without either good deeds or knowledge.

Furthermore, some Jews see the Four Species as symbolizing the human body. The *lulav* denotes the spine; the *etrog* represents the heart; the willow is symbolic of lips; and the myrtle depicts the eyes. Together, they form a shape very similar to a complete person, symbolizing the unity of the Jewish People.

To prevent the willow and the myrtle from drying out, it is wise to wrap them in a damp paper towel and store them in the refrigerator. Furthermore, you should be careful that the *etrog* does not lose the tiny stem at its tip, which would make it halachically unusable. To keep the *etrog* in one piece, it is customary to store it in a decorative box with a soft lining.

Shemini Atzeret

As soon as you finish celebrating Sukkot, you are on to the next holiday. Shemini Atzeret is a day dedicated to the spiritual component of these festival days and the relationship between God and the Jews. Shemini Atzeret is the Assembly of the Eighth Day: *shemini* means "eighth," referring to the eighth and final day of Sukkot, and *atzeret* translates as "solemn assembly."

Atzeret also translates as "holding back," suggesting another dimension to Shemini Atzeret. Indeed, the day represents a holding back from ending the festival days of Sukkot. The purpose for this extension is to bring the period of Sukkot to a state of completion or perfection. This eighth day, Shemini Atzeret, is dedicated to achieve this purpose.

Historically, Shemini Atzeret was the day of sacrifices for the benefit of the People of Israel. Since the Israelites were primarily farmers in an arid land, a special prayer for rain was made on this day. As we shall see, this prayer remains part of the liturgy on Shemini Atzeret.

FACTS

Like Shavuot, which marks the closure of Pesach, Shemini Atzeret could have occurred seven weeks later. However, a *midrash* explains that rather than requiring the Israelites to travel back to Jerusalem during the rainy season, God allowed the closure of Sukkot to be observed as an added day when the weather was more favorable.

Observances of Shemini Atzeret

Since Shemini Atzeret is a festival day in its own right, traditional rituals like lighting candles, saying the *Kiddush* over the wine, and saying grace after the meal, are performed at home on the eve of the holiday.

In keeping with the festival's historical significance as a day when God's intervention is sought for a good harvest ahead, a special prayer for rain, called *Geshem,* is recited during the *Musaf* service. While chanting *Geshem,* the cantor traditionally dons a white gown and chants a melody similar to that for the Days of Awe. Shemini Atzeret is also an appropriate time for reciting the *Yizkor,* the memorial prayer for the dead.

Rejoicing in the Torah

Several times a week, the Jews read a prescribed portion of the Torah, which is divided so that the reading may be completed in a year. Simchat Torah, which follows Shemini Atzeret, is a joyous holiday that marks the juncture at which the Jews complete the cycle of Torah readings each year.

To be even more precise, Simchat Torah is the second day of Shemini Atzeret. These special days occur on the twenty-second and twenty-third of *Tishri*. However, in Israel, as with all two-day holidays except Rosh Hashanah, Shemini Atzeret is observed for one day and thus includes Simchat Torah.

Simchat Torah is the "Celebration of the Torah" or "Rejoicing of the Torah." On this day, the congregation reads the last chapters of Deuteronomy, denoting the completion of the cycle in the Reading of the Torah. However, immediately thereafter, the first chapter of Genesis is read to signify the continuing cycle of worship and to demonstrate that so far as the Torah is concerned, there is neither beginning, end, nor a time when the Jews are not engaged in the Reading of the Torah.

The honor of reading the final verses of the Torah is called *chatan Torah* (the bridegroom of the Torah). The honor of reading Genesis is called *chatan Bereshit* (the bridegroom of Genesis). Should this honor fall upon a woman, the word for "bride" would have to be substituted.

Synagogue Services on Simchat Torah

Simchat Torah is primarily celebrated in the synagogue. On the eve of the holiday, when the *Ma'ariv* service is held, the congregation reads selected verses known as *Ata Horayta* ("you have been shown"), which recount how God revealed Himself to the Israelites at Mount Sinai. Upon completion of *Ata Horayta*, everyone in the synagogue looks toward the Ark, and the Torah scrolls are then removed.

Dancing with the Torah Scrolls

At this time, every member of the congregation is afforded an opportunity to dance and parade with the Torah scrolls, an act of honor and reverence for the Torah. (In most non-Orthodox synagogues, this honor also applies to women.) This custom is accomplished by conducting seven *hakafot* (revolutions), similar to the *hoshanot* made during Sukkot. Very large congregations add *hakafot* until every member of the congregation has had the opportunity to march with the Torah scrolls.

The *hakafot* are performed with one member leading those carrying the Torah scrolls in a circuit around the synagogue. As the Torah scrolls pass, each congregant kisses the scrolls. The rabbi then leads the congregation in reciting special prayers. Once the procession is completed, the next *hakafa* begins. After services, refreshments may be served. Marking the joyous nature of the holiday, honey cake and apples are traditionally on the menu.

FACTS

In many congregations, children are invited to join in the *hakafot*. Some youngsters may carry miniature Torahs while others bear banners or flags with apples placed on the top. Following the processions, the children are often rewarded with treats.

During morning service on the following day, the congregation again performs seven *hakafot* with the Torah scrolls. Once again, everyone is afforded an opportunity to carry the Torah scrolls and participate.

Special Attention to Children

Children receive an unusual amount of attention during the Simchat Torah services because the responsibility of the Reading of the Torah will soon fall upon their shoulders and the shoulders of the generations that will follow them. Consequently, with all the parading, flag waving, honey cakes, and apples, there is much for children to enjoy on Simchat Torah.

Making *Aliyah*

The morning service also has a special *Amidah* (silent recitation) and *Hallel* (psalm of praise). Each member of the congregation (in Orthodox synagogues, each man) is then given an *aliyah,* the blessing before the Torah reading.

The last *aliyah,* which is reserved for children, is called *kol ha-ne'arim* (translates as "all the boys," though some congregations include girls in

this honor). At this time, all the children in the congregation are called up to the *bimah*. A large *tallit* is spread over the children's heads to form a canopy. Led by an adult, the children recite the blessings over the Torah.

Making *aliyah* during services

Photo courtesy of © 2001 Brand X Pictures

In some congregations, Simchat Torah is also an appropriate time for consecration services. During this time, the congregation welcomes new students to the synagogue's religious school. Generally, the youngsters receive a blessing from the rabbi and perhaps a gift, like a small prayer book or miniature Torah scroll.

ALERT

Kol ha-ne'arim is reserved for children only, meaning anyone under the age of thirteen. Children who are bar or bat mitzvah are considered adults and are entitled to their very own *aliyah;* they should not participate in *kol ha-ne'arim.*

CHAPTER 12

Chanukah: the Festival of Lights

Though a minor festival in Judaism, Chanukah is replete with religious significance, historical facts, and the type of drama to make an average Hollywood movie seem uneventful in comparison. This chapter investigates the story behind this holiday of miracles and examines the Jewish traditions associated with it.

The Story of Chanukah

The story of Chanukah is a combination of fact and legend, with a little miracle thrown in. To understand the circumstances in which this story took place, a brief history lesson will be helpful.

Historical Background

After the death of King Solomon, the kingdom of Israel split in half: Israel (consisting of the Ten Tribes) and Judah (comprised of the tribes of Judah and Benjamin). Near the end of the First Temple Era, the Assyrians conquered Israel, and the Ten Tribes were dispersed (hence the phrase "the Ten Lost Tribes of Israel"). Later, in 586 B.C.E., Babylon conquered the kingdom of Judah and destroyed the First Temple.

FACTS

In Hebrew, "Judah" is *Yehudah,* so the people of Judah were called *Yehudim.* The Greeks used the word *Iudea;* later, when the Romans replaced the Greeks in control of that part of the world, they changed *Iudea* to *Judea.* Thus, the people became known as Judeans and their religion as Judaism.

After the Babylonian exile, many Jews returned to Judea and rebuilt the Temple. In their absence, the region had come under the control of the Persian Empire, but this did not last for long. In 338 B.C.E., Philip of Macedonia successfully invaded Greece. Two years later, after the death of Philip, his son, Alexander the Great, conquered territories from Macedonia and Greece and across the Persian Empire, including Egypt and Israel.

The Jews did not resist the army of Alexander when it arrived in Jerusalem. Alexander was a benevolent ruler who attempted to create a universal culture that blended Greek religions and Eastern philosophy. This culture, known as Hellenism, soon made its presence felt in the hills of Judea.

Hellenism: Jew Versus Jew

Many Jews eagerly embraced Hellenism, which permeated many levels of the Jewish community. To these Jews, known as the Hellenists, Greek culture represented the future and success. Many of them spoke Greek, especially those in the higher classes, and even translated the Hebrew Bible into Greek. Furthermore, they abandoned some aspects of Judaism by claiming that only the written Torah, not the Oral Law, need be followed.

On the other hand, many Jews saw Hellenism as anathema. While acknowledging the beauty and accomplishments of Greek religion and culture, the Jews who rejected Hellenism believed Greek values to be superficial and inconsistent with Judaism. Consequently, they argued, Judaism and Hellenism were mutually exclusive.

A schism developed within the Jewish population that pitted these two rival camps against one another. Eventually, the Hellenists became known as the Sadducees, while the reactionary rabbis and priests became known as the Pharisees (as you might remember from Chapter 2). The Sadducees wielded power and money to gain influence with the Greek rulers. Ultimately, they secured control of the position of high priest and the *Sanhedrin* (the highest Jewish court).

Fertile Soil for Rebellion

When Alexander the Great died, his empire was divided among his generals: Antigonus, Seleucus, and Ptolemy. Ptolemy and his successors, who were proponents of Hellenism, ruled Egypt and Israel. However, the Ptolemaic dynasty was relatively weak. In 199 B.C.E., Israel came under the control of the Seleucid dynasty. The new government issued decrees that limited the practice of Judaism, including prohibitions on Sabbath observance, the study of the Torah, and male circumcisions. Violations of these laws were punishable by death. In addition, symbols of the Greek religion and its gods were placed inside the Temple.

In 167 B.C.E., the Greek king Antiochus IV undertook even harsher actions in an attempt to force the Jews to officially adopt Greek practices. His edicts included the banning of all practice of Judaism, the placement of a Hellenist (a Sadducee) in control of the Temple, desecration of the Temple by requiring the sacrifice of pigs on the altar, and killing those who refused to obey.

The time was ripe for rebellion. The only question was when the kindling would ignite and burst into flames.

The Maccabean Rebellion

Mattityahu (Mattathias) was an elder and religious leader of the distinguished Hasmonean family who lived in Modiin when the Greek army arrived to establish a religious altar. Mattityahu received an order to offer a sacrifice to a pagan god, but he refused. Before another Jew, a Hellenist, could carry out this task, Mattityahu killed him. Turning his fury upon the Greeks, Mattityahu attacked the soldiers, but the first drop of blood spilled in this rebellion for religious freedom was that of a Jew at the hands of another Jew.

FACTS

Mattityahu and his five sons became known as the Maccabees, which in Hebrew means "men who are as strong as hammers." Though much smaller than the mighty Greek armies, the Jewish forces under the command of Judah Maccabee ultimately triumphed. On the twenty-fifth day of Kislev (the first day of Chanukah), the Maccabees reclaimed the Temple. It was a victory of the oppressed over the oppressors.

The Chanukah Miracle

When the Jewish forces recaptured the Temple Mount, they wanted to rededicate the Temple. (In fact, *Chanukah* is the Hebrew word for "dedication.") Part of the rededication ceremony required lighting the Temple Menorah, but the Jews could find nothing more than a small quantity of suitable oil, enough to last for one day.

The day after the battle for the Temple Mount, a rider was dispatched to Mount Ephraim, where olive trees grew that provided the oil for the Menorah. It would take three days to reach his destination and three days to return, plus the day needed to press the oil. Meanwhile, there was no way the oil found in the Temple would last that long—but it did. The small quantity of oil burned for eight days, until the messenger returned with new oil suitable for the Menorah.

ESSENTIALS

Chanukah celebrates the miracle of the oil, not the political victory of the Maccabees, who did not regain other land or political independence. The Maccabean Revolt was fought over religious freedom—not over land or political sovereignty.

Interestingly enough, the episode of the oil that burned for eight days is not even mentioned in the Book of the Maccabees. Instead, the narrative of the miracle of the oil is recounted in the Talmud. While some believe that the miracle was God's work, there are those who feel that it is merely a lovely legend.

The Meaning of Chanukah

The religious leaders, consisting of judges and rabbis who comprised the *Sanhedrin,* realized at once that something very important had occurred when the Jews reclaimed the Temple Mount. They began Chanukah celebrations the very next year. However, it apparently remained a minor holiday. In the Mishna that was compiled several hundred years after the event, there is little reference to Chanukah, perhaps because it was written at a time when Rome governed Jerusalem and rebellions were not tolerated. This point also supports the contention that the rabbis added the miracle of the oil in the Talmud to emphasize God's involvement and discourage political activism.

FACTS

It was not until the first century of the Common Era that the Jewish historian Josephus retold the Chanukah story, which subsequently became popular in the Middle Ages. Indeed, it was Josephus who first referred to Chanukah as "the feast of lights."

Regardless of how the Chanukah story made its way down through the ages or how much is fact (and there is indeed much fact) or legend or even fiction, Chanukah is imbued with a great deal of meaning on a number of levels.

Religious Significance of Chanukah

Clearly, Chanukah is a religious holiday that celebrates the rededication of the Temple and thanks God with praises, study, and the lighting of the Menorah. Chanukah commemorates a battle for religious liberty, the freedom to practice Judaism. Numerous scholars, rabbis, and historians have postulated that Chanukah was the first organized rebellion ever undertaken for the sole sake of religious freedom.

The Jews strove for the freedom to worship God, and it appears that He helped them in their endeavor. After all, how else could such a tiny, ill-equipped, poorly trained force led by a family of priests overcome the awesome might of the Greek Empire? Then there is the matter of the miracle of the lights. How is it possible for an amount of oil that could scarcely last for one day to keep the Temple Menorah illuminated for eight days?

Some have suggested that the Maccabee rebellion was motivated by the desire to regain land, but nothing could be further from the truth. The Maccabees belonged to the Hasmonean family of priests. Since priests could not own land, there could have been no land for the Maccabees to reclaim!

The Chanukah Menorah

The most significant rite of Chanukah is the lighting of the menorah, a ceremony performed in memory of the Menorah used in the Temple. The Chanukah menorah, also called *Chanukiah,* has spaces for eight candles all in a row, plus an additional ninth space above the other branches. This last space houses the *shamash* (the "servant" candle). Any other type of candelabrum (including electrical ones) is not kosher for this holiday.

How to Light the *Chanukiah*

The Chanukah menorah

Photo courtesy of Joshua Marowitz

Two blessings are recited each night of Chanukah. An additional blessing, the *Sheheheyanu*, is recited on the first night, and there is a specific order for lighting Chanukah candles. On the first night, you light one candle at the far right of the menorah. (On each subsequent night, an additional candle is set to the left of the candles lit the previous night.) Then you light the *shamash* and use it to light the other candles, going from left to right. When all the candles are burning, you return the *shamash* to its holder.

QUESTIONS?

Who lights the Chanukah menorah?
Everyone in the home should light the menorah, though a married woman may be included in her husband's lighting since they are viewed as an inseparable unit (just as the woman lights *Shabbat* candles on behalf of the entire family). Ideally, every person has his or her own menorah.

You may wonder why you light the candles from left to right, or why you don't start with eight candles and remove one for each night. If you have these thoughts, you are in good company. In fact, a famous debate over this topic occurred between the schools of two esteemed sages, Hillel and Shamai. The House of Shamai proposed that eight candles be lit on the first night, with one removed on each subsequent night, while the House of Hillel believed in just the opposite, saying that as we increase the light, we increase the holiness in the world. As you can see, the House of Hillel prevailed. As to why the candles are lit from left to right—well, it's to honor the newest candle first.

Part of the purpose of lighting the Chanukah menorah is to publicize the miracle of Chanukah and share it with the world. Therefore, it is customary for menorahs to be placed in front of a visible window or even set outside the front door. In Israel, some homes are constructed with cut-outs in the wall next to the front door for the Chanukah menorah to be displayed.

ALERT

Since Chanukah is eight days long, the holiday encompasses at least one *Shabbat*. Do not light the Chanukah menorah after the *Shabbat* candles since that would violate the *mitzvot* of *Shabbat*. Recite the blessings, light the Chanukah menorah, and then light the *Shabbat* candles.

Gifts, Games, *Gelt*, and More!

Following the lighting of the menorah, families sing songs that celebrate the Chanukah story. Perhaps the most well known of these songs is *Ma'oz Tzur,* or "Rock of Ages" (literally translated as "Mighty Rock").

Celebrating
Chanukah

Photo courtesy of © 2001 Brand X Pictures

At this time, children receive Chanukah *gelt* (a Yiddish term for "money") or candy money. Giving other types of gifts, often one on each night of the festival, is a relatively new tradition practiced by American Jews, a likely reaction to Christmas celebrations, which occur about the same time of the year.

Popular food dishes that appear during Chanukah are *latkes* (potato pancakes) and *sufganiot* (fried jelly doughnuts), fried in oil as a reminder of the miracle of the oil that lasted for eight days.

Gambling Allowed

During Chanukah, people also play the dreidel game, gambling with pennies, candy coins, or other small stakes, since children love to participate. The dreidel is a four-sided spinning top, and each side contains a Hebrew letter:

The dreidel

Photo courtesy of Joshua Marowitz

- נ *(nun)* for *nes*
- ג *(gimmel)* for *gadol*
- ה *(heh)* for *hayah*
- ש *(shin)* for *sham*

Together, these four words make up the phrase *nes gadol hayah sham* (a great miracle happened there). In Israel, dreidels substitute the Hebrew letter פ *(pei)* in place of *shin,* because *pei* denotes *po* (here). Another way of looking at these letters is that they stand for the Yiddish words *nit* (nothing), *gantz* (all), *halb* (half), and *shtell* (put), which are the rules of the game and determine what happens to the "pot" after a person spins the dreidel.

FACTS

According to *Kabbalah,* there is a deeper esoteric meaning to the four letters on the dreidel. The dreidel itself symbolizes Jewish history, and the four letters represent the four empires that tried to destroy the Jews: Babylon, Persia, Greece, and Rome.

Chanukah Services

Despite its religious implications, Chanukah is not very high on the list of religious holidays. Most of the observances are conducted in the home, yet Chanukah does make its presence known in the synagogue.

During morning services, the congregation recites *Hallel* (psalms of praise) and the special *Al Hanisim* ("for the miracles") prayer. The Torah portions read during Chanukah are taken from the Book of Numbers (from 7:1–8:4) and relate the story of rededication. On the *Shabbat* that falls during Chanukah, a special *Haftorah* is read from Zechariah 2:14–4:7. If the festival includes two *Shabbats*, the second *Haftorah* is Kings I 7:40–50. Some congregations add readings from the Book of the Maccabees or other works that express Chanukah themes.

ESSENTIALS

The reading from Zechariah 4:6 contains the following phrase that so fittingly reflects the Chanukah motif: "Not by might, not by power, but by My spirit says the Lord of Hosts."

CHAPTER 13
Celebrating Purim

The festival of Purim is a happy occasion. It's celebrated with more fun and frolic than during any other Jewish holiday. Purim commemorates a historical episode packed with court intrigue, convoluted plots, revelry and insobriety, a cast of characters possessed of every human trait from treachery to jealousy to courage, the near annihilation of the Jewish population, and, finally, its deliverance at the hands of a beautiful damsel.

The Story of Purim

The events recounted in the Purim narrative may or may not be authentic. Some scholars hold that Purim is a carryover from a pagan carnival held during the Babylonian New Year celebration. The carnival was an occasion filled with dancing and merrymaking, and many Jews could not restrain themselves from joining in the merriment. Realizing that any prohibition to participate would be fruitless, the rabbis added a Jewish flavor to the affair and rewrote it as the Esther-Mordecai-Haman legend.

FACTS

Some secular scholars have posited the possibility that the Purim story may have another historical basis apart from what is recounted in the Book of Esther. There might have been an attempt to murder the Jewish population during the reign of Xerxes (485–465 B.C.E.) or Artaxerxes II (403–358 B.C.E.).

However, such conjectures are no more or less likely than the possibility that the story of Purim (or some variation thereof) did in fact occur. Either way, Purim has become an integral part of the Jewish tradition. The way Jews have been observing Purim for more than two millennia is just as important as whether the historical event took place.

The Plot Develops

The tale of Purim unfolds 2,500 years ago, after the destruction of the First Temple, when the Jews lived in exile in Babylon. The court of Ahasuerus, the king of Persia, celebrated the expansion of the Babylonian empire with a six-month feast. Although the Jewish rabbis forbade the Jews from participating, most Jews joined in the festivities. During one of the many feasts, the tipsy Ahasuerus sent for his queen, Vashti, to appear at the party. For whatever reason—one version has it that she was too modest to dance in front of the king and his company, while another suggests she was vain and didn't want to appear because of a blemish on her face—Vashti refused to oblige the king. The refusal cost Vashti her life.

Seeking a new queen, Ahasuerus staged a beauty contest, and picked Esther as a winner. Following the advice of her uncle and guardian, Mordecai, Esther kept her Jewish identity to herself and married King Ahasuerus. Soon thereafter, Mordecai uncovered a plot to assassinate King Ahasuerus and thwarted the conspiracy, but he was not rewarded.

Esther's real Hebrew name was *Hadassah*. The Persians at the King's court called her Esther, comparing her to the divinity known as Ishtar/Astarte/Easter, who personified beauty to the Persians. Another possibility is that the word "Esther" came from the Hebrew root that means "hidden," which is a major motif of the Purim story.

Meanwhile, an ambitious and ruthless advisor named Haman steps into the spotlight when King Ahasuerus appoints him chief minister. Haman issues a proclamation that all must bow before him, and he wears an idol around his neck to bolster the legitimacy of this edict. When Mordecai refuses to prostrate himself before Haman (because Jews are forbidden to bow to any person or icon), he incurs Haman's enmity. The best way to dispose of Mordecai, Haman concludes, is to get rid of both him and his entire race. Convincing Ahasuerus that the Jews are a strange and separate people and that they pose an internal threat, Haman obtains the king's permission to have them slaughtered.

The king issues a secret decree that authorizes the populace to rise up and murder the Jewish population. The day of the genocide is established by the casting of lots *(purim),* and it is set as the thirteenth day of *Adar.* Everything is in place for the massacre of Persia's Jews.

The Plot Thickens

When Mordecai learns of his people's fate, he goes to Esther to tell her she must plead their case to Ahasuerus. After some vacillation, Esther agrees. However, to approach the king uninvited is a dangerous mission, so Esther fasts and prays for three days.

Esther then pays a visit to the king. She invites both Ahasuerus and Haman to a special banquet. Haman construes the invitation as a sign of royal favor. Sure of his power, and thinking that revenge is close at hand, Haman orders that gallows be erected upon which he will hang Mordecai.

Meanwhile, King Ahasuerus remembers the time that Mordecai revealed the assassination plot. He also learns that Mordecai was never rewarded. At the banquet, Ahasuerus asks Haman how a man who saved the king's life should be compensated. Haman, thinking the king is referring to no one other than himself, suggests lavish gifts and honors. The king agrees, and Haman discovers that he must carry out the king's orders and reward Mordecai.

Then Ahasuerus asks Esther what she would like from him. Her response is to spare her life and the lives of her people. The perplexed sovereign asks what could his beloved queen possibly be talking about? Esther explains that the royal edict, which calls for the death of the Jewish people, also calls for her death because she is a Jew.

Deliverance

Ahasuerus is furious with Haman, and, ironically enough, he orders that Haman and his sons be hanged on the very same gallows Haman had erected for Mordecai. Mordecai is appointed to Haman's former position of chief minister and sets out to find a way to thwart Haman's plot. Although the original decree cannot be rescinded, the king authorizes Mordecai to send out another decree that allows the Jews to defend themselves.

FACTS

In cities that were enclosed by a wall, such as Jerusalem, Purim is celebrated a day later. According to the Book of Esther, the Jews of Shushan (an enclosed city) fought for an extra day, and did not celebrate until a day later.

On the day of the attack, those who choose to rise up against the Jews are met with fierce resistance. The mobs are vanquished, and the

Jews prevail—what would have been a day of tragedy in Jewish history instead turns into a day of jubilation. The next day, the Jews rejoice and celebrate their deliverance.

Purim in the Synagogue

Purim marks the deliverance of the entire Jewish community that lived in Persia 2,500 years ago. It is fitting, therefore, that it be celebrated as a community. Hence, the focus of this holiday lies in the synagogue.

On Purim, many people arrive at the synagogue in costume or participate in a Purim parade or carnival held at the synagogue. Most often, people dress in costumes representing one of the characters in the Purim story, but contemporary political and historical figures appear as well.

Pre-Purim Observances

The Sabbath preceding the month of *Adar* is a special Sabbath called *Shabbat Shekalim* (the *Shabbat* of shekels, or money). On this Sabbath, the service includes a special reading of an additional Torah portion dedicated to *tzedakah,* giving to charity (Exodus 30:11–16), and a special *Haftorah* reading from II Kings 11:17–12:17, which deals with collection of money for repairs to the Temple.

The Sabbath immediately before Purim is called *Shabbat Zachor,* the Sabbath of Remembrance. The Torah portion read on *Shabbat Zachor* recounts the Exodus from Egypt and how the Hebrews were attacked by Amalek (the grandson of Esau) just after they emerged from the parted Red Sea. The *Haftorah* for this day, I Samuel 15:1–34, relates how King Saul spared the life of Agag, the sovereign of the nation of Amalek. For this act of mercy, Saul was severely criticized by the Prophet Samuel, who took it upon himself to kill the Amalek king. However, before Samuel took Agag's life, King Agag sired a child, one of whose descendants would turn out to be Haman!

The day before Purim, the thirteenth of *Adar* (when the Jews fought the hordes determined to exterminate them), the Jews observe the Fast of Esther, which commemorates her three-day fast before walking in unannounced to meet King Ahasuerus. Like all days of fasting, other than Yom Kippur and Tisha B'Av, the fast lasts from dawn until nightfall.

Synagogue Observances on Purim

On Purim, each congregation hears the reading of the Book of Esther, commonly referred to as the Megillah ("scroll"). The text was edited between the fifth and fourth centuries B.C.E. by the Men of the Great Assembly, of which Mordecai was a member. It is believed the Megillah is largely based on letters written by Mordecai and Esther.

Although the Book of Esther is usually called the Megillah, in fact it is one of five *megillot* that are read on different holidays. In addition to the Book of Esther, the *megillot* include the Song of Songs (read on Passover), the Book of Ruth (Shavuot), Lamentations (Tisha B'Av), and Ecclesiastes (Sukkot).

The Megillah is chanted with its own melody. During the reading, it is customary to boo, hiss, or rattle noisemakers each time the reader says the name of Haman. The purpose of this practice, called "banging Haman," is to blot out Haman's name.

The Purim Parades

After the reading of the Megillah, many synagogues organize Purim parades or stage humorous plays called *Purimspiels*. Anything goes in such plays—and the sillier the better! Children enjoy these activities, especially after having sat through the lengthy reading of the Megillah.

Why do people dress in costumes on Purim?
While there are several explanations for dressing in disguises or costumes, the best answer is perhaps that this custom recalls how God saved the Jews while remaining hidden. Dressing in disguises and costumes reminds us how, acting behind the scenes, God delivered the Jews from annihilation.

The Hidden Face of God

Perhaps the most noteworthy point about the Book of Esther is that, unlike any other great Jewish tome, it never mentions God—not even once! As you might recall, "Esther" shares a root with the Hebrew word for "hidden." Even though God remains hidden in the story of Purim, it is believed that He engineered the events that the story describes. In Hebrew, the "hidden face of God" is called *hester panim,* a concept that Purim celebrates. Although it may appear that humans control their own destinies, God is the architect of all that goes on, controlling events in ways that are not often apparent.

FACTS

Other occasions when the Jews have been delivered from mass destruction sometimes get the title *Purim Katan* (small Purim). One well-known *Purim Katan* was the Wintz Purim of 1614, when the Jews of Frankfurt-am-Main were driven from the city by a mob led by Wintz Fettmilch. When the emperor intervened, the Jews were allowed to return to their homes.

The Power of the Individual

Another way of looking at Purim, not necessarily inconsistent with the notion that God controls events from behind the scenes, is that Purim is a story of survival. It exemplifies the human capacity to change history and events. When Mordecai learns of Haman's plot and the king's decree, he immediately takes action and approaches Esther. Despite her fears, Esther gathers her strength and courage, fortifying herself by fasting and praying to God. In the end, her actions save her people.

Mordecai and Esther performed boldly. They prayed to God and fasted, but they also took action. Moreover, while the entire Jewish community worshiped and fasted, repenting their previous participation in the festivals that had been forbidden by the rabbis, when the mobs rose against them, they fought for their lives and prevailed. Esther, Mordecai, and their fellow Jews serve as models that modern Jews can certainly strive to emulate if and when we should ever find ourselves in similar circumstances.

Purim Customs and Traditions

In addition to services performed in the synagogue, Jews observe a number of traditions and customs during the Purim holiday. Though practices vary, the common thread woven through all of them is the emphasis on the celebration of Purim as a day to rejoice and commemorate the deliverance of the Jews from the hands of Haman. Although no formal ruling prohibits work on Purim, Jews do try to take the day off in order to fully observe the holiday.

A Day to Imbibe

On Purim, it is a *mitzvah* to eat, drink, and be merry. In fact, tradition encourages Purim partiers to keep drinking until they can no longer distinguish between "blessed be Mordecai" and "cursed be Haman"! Of course, nobody needs to drink so much as to become seriously ill or violate other *mitzvot,* but otherwise, feel free to imbibe the finest kosher wine or Maccabee beer, and know you are carrying out a *mitzvah*. And although it is not officially a *mitzvah* yet, be sure to find a designated driver!

Holiday Food

Many Jewish holidays boast special and sumptuous foods prepared for a particular historical or symbolic reason, and in this regard Purim is no different. A festive meal is appropriate at dinnertime following evening synagogue services, and another one the following day, after the morning service. However, the primary holiday meal is served late in the afternoon after *Mincha* (the afternoon service). This meal is called the *Purim Seudah*. At this meal, observant Jews should eat bread and at least one cooked food, drink at least one cup of wine, and dine on anything else they desire.

Hamentaschen, traditional Purim pastries

Photo courtesy of Joshua Marowitz

The traditional food eaten on Purim is a delightful pastry called *hamentaschen* (Yiddish for "Haman's pockets") or *oznei Haman* (Hebrew for "Haman's ears"). These pastries are triangular cookies that are usually filled with fruit jam or poppy seeds. The three-corner shape of these cookies represents the type of hat Haman is said to have worn, or perhaps his funny-shaped ears.

Performing *Tzedakah*

As you already know, *tzedakah* is an integral part of Judaism. Several *tzedakah* traditions are practiced specifically during Purim. For instance, a special *mitzvah* originates from a passage in the Megillah, which quotes Mordecai's declaration that Purim is a time "of feasting and gladness and of sending food to one another, as well as gifts to the poor."

As a result, it is now a Purim tradition to send baskets or packages of food to friends and relatives. These packages of food are called *mishloach manot* in Hebrew and *Shalach-manos* in Yiddish (in both cases, a literal translation is "sending out portions"). These packages may be as simple or as elegant as you wish, but they must contain at least two different types of food that are prepared and ready to be eaten.

Mordecai also instituted the practice of *Matanot L'evyonim* (gifts for those in need), which requires making gifts to the poor and donations to charitable organizations. In fact, you should give charity to anyone who asks, with the hope that God will act likewise in responding to your prayers.

CHAPTER 14

Passover: a Story of Liberation

Passover celebrates the Exodus of the Jews from Egypt, perhaps the most pre-eminent event in Jewish history. Passover's essential message is one of freedom in every connotation—not only freedom from slavery but also freedom to think, believe, and pray as one chooses. Today, Passover remains the most widely observed Jewish holiday.

The Background of the Story of Passover

The Passover narrative is recounted in Exodus, the second book of the Torah. It begins with the death of Joseph and the appearance of a new pharaoh in Egypt. However, to fully appreciate the events, it is important to know more about Joseph and exactly how the Israelites came to be a nation of slaves in Egypt.

ESSENTIALS

The Hebrew word for Passover is *Pesach,* derived from the Hebrew root *peh-samech-chet,* which means to pass through or over, or to spare. The holiday has other less commonly employed names as well: *Hag Ha-Aviv* (the holiday of spring), *Hag Ha-Matzot* (the holiday of unleavened bread), and *Z'man Heiruteinu* (the season of our liberation).

Joseph's Story

This is not the place to do justice to the saga of Joseph, son of Jacob (also called Israel) and great grandson of Abraham. But a summary of Joseph's extraordinary adventures is important. Without these occurrences, the Israelites never would have found themselves in Egypt in the first place.

Jacob had twelve sons (hence the twelve tribes of Israel), and Joseph was his favorite. His brothers were jealous, but Joseph did nothing to assuage this jealousy and made it worse by doing such things as preening about in his "coat of many colors," a special present from his father. As a result, his brothers sold him into slavery, telling Jacob that a wild animal killed Joseph.

Eventually, Joseph became a favored servant to a wealthy Egyptian family. When he rejected the licentious advances from his master's wife, she accused Joseph of attacking her, and Joseph found himself in prison. While incarcerated, Joseph earned a reputation as an interpreter of dreams. This talent came in very handy when Joseph was summoned to explicate Pharaoh's dreams. Joseph successfully deciphered the dreams, predicting a great famine and advising Pharaoh how to prepare for it.

When Joseph's prophecy proved true, Pharaoh was grateful and Joseph was catapulted to a position of great authority in Egypt.

Israel Comes to Egypt

Meanwhile, the famine ravaged Canaan, and Jacob dispatched his sons to Egypt to buy grain. When they reached their destination, the person in charge of the grain supplies turned out to be none other than their brother Joseph! At first, the brothers did not recognize Joseph, but when Joseph concluded that his brothers were truly repentant for what they had done to him, he revealed himself and an emotional family reunion followed.

Upon hearing that his father, Jacob, was still living, Joseph instructed his brothers to bring him to Egypt. Naturally, Jacob was thrilled to hear that his favorite son was alive. Jacob's entire family gathered all their belongings and made the journey into Egypt, settling in a district known as Goshen.

FACTS

When Jacob and his clan entered Egypt, they numbered seventy men and women. Since Jacob was also called Israel, his descendants referred to themselves as the Children of Israel. In time, these people became a mighty nation. It was their dramatic population growth that would prove extremely perilous to them in later years.

The Passover Narrative

Though they thrived, the Israelites remained a separate people. They maintained their identity largely by speaking their own language, wearing distinctive clothing, using Semitic names for their children, and not inter-marrying.

Once Joseph died, however, the Israelites fell out of favor with the pharaoh. Their growing numbers threatened the power structure in Egypt. Things no longer boded well for the Israelites.

Slaves in Egypt

In an effort to keep the Israelite population in check, the Egyptians enslaved the Hebrews, assigning them harsh work under cruel conditions. Things became even more precarious when Pharaoh was informed by astrologers that an Israelite male child born at that time would grow up to overthrow him. As a result, Pharaoh decreed that every Israelite male newborn be drowned in the Nile River.

Not willing to accept the decree as a *fait accompli*, Amram and Yochebed placed their baby boy in a basket and floated him down the Nile. The boy's sister, Miriam, followed the basket at a safe distance. She saw Pharaoh's daughter, Bityah, find the basket and lift it from the river. Bityah called the baby boy Moses because he was drawn from the Nile.

Moses and the Exodus

Moses grew up as a prince in Pharaoh's palace. One day, he saw an Egyptian overseer striking a Hebrew slave. When the overseer would not stop the beating, Moses killed him. Fearing for his life, Moses fled to Midian, where he married Tziporah, the daughter of Jethro, a Midianite priest. Moses became a shepherd and was content with his life until one day, when he was tending to his flock he came upon a burning bush that was not consumed by the flames. It was then that God spoke to Moses, instructing His reluctant emissary to go into Egypt and tell Pharaoh to let the Israelites leave.

Along with his brother Aaron, Moses conveyed God's demand to Pharaoh, but Pharaoh was angered and only made things worse for the Hebrews. To demonstrate the power of God, ten plagues were visited upon the Egyptians:

1. Blood
2. Frogs
3. Lice
4. Wild beasts
5. Pestilence
6. Boils
7. Hail
8. Locusts
9. Darkness
10. Slaying of the firstborn

Before subjecting the Egyptians to the final plague, the slaying of the firstborn males, God directed Moses to instruct each Israelite family to slaughter an unblemished lamb before sundown. They were to smear the blood of the lamb on doorposts and thresholds and then prepare the lamb for their dinner.

During this meal, the original *seder,* the Israelites ate the roasted lamb, unleavened bread (because there was not sufficient time for the dough to rise), and maror (bitter herbs). While they recounted the many miracles God had performed for them, God passed through Egypt, slaying every firstborn male. Because the Israelites' houses marked with the smeared blood of the sacrificial lamb were passed over, the holiday that celebrates the Jews' eventual liberation from Egypt is known as Passover.

Into Freedom

The following day, Pharaoh ordered the Israelites to immediately leave Egypt. Under the leadership of Moses, somewhere between two and three million Israelites departed from Egypt. Indeed, the Israelites were a prolific people!

FACTS

Many scholars believe that Ramses II (1300–1234 or 1347–1280 B.C.E.) was the Pharaoh who enslaved the Israelites. Ramses was known for his deployment of slave labor to construct his building projects. However, it is likely that the enslaver was Ramses's son, Merneptah, who was the pharaoh at the time of the plagues and the exodus of the Israelites from Egypt.

Pharaoh soon regretted his decision. He sent his army to pursue the Israelites, catching up with them at the Sea of Reeds (also known as the Red Sea). With the sea directly ahead of them and Pharaoh's mighty army at their backs, the Israelites were trapped, but God parted the water and allowed the Israelites to pass through. When the Egyptian army pursued, the water fell back and they all drowned. Gathered together, Israelites sang songs of praises to their God (Exodus 15:1–20).

The Israelites encountered more challenges before they reached Mount Sinai, where God gave Moses the 613 *mitzvot* (including the ten known in the Christian world as the Ten Commandments). The Hebrews wandered in the desert for forty years, until they entered the Promised Land as a free people.

The Passover Holiday Takes Shape

During the centuries following the Exodus from Egypt, the Israelites were consistent neither in their observance and adherence to the commandments nor in their relationship with God. As a consequence, Passover was sometimes celebrated and sometimes not. After the destruction of the First Temple, the Jews did observe Passover while in exile in Babylon, but without the paschal offering (sacrificial lamb). In 516 B.C.E., when some Jews returned to Israel and rebuilt the Temple, the traditional observances at the Temple resumed.

During the era of the Second Temple, Jews once again made pilgrimages to Jerusalem and celebrated the holiday with festive meals, merriment, and study. The Pharisees added to the religious observances by establishing the *seder* and instituting the drinking of wine, reclining, and leisurely discussing the narrative. Outside Jerusalem, Passover was observed in the home and at synagogue, and new customs were added to the *seder*.

After the destruction of the Second Temple, Diaspora Jews developed the *Haggadah,* a book that recounted the story of Passover and included biblical passages, *midrashim,* poems, and various ceremonies that are performed during the Passover *seder*.

Over the years, Passover evolved into a holiday celebrated primarily in the home. Its message of freedom has remained relevant for the Jews in the Diaspora and for people everywhere. Perhaps this is why it is the most widely celebrated Jewish holiday today.

Passover Preparations

In preparation for Passover, your home must be rid of all *chametz*. Exactly what is *chametz*? It's anything that is made from the five major grains (barley, wheat, oats, rye, and spelt) that has not been completely baked within eighteen minutes after coming into contact with water. Observant Ashkenazic Jews also avoid rice, corn, peanuts, and beans, since they are commonly used to make bread. But if you think making your home "*chametz* free" is an easy job that you can complete just before Pesach begins, you had better think again. You'll need days, if not weeks, to accomplish this task.

FACTS

An additional reason that observant Ashkenazic Jews avoid rice, corn, peanuts, and beans during Passover is that these were often processed alongside wheat and there was a fear that wheat that had been exposed to water (making it *chametz*) might have been mixed in.

Not only must you make certain that all *chametz* is removed from your house, but you may not use any utensils, dishes, pots, and pans that had come into contact with *chametz*. Therefore, some families have an extra set of Passover kitchenware while others might utilize paper products during the holiday.

The entire home, and particularly the kitchen, must be cleaned and scrubbed and made *chametz*-free. Once you are satisfied that everything is in order, a formal search, called *bedikat chametz,* usually takes place on the night before Passover. Any *chametz* that is found is carefully set aside, wrapped, and burned the following morning.

ALERT

You had better be prepared if Pesach begins on a Saturday night. The process of making your home *chametz*-free is made more difficult when this occurs because some of the things you must do would violate *Shabbat* so they will have to be attended to well in advance.

Another ritual observed at this time is *mechirat chametz,* the sale of *chametz* to a gentile or a rabbi acting with power-of-attorney. In fact, those who sell their *chametz* intend to repurchase it after Passover. This rite usually takes place when the *chametz* discovered from the search is burned. It is customary that a renunciation of ownership is declared regarding any *chametz* that has not been detected.

Grocery Shopping

In addition to buying food that is marked kosher for Passover, you want to have a good supply of *matzah* on hand. *Matzah* is a grain product

Matzah, a special bread eaten during Passover

Photo courtesy of Joshua Marowitz

made of flour and water that is baked quickly so that it does not rise. Enriched *matzah,* called *matzah ashirah,* contains egg, milk, honey, wine, or fruit juice. It is only permitted on Passover for someone who has difficulty digesting regular *matzah.*

You also need to prepare special dishes for the Passover *seder.* There are some things you may want to add that are normally not on your shopping list. You'll need to prepare *karpas* (made from watercress, celery, potatoes, parsley, or cabbage), bitter herbs, *charoset* (a mixture of ground almonds or other nuts, cinnamon, and apples), drumsticks or shank cuts, and hardboiled eggs. You will also need to purchase kosher red wine and/or grape juice, kosher salt, and holiday candles. For the meal itself, feel free to purchase whatever you wish, although the food should be kosher. Ashkenazic Jews generally eat a traditional meal of gefilte fish and *matzah* ball soup, followed by roast chicken, turkey, or brisket of beef.

Pre-Passover Synagogue Observances

Passover is preceded by three special Sabbaths. *Shabbat Parah* occurs two weeks before the month of *Nisan* and on this *Shabbat,* the Torah portion (Numbers 19:1–22) explains the purification process involving the sacrifice of the *Parah Adumah* (red cow).

The Sabbath immediately preceding *Nisan* is *Shabbat Ha-Chodesh*. The Torah portion read that day (Exodus 12:1–20) recounts the commandments of the Passover sacrifice and preparations for departing from Egypt. The third Sabbath takes place just before Passover and is called *Shabbat Ha-Gadol* (the great Sabbath). The *Haftorah* read on this *Shabbat* (Malachi 3:4–24) refers to the final redemption of the Messianic Age that will be ushered in by Elijah: "Behold, I will send you Elijah the prophet. Before the coming of the great and terrible day of the Lord" (Malachi 3:4–24).

There is an additional observance preceding *Pesach* that is not exclusive to either the synagogue or the home but applies to a particular category of Jews. On the day just before Passover, there is the Fast of the Firstborn, when all firstborn males commemorate the fact that while their Egyptian counterparts were slaughtered, God spared the firstborn Jewish males. Should this day occur on Sabbath, the fast is made on Thursday.

Synagogue Services

The first day of Passover is *Yom Tov* ("the good day"). During this day (two days for the Orthodox outside of Israel), work, travel, and other everyday activities are not permitted.

FACTS

Liturgy services during Passover are similar to those for other festivals but with a few distinctive features. During the *Musaf* service on the first day, congregations recite a special prayer for the dew called *Tfilat Tal*. This prayer is the counterpart to *Geshem,* the prayer for rain that is made on Shemini Atzeret. On the last day of Passover, the liturgy also includes *Yizkor* (memorial service).

The Torah readings during the eight days of Passover are from all parts of the Torah because of the numerous times the Exodus and Passover narrative are mentioned. Torah portions are read from the following

Books: Exodus (first, third, fourth, fifth, and seventh days), Leviticus (second day), Numbers (sixth day), and Deuteronomy (eighth day).

Passover at Home

During the periods of the First and Second Temples, Passover centered on pilgrimages to Jerusalem because each family had to sacrifice a paschal lamb at the Temple. After the destruction of the Second Temple and the dispersal of the Jews, the focus shifted to the synagogue and even more to the home. Today the injunction to remember and to tell the Passover story is carried out primarily in the home at a function called the *seder*.

The *Seder*

The *seder* is a Passover meal and the related ceremonies that are celebrated on the first night of Passover (though many Diaspora Jews

A *Haggadah* used to conduct the Passover *seder*

Photo courtesy of Joshua Marowitz

also hold a second *seder* on the second night). The word *seder* is Hebrew for "order" or "order of the service," so the order and specifics of the *seder* ceremonies hold great importance.

Conducting a *seder* is not as hard as you might think. All you have to do is follow the *Haggadah*, a book relating the story of the Exodus that contains the order of the *seder*. The title *Haggadah* comes from the Hebrew *l'hagid* ("to tell"), and the *Haggadah* is the telling of the Exodus story that is central to the celebration of Passover.

It is likely that the first *Haggadah* was published in the eleventh century; the first illustrated *Haggadah* appeared in 1482 in Spain. The *Haggadah* has been published in thousands of editions. Today, *Haggadot* come in a wide variety of traditional, secular, feminist, mystical, and vegetarian versions. Some families have even produced their own *Haggadot*.

Setting the *Seder* Table

In order to follow the *Haggadah*, you prepare in advance by setting the *seder* table. Most of the objects present on the *seder* table are highly symbolic and play a ceremonial role in the dinner. Here's what a *seder* table should include:

- A special *matzah* cover with dividers for three pieces of *matzah*.
- Sufficient wine and/or grape juice (enough for four cups per person).

QUESTIONS?

Why do Jews drink four cups of wine during the *seder*?
The four cups of wine represent the four promises made by God to the Israelites: that He will free them from the burdens of bondage, deliver them from slavery, redeem them with an outstretched arm, and take them to be "My people" (Exodus 6:6–8).

- Napkin or doily to cover the middle piece of *matzah* (the *afikoman*).
- A *kiddush* cup for everyone and one special goblet to serve as the cup of Elijah.
- A pitcher and bowl for washing hands.
- At least one bowl filled with salt water that will be needed for dipping.
- Cushioned chairs or pillows on each chair so that everyone can recline and be comfortable during the *seder* (a symbol of freedom and wealth).
- One *Haggadah* per person (preferably uniform).
- A *seder* plate (the contents of the *seder* plate will be examined in further detail).
- Flowers, though not required, are always appropriate for this special occasion.

The *Seder* Plate

Seder plate with traditional food items

Photo courtesy of © 2001 Brand X Pictures

The *seder* plate, or *ke'arah*, contains the five symbols of the *seder*. While you can use any dish at all, you may want to purchase a special *seder* plate and use it for future Passovers. The five food dishes that will appear on the *seder* plate are:

- *Karpas*, a green vegetable (usually parsley, watercress, or celery) that symbolizes the greenness of spring; during the *seder*, the *karpas* is dipped into the salt water.
- *Charoset*, a mixture of chopped nuts, apples, wine, and cinnamon, reminiscent of the mortar used by the Hebrew slaves when they toiled in Egypt.
- *Maror*, bitter herbs or horseradish, a dish that represents the bitterness of slavery.
- *Beitzah*, a roasted (hardboiled) egg that symbolizes the continuity of life and the commencement of spring.
- *Zeroa*, a roasted shankbone that represents the sacrifice of the paschal lamb.

You are now ready to join in with family and friends to conduct the Passover *seder*. As a matter of fact, it is considered a *mitzvah* to invite guests to the *seder*, so the more the merrier!

The Order of Ceremonies

After lighting the holiday candles, begin the *seder* with the blessing over the first cup of wine. After you drink the wine, pour a second round. Then, wash your hands in preparation for dipping the *karpas* in salt water (the *karpas* is eaten as a symbol of the tears shed by the Hebrew slaves in Egypt).

Next, perform *yahatz,* a ceremony that requires breaking a piece of the *matzah* (the middle piece from the special three-layered *matzah* covering). After the *matzah* is broken in half, the larger piece becomes the *afikoman,* a piece that you hide from the children (before the end of the *seder,* the children will participate in the search for the *afikoman*).

At this point, it is time to relate the Passover narrative, which begins with the youngest child present at the table asking the Four Questions. During the course of the narration, as the gathered recite the ten plagues, each person removes ten drops of wine from their cup. One interpretation for this custom is that it serves as a reminder that when other people suffer, our joy is diminished. The participants then drink the second cup of wine and a blessing is made.

Again, everyone washes their hands, this time while reciting a blessing. A *motzi* is made over the *matzah* and a second blessing is said for the specific *mitzvah* of eating *matzah.* Then, each person dips the *maror* (bitter herbs) in the *charoset.*

ESSENTIALS

The *maror* and *charoset* are sandwiched between pieces of *matzah* in a *Korech,* a custom introduced by the sage Hillel. With this surprisingly delectable treat tantalizing your taste buds, you will be pleased to learn that the time for dinner has arrived!

After the meal, the children search for the *afikoman.* Usually, when the children find the *afikoman,* they receive gifts as a ransom to allow the *seder* to continue. (An alternative custom is for the children to hide the *afikoman* for the parents to find.) Everyone eats a piece of the *afikoman* and the *seder* proceeds with the after-meal grace and the drinking of the third cup of wine. As the fourth and final cup of wine is poured for each guest, a special cup is filled for the prophet Elijah. As the door is opened to welcome Elijah, a blessing praising God is made over the wine that is then consumed.

The final part of the *Haggadah* contains songs and praises to God and the remainder of *Hallel* is recited. The *seder* is concluded with a poem and song, ending with the words *Le shana ha-ba'ah b'Yerushalayim* (next year in Jerusalem).

CHAPTER 15

Shavuot, Tisha B'Av, and Tu B'Shevat

The last three holidays in the annual cycle are Shavuot (the Festival of Weeks), Tisha B'Av (a day that commemorates the destruction of the Temple), and Tu B'Shevat (a New Year's day for trees). These holidays, each in its own way, commemorate the history and culture of the Jewish people.

The Festival of Weeks

In Hebrew, *shavuot* means "weeks," which is why Shavuot is also known as the Festival of Weeks. In fact, Shavuot occurs exactly seven weeks after the second day of Passover, a time period that represents the interval when the Israelites left Egypt but had not yet received the Torah.

FACTS

Shavuot is known by many names: *Hag Habikkurim* (the Festival of the First Fruits), *Hag Matan Torateinu* (the Festival of the Giving of Our Torah), and *Hag Hakatzir* (the Feast of the Harvest). Because Shavuot falls on the fiftieth day from the second day of Passover, it is sometimes known as Pentecost (a Greek term that has become famous thanks to its importance in Christianity).

Shavuot commemorates the day when Jewish tradition says God revealed the entire Torah to Moses on Mount Sinai. That is why the period between Passover and Shavuot is considered to be a time of solemnity. During certain segments of this period, tradition forbids marriage ceremonies and the playing of live music. The devout avoid cutting their hair, for this is a season for preparing oneself to receive the Torah, a time for study and meditation.

An Agricultural Holiday

Despite the deeply religious significance of Shavuot, the Torah itself first mentions Shavuot as an agricultural festival marking the transition between the barley harvest and the start of the wheat-ripening season. Before the destruction of the Temple, Jews used this brief respite from work to travel to Jerusalem, to celebrate and offer sacrifices at the Temple. After the destruction of the First Temple, many pilgrims continued to come from Babylon. Communities that could not send all their members dispatched a representative delegation.

After the razing of the Second Temple in 70 C.E., pilgrimages to fulfill the earlier purpose of Shavuot became impossible. Hence, the focus of the holiday shifted from its dual agricultural and spiritual importance to emphasize the spiritual aspect.

Customs and Traditions of Shavuot

Like all Jewish holidays, Shavuot begins the night before. At home, Jews conduct the customary candle-lighting ceremony and blessings, making *Kiddush* over wine or grape juice and the blessing over the bread (usually two loaves), before going on to have a festive holiday meal.

Tradition holds that you should have at least one dairy meal during Shavuot. One explanation for this custom is that it serves as a reminder of God's promise to deliver the Israelites into a land flowing with milk and honey (Exodus 3:8). Another reason offered is that when they received the Torah (which includes the dietary laws), the Israelites did not yet have separate meat and dairy dishes and thus had to eat only dairy until they could have proper utensils. A more symbolic explanation is that the Jews eat dairy because the Israelites were as innocent as newborns whose only food is milk.

Just like Passover and Sukkot, the other two pilgrimage festivals when Jews traveled to Jerusalem to celebrate and give thanks at the Temple, Shavuot is laden with both historical and agricultural importance. Unlike those other two festivals, Shavuot is not a lengthy holiday and only lasts for one day (or two days, in the case of more traditional Diaspora Jews).

It is common practice on Shavuot to decorate both the home and synagogue with flowers, plants, and tree branches, perhaps because foliage is reminiscent of Mount Sinai, which was forested and lush with greens. Plants also serve as a reminder that Pharaoh's daughter found Moses among reeds in the Nile.

Tikkun Leil Shavuot

Perhaps the most important tradition of Shavuot has to do with the custom of staying awake most of, or even all of, the night to study the Torah. This practice, called *Tikkun Leil Shavuot,* began sometime in the sixteenth century in Safed, Israel, a Kabbalistic center. People frequently gather to study in the synagogue, but the location is not important.

ESSENTIALS

The word *tikkun* comes from the verb *letakein* ("to fix or rectify"). A Midrashic interpretation suggests that the reason for this ancient practice of staying awake all night studying on Shavuot is to symbolically "rectify" the fact that the Hebrews overslept on Shavuot morning.

Synagogue Services

During Shavuot, morning Torah readings include the revelation at Mount Sinai and the giving of the Ten Statements (Exodus 19:1–20:23), and the portion involving the Ten Statements is recited in a special chant.

Reading
the Torah

Photo courtesy of © 2001 Brand X Pictures

In many Ashkenazic synagogues, the service includes a liturgical poem titled *"Akdamot Milin."* Written in Aramaic by Rabbi Meir ben Isaac of Worms, Germany, in the eleventh century, this poem exalts Israel's attachment to the Torah and describes what conditions will be like during the time of the Messiah. In Sephardic synagogues, it is the practice to recite a *piyyut* (religious poem) called *azharut,* which lists the 613 *mitzvot. Yizkor,* the memorial service, is recited on the first day or on the second day for those who observe two days.

On Shavuot, congregations also read from the Book of Ruth, which relates the inspiring story of a Moabite woman who, after the death of her Jewish husband and her father-in-law, voluntarily chooses Judaism in order to be with her mother-in-law. Likely as not, you will have heard some version of Ruth's famous unselfish pledge to her mother-in-law: "For wherever you go, I will go; wherever you lodge, I will lodge; your people will be my people and your God my God" (Ruth 1:16).

The saga of Ruth is recounted on Shavuot for two reasons. First, part of the story happens during the barley and wheat harvests. Second, Ruth voluntarily accepts the Torah, the first recorded convert to Judaism. What is more, Ruth becomes the great-grandmother of King David.

Like the Israelites at the foot of Mount Sinai, Ruth freely accepted the Torah and Judaism. The concept of being given the Torah and opting to embrace it remains relevant today because, as a *midrash* explains, the Sinai experience touches all Jews since all Jews—past, present, and future—were present at Sinai.

Given that Shavuot marks the giving of the Torah, many Reform, Reconstructionist, and Conservative congregations hold Confirmation services on Shavuot (see Chapter 17). This is an occasion that recognizes the completion of a course of study for those who continue past bar mitzvah and bat mitzvah for several more years of Jewish education.

FACTS

Minor holidays that occur around the time of Shavuot are *Yom Ha-Atzma-Ut,* the day the modern State of Israel came into existence (May 14, 1948); *Yom Ha-Zikaron* (Remembrance Day for those who died defending the State of Israel); *Yom Ha-Shoah* (Holocaust Remembrance Day); and *Yom Yerushalayim* (Jerusalem Day), which commemorates the recapture of the old city of Jerusalem on June 7, 1967, and the reopening of access to the Western Wall.

A Day of Mourning

Most revealing about Tisha B'Av is its name. It is simply a date, the ninth day of the month of *Av.* This day is consecrated not because it is a harvest festival or because a milestone has been reached in the reading of the Torah. Rather, it is a date memorializing the worst misfortune to have befallen the Jewish people—the destruction of the Temples.

FACTS

According to the Jewish tradition, both the First and the Second Temples were destroyed on the same date—the ninth of *Av.* The Babylonians laid the First Temple in ruins in 586 B.C.E., and the Romans decimated the Second Temple in 70 C.E. The destruction of the Second Temple commenced the Diaspora, a time period that lasted until the establishment of the modern State of Israel in 1948.

The destruction of the Second Temple was not the last tragedy to occur on Tisha B'Av. On this day in 1290, King Edward ordered the expulsion of the Jews from England. Two hundred and two years later, in 1492, the Jews were expelled from Spain. That is why Tisha B'Av is a day when it is appropriate to mourn the afflictions that have befallen Jews over the centuries.

The remains of the Temple known as the Western Wall

Photo courtesy of © 2001 Brand X Pictures

Tisha B'Av Fast and Other Practices

Given the plaintive nature of the day, it is not surprising that Tisha B'Av is a day of fasting. With the exception of Yom Kippur, this is the only fast day that lasts from sundown to sundown. (All the other days of fasting begin in the morning and end at night.)

Tisha B'Av is the culmination of a three-week period of mourning that begins with the fast of the seventeenth day of *Tammuz* (which commemorates the first breach of the walls enclosing Jerusalem). This period has certain restrictions: weddings and parties are not permitted, people do not cut their hair or wear new clothing. From the first through the ninth of *Av* (except on *Shabbat*), observant Jews also abstain from meat and wine.

FACTS

If Tisha B'Av should fall on a Saturday, *Shabbat* takes precedence. Therefore, the fast is postponed until Saturday night through sundown on Sunday. In such an event, you need not eliminate bathing altogether and may do so the following day (though not the following night).

The restrictions on Tisha B'Av are similar to those on Yom Kippur, but also incorporate certain practices associated with mourning. On this day, avoid the following:

- Eating or drinking
- Washing or bathing (though you may wash your fingers up to the knuckles)
- Shaving or wearing cosmetics and lotions
- Wearing leather shoes
- Having sexual relations
- Working (at least until noon) or doing any pleasurable activity
- Smiling, laughing, having idle conversations, or greeting others
- Sitting on regular chairs (instead, you should sit on a low stool or on the ground)
- Studying the Torah (with the exception of certain subjects related to mourning, since the study of Torah is a joyful experience)

By fasting, carrying out traditional rituals of mourning, and attending prayer services that to some extent have been customized to reflect the gravity of the day, you create the milieu for remembering some infamous times in Jewish history. In this fashion, you strengthen the links with the Jews of the past.

ALERT

Do not greet anyone on Tisha B'Av. If someone is unaware of this *mitzvah* and greets you, explain the law and why you do not respond, or simply reply in a low voice and with a somber demeanor.

Synagogue Services During Tisha B'Av

Following the typical evening *Ma'ariv* service, the congregation reads from the Book of Lamentations, where the prophet Jeremiah describes the destruction of the First Temple. In some congregations, the congregants sit on the floor during the reading. Following Lamentations, they recite prayers of mourning.

To give added emphasis to the unique nature of this day of mourning, it is customary to remove the curtain from the Holy Ark where the Torahs are kept and to drape the Ark in black. In some synagogues, the main lights are turned off and prayers are recited by candlelight. On the morning of Tisha B'Av, at *Shacharit* prayers, men do not wear *tallit* and *tefillin*. While small *tzitzit* are donned, no blessing is made.

The New Year for the Trees

Like Tisha B'Av, the name of the holiday Tu B'Shevat denotes the date on which it falls—the fifteenth day of the month of *Shevat*. Tisha B'Av is also known as *Rosh Hashanah L'Ilanot* (New Year for Trees), which is exactly what this holiday is about.

Leviticus 19:23–25 states that the fruit from trees may not be eaten during the first three years. The fruit of the fourth year belongs to God, but after the fourth year, the fruit may be eaten. The purpose of Tu B'Shevat is to calculate the age of trees for tithing, because it is the boundary date for determining the age of trees. This date was probably selected to mark the end of the rain season in ancient Israel.

On a more spiritual level, Tu B'Shevat is a time for prayer and judgment regarding trees. The premise is that whenever any of God's creatures begins to grow, God contemplates its future. Therefore, it is proper to pray on behalf of that creature—animate or inanimate.

Plant a Tree for Tu B'Shevat

The best way to celebrate Tu B'Shevat is to plant a tree. In fact, this is a prevalent practice in Israel, where trees play an important ecological role, reclaiming the desert and providing shade in an arid, sandy terrain.

With the founding of the State of Israel, it became a common custom for Jewish children in other countries to collect funds to be sent to Israel for the planting of trees and the establishment of forests. Although not as widespread, this tradition continues today.

Another custom that celebrates this holiday is eating fruits, particularly fruits that are native to Israel, such as grapes, figs, pomegranates, olives, and dates, for which the Torah praises the land of Israel. You may want to make these fruits the center of a special meal or even a Tu B'Shevat *seder,* with recitations, songs, and wine. In fact, having a *seder* on Tu B'Shevat is becoming very popular in many Jewish communities, a practice that is fast becoming a new tradition.

CHAPTER 16

A New Life

Judaism attaches great importance to human life. Indeed, there is a Jewish adage that "with each child, the world begins anew." What event could be more beautiful and sacred than the arrival of a new life into this world of ours? When such an occasion presents itself, the Jewish people have much to celebrate.

A Child Is Born

According to Judaism, a child's soul exists prior to its birth, but its life begins at the time of birth—more specifically, when the child is halfway emerged from the womb. The new soul that enters the world is considered to be pure and chaste. The concept of original sin is foreign to Judaism. Of course, the Jews recognize that people commit sins as the years go by, but they believe that humans begin their lives with a clean slate.

FACTS

After giving birth, a woman is considered *niddah* (see Chapter 6). She and her husband must abstain from sexual relations for seven days if she had a male child and fourteen days if the child is a girl (Leviticus 12:2). During the time of the Temple, the periods of abstinence were forty days and eighty days for a baby boy and girl, respectively.

After the birth of a child, the father is given an *aliyah* (the honor of making a blessing over the Torah). A blessing is recited at that time for the health of the new mother and baby. As we shall see, this may also be an occasion when a baby girl is named.

Name-Giving Traditions

The naming of a new child is a very important event, since the name a person bears reflects that person's basic nature. Ashkenazic Jews name their children in remembrance of a recently deceased relative. This tradition honors the memory of the departed but also follows a superstition that a child should not be named after someone who is living.

On the other hand, Sephardic Jews name their children after living relatives. Note that they generally do not name a son after the father or a daughter after the mother. Should you decide to follow this practice in naming your child, honor someone other than yourself! For instance, it is perfectly proper to name a child after a grandparent.

A Hebrew Name

Although no formal Jewish commandment specifies the necessity of a Hebrew name, most Jewish parents give their child a Hebrew middle name. The Hebrew name is used by the child during important occasions and ceremonies, such as being called to the Torah for an *aliyah* or identifying the bride and groom in the *ketubah.*

The formal Hebrew name comes with the word *ben* (son of) or *bat* (daughter of) and the father's name (though some non-Orthodox families may include the mother's name). For instance, Shmuel ben Yosef is the full name of Samuel, the son of Joseph. If the child is a *kohein,* the title *ha-Kohein* are added; if the child is a Levite, the title *Ha-Levi* will follow.

The Covenant of Circumcision

While there are no formalities governing how a child's name is determined, specific ceremonies do exist for naming children. They differ depending on the gender of a child. Male children must undergo the circumcision ceremony known as the *bris* (or *brit,* as it is pronounced in Israel). The Covenant of Circumcision *(Berit Milah)* occupies a principal place in Judaism.

FACTS

Jewish circumcision is unique because it takes place so early— on the eighth day of the male child's life. In some cultures, circumcision is not performed until the boy is four or five years old. In other societies, circumcision does not take place until puberty or marriage.

History of Circumcision

The Jews were not the first people to practice circumcision. It was a custom among the ancient Egyptians, Ethiopians, Syrians, and Phoenicians, and appeared in parts of Africa, India, Australia, Indonesia, and the Philippines. On closer shores, most Eskimos and Native Americans also circumcised their male children.

Meaning of Circumcision

Berit milah is probably the most observed commandment in Judaism. It is the first *mitzvah* from God that applies specifically to the Jewish people. In Genesis 17:10–12, God said to Abraham, "As for you, you and your offspring to come throughout the ages shall keep My covenant. . . . Every male among you shall be circumcised. You shall circumcise the flesh of your foreskin, and that shall be the sign of the covenant between Me and you. And throughout the generations, every male among you shall be circumcised at the age of eight days."

QUESTIONS?

Who circumcised Abraham?
The covenant between God and the Jews was made with Abraham. Since until that time his people did not practice circumcision, Abraham was uncircumcised. It is written in the Torah (Genesis 17:24) that Abraham circumcised himself—at ninety-nine years of age!

While there may be health benefits to circumcision, this has nothing whatsoever to do with the practice in Judaism that is carried out to satisfy this *mitzvah*, which marks an outward sign of the covenant between God and the Jewish people. God's command couldn't be clearer. Since it specifies that the rite be performed on the eighth day from birth, this is when the *berit milah* is scheduled.

Questions about Circumcision

Until recently, the medical community believed that circumcision had many health benefits. Although some recent studies have called the validity of these beliefs into question, there is no strong evidence to indicate any harmful side effects of circumcision.

Those Jews who choose to circumcise their child also need to decide whether a *mohel* or a physician should perform the operation. The *mohel* is a specialist trained both in the medical and the religious aspects of the *berit milah*. However, the *mohel* is usually not a physician. In recent years, more circumcisions have been performed in the hospital rather than in the home by a *mohel* or in the synagogue, as is the custom of Sephardic Jews. However, a medical circumcision does not fulfill the *mitzvah*. More traditional and observant Jews consider the removal of the foreskin to be a religious ritual. Therefore, it must be performed by a *mohel*.

FACTS

The *mohel* uses a double-edged knife to make certain the cut is swift and clean. If the knife were not double-edged and the blunt side was used by mistake, the baby would endure unnecessary pain. And just to be sure, the *mohel* usually comes prepared with two knives—in case one is dull!

Today, there are three alternatives to having a *mohel* perform the circumcision. You can have a doctor carry out the medical procedure with a rabbi conducting the religious component. You may find a physician who has been trained in the religious aspects of circumcision. Or, after a physician performs the circumcision, arrange for a *mohel* to conduct the *berit milah* anew. In such a case, the *mohel* will only take a symbolic drop of blood to satisfy the physical requirement (a ritual known as *Hatafat Dam Berit*).

The *Berit Milah* Ceremony

Custom has it that you do not actually invite your friends and family to the *bris*. Instead, inform everyone when the event is scheduled with the understanding they may come if they wish.

As the ceremony begins, the parents bring the baby into the room and carefully place it on the special chair set aside for the prophet Elijah, who is said to watch over all circumcisions. The baby is then picked up and laid on the lap of the *sandek* or godfather (often the grandfather) who is seated on another chair.

Several blessings and prayers are made before, during, and after the circumcision. Following the circumcision, a blessing is made over the wine and a drop is placed on the baby's lips. At this time the baby boy is given his formal Hebrew name.

As with all joyous events, a festive meal follows. In some circles it is traditional to include wine and sponge cake on the menu. The baby boy now has a name and has fulfilled the *mitzvah* to mark the covenant of the Jewish People with God.

It's a Girl!

There is no female version of the *berit milah*. While some think this means that girls receive the short end of the stick when it comes to being welcomed into the world in accordance with Jewish tradition, another way of looking at it is that they get off easy! While there are no explicit rituals or *mitzvot* associated with the birth of a girl, customs and traditions have evolved to celebrate this important occasion.

Naming a Baby Girl

Traditionally, a baby girl receives her name either when her father is honored with an *aliyah* on the first Sabbath after she is born or during any Torah reading. A prayer is said at this time for the health and well-being of the mother and child. If the mother is present, she recites a special prayer of thanksgiving.

SSENTIALS In naming a baby girl, the prayer recited by Ashkenazic Jews begins with the patriarchs: Abraham, Isaac, and Jacob. When Sephardic Jews name a baby girl at a Torah reading, the blessing that is customarily made begins with the matriarchs: Sarah, Rebecca, Rachel, and Leah.

In Reform congregations, it is the common practice to name a baby girl during a Friday evening or Saturday morning service where the parents are in attendance with their friends and family.

However, a baby may be named in places other than the synagogue. Some parents prefer to name their baby girls in their home and invite family and friends to participate in a festive celebration of a new life. This ceremony is called a *Berit Ha-Chayim* (the Covenant of Life) or

Berit Ha-Bat (the Covenant for a Daughter). During this ceremony, the baby girl is given her name.

Redeeming the Firstborn Son

One of the 613 commandments proclaimed by God is that every firstborn male among the Israelites belongs to God and must be sanctified. In some cultures during biblical times, this would have required nothing less than a physical sacrifice of the newborn baby. However, God decreed an additional *mitzvah* by providing for the redemption of the child.

Why the Firstborn?

The idea of "first" has always held a special position in Judaism. For instance, the Torah specifies that the first fruits and firstborn kosher animals had to be brought to the priests at the Temple. The first of all things belong to God, and this principle applies to children as well.

Another explanation has to do with the Exodus from Egypt, when God spared the firstborn Jewish males from the final plague. Because the Jews are indebted to God for the firstborn males, they should be redeemed.

Who Must Be Redeemed

Redemption of the firstborn pertains only to a small percentage of Jews. First of all, the *mitzvah* specifically states it applies only to males. Redemption is therefore not appropriate if the firstborn is a girl. One rationale for this distinction is that the tenth plague never placed the lives of firstborn females in jeopardy.

In fact, if the firstborn to a family is a girl, any children thereafter are not subject to redemption. Moreover, the mother of the firstborn male child must be Jewish. Otherwise, according to traditional Judaism that follows the matriarchal bloodline, the child is not Jewish and is not subject to this commandment. The family lineage also plays a role when it comes to this ritual. If either the father or mother is a *kohein* or Levite, then redemption is not necessary.

Things get even more technical because the *mitzvah* specifically refers to the firstborn as one who "opens the womb." Therefore, a child delivered by cesarean section does not fall within the definition and is not redeemed. The question then arises regarding any subsequent children born to the mother in the traditional fashion. While there is no complete consensus, most believe redemption would not apply in such instances. In cases of miscarriage or stillbirth, there is no redemption for any ensuing children. As for twins, the first one out of the gate gets redeemed!

The *Pidyon Ha-Ben* Ceremony

Pidyon Ha-Ben literally means "redemption of the son." Some families have developed a parallel ceremony for firstborn girls, called *Pidyon Ha-Bat*. The ritual must take place on the thirty-first day of the child's life or as soon as possible thereafter. Since a monetary transaction is involved, the ceremony may not occur on *Shabbat* or on any biblical holiday. While it is traditional for Ashkenazic Jews to conduct the ceremony during the day, Sephardic Jews usually perform it at night.

FACTS

If the mother is Jewish but the father is not, the firstborn male should be redeemed by the mother. However, it is advisable for the boy to perform the redemption again after reaching the age of thirteen without reciting the customary blessings.

While it is not necessary, it is desirable to have a *minyan* (ten Jewish adults) during the ceremony, but the father of the child and a *kohein* must be present. Appropriate blessings are made for washing the hands and breaking the bread. At this time, the redemption is made and then the meal is eaten.

In preparation for the ceremony, the appropriate sum of money is set aside on an ornate tray (preferably silver). In the Torah, the amount to be paid was set at five *sela'im* (equal to about 100 grams of silver). Today, this sum translates to about four or five dollars, preferably in silver dollars.

Traditionally, the baby is placed on another tray and the father carries his son to the *kohein*. As he holds the boy on the tray, the *kohein* performs a brief ritual, which includes blessings and recitations. During the ceremony, the father hands over the money to the *kohein* and the *kohein* blesses the child. A blessing is made over the wine and the gathered people enjoy a festive meal.

A Jewish Look at Adoption

It is a *mitzvah* to get married and have children. If a married couple is physically unable to have children, the commandment to be fruitful and multiply may be satisfied by adopting a child. Jewish law does not directly address the matter of adoption, nor is there a formal adoption ceremony (although several beautiful prayers and blessings have been written for such an occasion).

But what happens when a Jewish couple adopts a child born of a gentile mother? The answer is that the child must undergo the conversion process, although many Reform rabbis will forego this requirement so long as the child is raised as a Jew and given a Jewish education.

SSENTIALS

In most respects, all obligations parents have toward their natural children apply to adoptive children and, vice versa, concerning the child toward the parents. The child becomes a part of the Jewish community and is welcomed like all Jewish children with a *bris*, a *Pidyon Ha-Ben* (if applicable), and a naming ceremony.

Conversion Procedure

The conversion procedure for a child is not as rigorous as that of an adult. Although the conversion process does vary according to the branch of Judaism to which the family adheres, it will generally include the following:

*   Approval by a rabbinic court
*   Circumcision performed with appropriate ceremony
*   Immersion of the child in a *mikvah* (ritual bath)
*   A commitment the child will receive a Jewish education

Judaism and Abortion

Judaism's position on this very sensitive issue incorporates some ideas that will probably please just about everyone and other ideas that will likely displease each one of them. Unlike some other religions that completely ban abortion under any circumstances, Judaism has always allowed abortions—in fact even required abortions—to preserve a life. You already know that Judaism holds each and every life to be sacred. When the life of a woman is in jeopardy, it is clear that the pregnancy must be terminated.

However, when it comes to this controversial topic, there is no unanimity among the respective movements of Judaism beyond this clear maxim. The traditional point of view is that abortion is not permitted other than when the woman's life is in danger. But what about the woman's health? And what about when the risk to health becomes so serious that it could become life-threatening?

More liberal branches of Judaism will take the emotional health and well-being of the woman into account as well. However, as far as a woman's having the absolute right to abortion for any reason or no reason at all, it is not likely you will find an organized branch of Judaism to support this position.

CHAPTER 17

Bar Mitzvah, Bat Mitzvah, and Confirmation

As Jewish children grow up, they are introduced to Judaism, the Hebrew language, Jewish celebrations and rituals, the Jewish history and traditions, and, of course, to the Torah. Bar mitzvah, bat mitzvah, and (to a much lesser extent) Confirmation mark the way of each Jewish child along the road to adulthood and the assumption of one's place in the Jewish community.

The Meaning Behind Bar and Bat Mitzvah

Bar mitzvah literally translates as "son of the commandment" (*bar* is Aramaic for "son"), and *bat mitzvah* (pronounced *Bas mitzvah* by the Ashkenazim) means "daughter of the commandment," since *bat* is Hebrew and Aramaic for "daughter."

Bar mitzvah and Bat mitzvah are nouns. To say one is "bar mitzvahed" or "bat mitzvahed" is incorrect and is a common mistake. Moreover, there is no such thing as "having a bar or bat mitzvah." A young man or woman cannot "have" themselves be a son or daughter of the commandment.

According to Jewish law, children should be taught the ways of Judaism. They are encouraged to observe as many of the rituals and obligations as they can, but they are not required to comply with the *mitzvot* until they become adults—that is, until the bar or bat mitzvah. Once they become adults in the eyes of Jewish law, the duty arises to abide by God's commandments.

Becoming a Bar or Bat Mitzvah

Possibly the most pervasive misunderstanding Jews have about Judaism is the notion that in order to become a bar mitzvah or bat mitzvah, they must do so in a ceremony conducted in the synagogue. The reason for this error goes to a misreading of what bar mitzvah and bat mitzvah mean.

In Judaism, one does not have the option of deciding whether or not to be bound to the commandments. It is a responsibility that comes with the covenant God made with Abraham and the Jews for all generations to follow. It is automatic. It just happens.

At the age of thirteen, a boy becomes a bar mitzvah. From then on, he is expected to keep all the *mitzvot* Jewish men are required to fulfill. At the age of twelve, a girl becomes a bat mitzvah, which means that she is now obligated to carry out all of the *mitzvot* pertaining to Jewish women. (The reason girls assume this responsibility at a younger age probably has to do with the fact that girls mature faster than boys at this time of their lives.) Again, no ceremony is required in the case of either gender. Rituals and practices are not needed. And a festive party is clearly an extraneous bonus.

Becoming a bar mitzvah also confers certain rights under Jewish law. (Some of these laws may also apply to girls who are bat mitzvah, depending upon the branch of Judaism involved.) These rights include the following:

- The right to participate in or lead a religious service
- The right to count toward a *minyan*
- The right to enter into binding contracts
- The right to provide testimony in religious courts

Note that while the ages of twelve and thirteen for a girl and boy, respectively, mean they are adults insofar as fulfilling *mitzvot,* this does not suggest that they are adults in every sense of the word. For example, according to Jewish law, marriage should take place no earlier than at sixteen years of age, and the suitable age to enter the work force is considered to be twenty.

QUESTIONS?

What about a convert to Judaism?
Whatever process (Orthodox, Reform, or Conservative) is undertaken to become a Jew, an education in Judaism and a willingness to accept its commandments is a prerequisite for the conversion. Therefore, upon converting, one becomes a son or daughter of the commandment (bar mitzvah and bat mitzvah).

Cause for Celebration

Although no specific ceremony is required for becoming a bar mitzvah or a bat mitzvah, a ceremony of celebrating this rite of passage does exist. It generally takes place after the boy or girl has completed several years of Hebrew and Judaic studies. In fact, bar mitzvah and bat mitzvah ceremonies are beautiful events that mark an important occasion in a young person's life.

The Bar Mitzvah Ceremony

The bar mitzvah ceremony is not mentioned in the Bible or the Talmud, and the practice probably has its origins in the Middle Ages. Because the ceremony does not actually denote when the young man becomes a bar mitzvah, it can occur anytime after his thirteenth birthday. In fact, if studies and preparation have not been completed, it is wise to postpone the ritual.

A Torah scroll, unrolled

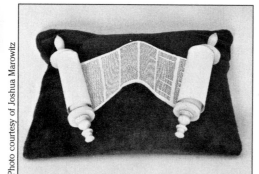

Photo courtesy of Joshua Marowitz

Because there are no *mitzvot* governing the ceremony, practices vary among the respective movements in Judaism and even from congregation to congregation. However, some common elements usually occur.

Probably the oldest and most universal aspect of the ritual is that it takes place during a *Shabbat* service soon after the boy's thirteenth birthday. During that morning, the young man is called to the Torah to recite a blessing and the weekly Torah reading.

In more recent years, the bar mitzvah generally chants the *Haftorah* portion (the concluding reading from the Prophetic section of the Bible). In addition, the bar mitzvah may read the entire Torah portion, conduct part of the service, lead the congregation in selected prayers, or make a speech.

ESSENTIALS

Unless the bar mitzvah is an Ashkenazic Orthodox Jew, the bar mitzvah ceremony will mark the first time he wears a *tallit* (ceremonial prayer shawl). Ashkenazic Orthodox men do not wear the *tallit* until they get married. Therefore, it would be inappropriate for an unmarried male to wear a *tallit* when *davening* (praying) in such congregations.

Furthermore, the rabbi may speak to the bar mitzvah boy about the significance of the occasion, and the congregation may present the boy with gifts such as books or ritual items. When the service is concluded, a feast or party may follow.

The Bat Mitzvah Ceremony

The first bat mitzvah ceremony took place on Saturday morning, March 18, 1922. On that *Shabbat*, Judith Kaplan, the twelve-year-old daughter of Rabbi Mordecai Kaplan (the founder of Reconstructionism), stepped up to the *bimah* of her father's synagogue, the Society for the Advancement of Judaism in New York. She recited the preliminary blessing, and read from the Torah portion. This was a startling, bold, and innovative event designed to support Mordecai Kaplan's objective for women to have equal standing with men in Judaism.

However, over the next two decades, few women participated in the bat mitzvah ceremonies. Probably because the Reconstructionist movement did not commence substantial growth until the late 1960s with congregations of their own, it was the Conservative movement that became responsible for the growing popularity of the bat mitzvah ceremony.

The Reform movement did not play an active role in this issue for the simple reason that it was questioning the necessity of even having bar mitzvah ceremonies. It was therefore not concerned with bat mitzvah ceremonies either. In the Reform movement, some boys and girls underwent a Confirmation ceremony (as described in the last section of this chapter).

By 1940, only a handful of Conservative congregations had adopted bat mitzvah rituals, but by the end of that decade, more than a third of the movement's member synagogues had established the ceremony. A mere twenty years later, this practice was the norm among Conservative congregations. However, during the formative years of this ceremony, the bat mitzvah did not read from the Torah and even today, some Conservative synagogues still refrain from this practice.

By the 1950s, only a third of Reform temples conducted a bat mitzvah ceremony but a decade later, it was widespread within the movement. Today, in Reform and Reconstructionist congregations alike, the bat mitzvah sings the blessings and reads from the Torah portion—in fact, the ceremony is essentially the same as a bar mitzvah.

ESSENTIALS

Bat mitzvah ceremonies are generally conducted after the girl reaches the age of thirteen. Most likely, this is because, while not signifying the end of a young person's Jewish education, a prescribed course of study must be completed before the ceremony is held. To coincide with the boys, the age of thirteen for the ceremony becomes convenient.

Among the Orthodox, there is no similar type of bat mitzvah ceremony in the synagogue since women are not called to the Torah. However, many Orthodox do celebrate the occasion of a girl becoming a bat mitzvah with a festive party or some type of ceremony.

Celebration Feasts

Following the religious ceremony, family and friends of the bar and bat mitzvahs participate in a social celebration, a *Seudat Mitzvah*—a feast that celebrates the fulfillment of a commandment. Although in this case the commandment was attained automatically upon reaching the appropriate age and not by way of the ceremony, a celebration is still in order.

The bar or bat mitzvah feast should be an opportunity to impress upon the young man or woman the responsibilities and obligations to fulfill the commandments that accompany reaching this milestone in their lives. But how many young people today even know the literal translation of bar mitzvah and bat mitzvah?

The decorum ought to reflect the seriousness of the occasion. A meal is always appropriate and there can be festive dancing and music. But this should also be a time for discussions about subjects of Jewish interest, particularly with the new son or daughter of the commandment in mind.

The Bar/Bat Mitzvah Affair

Have you heard of the Schwartz family who, not wanting to be outdone, planned to take their family and closest 200 friends on a safari to celebrate their son Joshua's becoming a bar mitzvah? Promptly following the service, the entire entourage was chauffeured to the airport and flown on a chartered plane to Africa. They disembarked and spent the night in lavish rooms at the best five-star hotel on the continent. Early the next morning, after an extravagant buffet breakfast (with lox and bagels, of course!), all were loaded into fifty Jeeps to make their way to the surprise destination.

About two hours into the journey, the caravan came to an abrupt halt and remained in place for some time. Finally, after what was becoming an interminable wait, a frustrated and agitated Mr. Schwartz demanded of the guide to explain what the holdup was in getting to the secluded wooded area where a grand fête was to be held. Sighing and scratching his bewhiskered chin, the unruffled guide replied, "Not long now, Sir, the Cohen bat mitzvah barbecue should be just about over."

FACTS

A wide array of presents is suitable to give to the bar and bat mitzvahs. Any one of the religious objects or special clothing items described in Chapter 7, such as a *kippah* or a *tallit*, would be an excellent choice. Another appropriate option is to give the bar or bat mitzvah a book about Judaism or Jewish history and culture. Money is also acceptable.

When it comes to the bar and bat mitzvah extravaganzas, one-upmanship has become almost routine. This is true, albeit to varying extents, for all the branches of Judaism, from Reform to Orthodox. Naturally, many parties are conducted tastefully and unpretentiously and do not overshadow the truly important part of the day, but one must wonder how many of these more modest celebrations are dictated by financial constraints. The fact is that although the bar and bat mitzvah galas were unheard of a hundred years ago, and although they form no part of Jewish tradition or culture, such spectacles have frequently become the focus of the bar and bat mitzvah ceremonies in contemporary American society.

What messages do such garish displays convey to the new son or daughter of the commandment? Do such affairs add to or detract from the *mitzvah* they are meant to celebrate? Can something better or more appropriate be done? People are beginning to ponder such issues, and answers are forthcoming.

Bring Back the "Mitzvah"

What better way is there to illustrate to the bar or bat mitzvah that becoming a son or daughter of the commandment means carrying out those *mitzvot* requiring our responsibility for those around us? More and more Jews are adhering to the concept of *tikkun olam* (repair of the world) and are making this part of the bar and bat mitzvah parties and feasts.

For example, why not deliver the leftover floral arrangements to a senior citizen home or a hospital? How about making sure all that extra food is sent to a homeless shelter? And speaking of the homeless and the poor, ask the guests to bring canned food and used clothing that can be distributed to those in need. Why not arrange to have a tree planted in Israel in honor of every person who is called to light a candle on the bar or bat mitzvah cake? And what better way to stress upon the bar mitzvah or bat mitzvah the importance of those *mitzvot* that require giving to those less fortunate than by setting aside a portion of the gifts received and donating them to charities the young man or woman selects?

ALERT

Clearly, there are many options and activities that can underscore and complement what it means to become a bar mitzvah or bat mitzvah. Lavish affairs do not do this. *Tzedakah* (charity) does.

Visit *Eretz Yisrael*

What could be more appropriate than a trip to *Eretz Yisrael* (the Land of Israel) to welcome a new son or daughter of the commandment! A land steeped in the history of the Jewish People, where the events recounted in the Bible come alive and where you can see the actual sites firsthand.

Israel is a nation populated with Jews of every ilk—Sephardic and Ashkenazic, religious and secular, hailing from countries all over the world, all coming together in the Jewish homeland.

Some people believe that rather than spending many thousands of dollars for an affair that's over in one night, the funds are put to better use to finance a trip for the entire family to Israel. This has become such a popular idea that you will have no difficulty joining an organized group from an array of organizations, synagogues, and tours—or you can customize your experience and go it alone. It's really very simple.

At the Western Wall

Sometimes, either in addition to or in lieu of a bar or bat mitzvah ceremony in your synagogue, you can hold the ceremony in Israel. Once again, religious organizations or travel agencies can easily help you make all the arrangements. Imagine having the bar mitzvah make the blessings over the Torah and read a Torah portion at the Western Wall!

Praying at the Western Wall

Photo courtesy of © 2001 Brand X Pictures

The Western Wall is under the auspices of the Orthodox, and when you are there, you have to abide by their rules. For instance, a girl cannot easily have a bat mitzvah ceremony at this site. The Orthodox do not conduct bat mitzvah ceremonies, and the area by the Western Wall is separated by gender.

FACTS

The Western Wall is the outer retaining wall of the Temple Mount in Jerusalem, all that remains of the Second Temple that was destroyed in 70 C.E. Also referred to as the "Wailing Wall," it is a holy place of prayer and devotion.

Climbing Masada

Fortunately, you have other locations to choose from. Another popular location to have a bar or bat mitzvah ceremony is at the mountaintop fortress at Masada. The fortress at Masada sits atop a rock mesa 1,300 feet over the Dead Sea. In 71 C.E., this site remained the last stronghold of the Jewish zealots after the Roman troops had destroyed Jerusalem and the Second Temple.

Some 1,000 Jewish men, women, and children defended Masada for two years against 15,000 Roman soldiers. At the end of those two years, rather than face slavery and defeat, the Jews chose to commit mass suicide as their final act of defiance. They left two women and five children to tell their tale.

SSENTIALS

There are numerous youth summer programs in Israel that combine education, sightseeing, and social activities. Some parents use the money received as bar/bat mitzvah gifts to send the young man or woman to Israel, where his or her Jewish identity can be reinforced. A trip to Israel is invaluable when it is part of the milestone in becoming a bar or bat mitzvah.

Overlooking the Dead Sea, Masada is a place infused with courage and history, and is very popular for holding bar and bat mitzvah ceremonies. At Masada, a more secular Jewish site and an emblem of the Jewish fight for independence, men and women need not separate.

Confirmation Ceremony

The Confirmation ceremony is a very recent addition to the rituals and events of Judaism. Interestingly, it is an outgrowth of a negative reaction to bar mitzvah and bat mitzvah ceremonies held in a synagogue.

In the mid–nineteenth century, as Reform Judaism moved away from traditional customs and observances, the bar mitzvah ceremony came into question. For a period of time, Reform temples even stopped holding bar mitzvah ceremonies altogether. In its stead, the Reform movement introduced group Confirmation ceremonies that marked the completion of a course of Jewish education for Jews anywhere between the ages of fifteen and eighteen. (This abandonment of the bar mitzvah ceremony by Reform congregations is why it fell upon the Conservative movement to promote the idea of a bat mitzvah ceremony once Mordecai Kaplan introduced the ritual.)

While the Reform movement eventually reinstated bar mitzvah ceremonies and added the bat mitzvah ceremonies as well, the concept of a group Confirmation service had become entrenched. In fact, Confirmation became adopted by the Conservative and Reconstructionist movements, some modern Orthodox congregations, and is widespread today. Confirmation provides young men and women with a unique opportunity to continue their Jewish education after they become a bar or bat mitzvah.

A Special Shavuot Celebration

This rite-of-passage occasion commonly takes place at the age of sixteen, following three additional years of Jewish education after the bar or bat mitzvah event. Typically, congregations hold this group ceremony on Shavuot. Together as a class, the young men and women often perform a cantata or drama. The service may include a Torah reading, special music, speeches, a blessing from the rabbi, and floral arrangements.

Friends and family fill the sanctuary, taking pride not so much in the ceremony itself but in the fact that the confirmands spent several additional years learning about Judaism and the history and culture of the Jewish people. Of course, this does not mean that they have reached the end of their Jewish education—there is always more to learn. Throughout each person's adult life, there are numerous forums and opportunities to study Judaism and the myriad of topics connected with the rich tradition of the Jewish people. Each Jew has not just the opportunity but also the responsibility to continue learning for the rest of his or her life.

CHAPTER 18

Marriage and Divorce

Did you know that God created man and woman as one being? It was only later that God removed Adam's rib to fashion woman as a separate person. Therefore, Judaism holds the union of a man and a woman in marriage to be a consecrated event that rejoins two souls, two separate beings, to once again become one whole.

The Meaning of Marriage

The Jewish tradition views marriage as the ideal state. In fact, the Hebrew word for the first part of the marriage ceremony is *kiddushin*—"holiness" or "sanctification." Marriage is sacred for two reasons. First, it fulfills the important *mitzvah* to procreate. Second, the physical union of husband and wife is considered sacred, in and of itself, because two beings become one.

A Holy Union of Soul Mates

The Hebrew word for "soul mate" is *zivug*, and this term illustrates how Judaism views each married couple—as soul mates. Although this idea is popular in contemporary culture, it has been well established in Judaism since the narrative of Adam and Eve.

According to the Talmud, when God created Adam, Adam had two faces. When God split him in two, one became Eve. God brought Eve to Adam, and they were reunited. Therefore, the joining of man and woman is the reunification of a sundered soul. It is also written in the Talmud that forty days before a male child is conceived, it is announced in heaven whose daughter he will marry. This perfect match is called *bashert* ("fate" or "destiny" in Yiddish).

FACTS

Since the first marriage is considered *bashert* and the husband and wife are viewed as soul mates, a question arises regarding second marriages following the death of a spouse or divorce. Because the Talmud instructs us that God also arranges second marriages, a subsequent marriage can be just as fulfilling and meaningful as the first.

Consequently, Judaism treats marriage as the means by which two human beings unite and reach a complete state that brings them closer to God. While the man and the woman retain their distinct identities, each one can become truly whole only when united with their significant other.

Because the union of husband and wife is sanctified, the married couple is deemed to have the opportunity and responsibility to make their home into a miniature sanctuary or *mikdat me'at*. This is why the home and the raising of children are central to Judaism and why the home has such a prominent role in the celebration of holidays and festivals. Recall that it is in the home that the Sabbath and other holidays are initially greeted with the lighting of the candles and the recitation of appropriate blessings.

Marriage as a *Mitzvah*

More than likely, you are acquainted with God's commandment to "be fruitful and multiply" (Genesis 1:28). To marry and have children is not considered an option. It is a *mitzvah,* and it is stated as a requirement in the *Shulchan Aruch,* the Code of Jewish Law. In order to fulfill this commandment, each couple must have at least one male and one female child.

The importance placed upon procreation is also emphasized in the Talmud, where it is written that when each person enters the world to come, he or she will have to answer the following three questions: Were you honest in your business dealings? Did you have a set time for Torah study? Did you raise a family?

Remember how Jacob entered Egypt with a band of seventy adults but the Israelites emerged from Egypt a little more than two centuries later some two to three million strong? You might think these numbers are a fabrication, but if you do the math, you will see that if the Israelites obeyed this *mitzvah,* the population that came forth from Egypt is well within the realm of the probable.

ESSENTIALS

The late American Jewish scholar, Rabbi Aryeh Kaplan, calculated that if a couple has at least two children and each of their descendants has two children, after 250 years, that couple will have more than 1,000 descendants. After 600 years, there would be over 16 million descendants!

Getting Married

Exactly how do you go about finding a soul mate? One view holds that there is really nothing special for you to do—once you get married, that person is ipso facto your soul mate. According to one *midrashic* story, marriages are arranged in heaven and, in fact, ever since creating the world in six days, God has been busy arranging matches!

Jews are not any different from other people when it comes to matters of the heart, and a person can grow impatient awaiting "true love." Sometimes, you must take matters into your own hands, either on behalf of yourself or for someone else.

The Mishna describes festivities that occurred in Jerusalem on the fifteenth day of *Av* and on the afternoon of Yom Kippur. On these occasions, single women dressed in white and danced in the vineyards, hoping to be chosen by one of the attentive men to become his bride. However, such activities as this did not always succeed and one (or one's parents) would grow weary waiting for "fate" to step in. And so, a profession of sorts arose to arrange marriages.

The Role of Matchmakers

For many centuries, even to the present (though employed much less frequently today), the task of finding suitable marriage partners was left to the *shadchan* (the marriage broker, or matchmaker) to arrange a *shidukh* or "match." The "profession" of a *shadchan* became very popular in the thirteenth and fourteenth centuries but then began to wane as the notion of romantic love began to gain the upper hand in choosing marriage partners. Even though these matchmakers were not necessarily the brightest or most scrupulous of people, the *shadchan* remained an important person, particularly in the *shtetls* of Eastern Europe, up until the nineteenth century.

FACTS

The word *shidukh* is Hebrew for "marital match." The Aramaic version of this word is *sheket,* which also means "quiet." That is, the term *shidukh* reflects tranquillity or peacefulness—the idea is that the match should prove serene and happy for all concerned and also bring some relief to the parents!

In contemporary society, the use of matchmakers is rare and is generally limited to more observant families. There are other paths to take to find a soul mate: people can visit Web sites on the Internet, scan the personals, contact dating services, go to social events, or follow up on that phone number provided by their mothers—there are many options to choose from.

Acquiring a Spouse

Once you find your *bashert,* Judaism imposes certain conditions to meet before the marriage ceremony can take place. The couple must undergo the engagement or betrothal period that is known as the *kiddushin,* derived from the Hebrew root *kodesh,* meaning "holy." This term reflects the idea that the man and woman have become consecrated to each other. However, in recent times *kiddushin* has merged into the actual marriage ritual and is held during the first part of the wedding ceremony.

Kiddushin requires that in order for a woman to be acquired and a marriage made, one of the following three conditions be satisfied (although, ordinarily, all three are fulfilled):

1. Payment of money or something of value
2. A written contract
3. Physical consummation of the relationship

Do not buy a wedding band that is jeweled, since it is customary that it be unornamented. This practice arose to avoid the possibility of acquiring a wife by fraud, since only an expert could discern the value of gems but anyone can see the worth of an unadorned ring.

The notion that a woman is "acquired" is probably troublesome to our modern way of thinking. However, Jewish tradition does stipulate that regardless of who proposed the match or what the parents may demand, a woman may be "acquired" only with her consent. In fact, the written marital contract is designed, for the most part, to protect the woman.

Today, the thing of value that is customarily offered is the wedding ring. It was never intended that this item have substantial value, since the purpose has nothing to do with buying or selling a woman. Rather, the woman's approval of this thing of value serves to indicate her acceptance of her future husband.

If there is to be a double ring ceremony, which is not required in Judaism, it is advisable for the bride to have a plain wedding band for the groom. With rings at hand, everything is ready for the marriage to take place.

The *Ketubah*

In addition to betrothal ceremonies, the couple must also sign the marriage contract (different from the betrothal contract previously mentioned). The marriage contract is called a *ketubah,* a term that comes from the Hebrew word *katav* (writing).

Ketubah, a Jewish marriage contract

Photo courtesy of Joshua Marowitz and Joshua and Ali Hurwitz

Ketubot range from standard printed certificates with blanks filled in to beautiful customized works of calligraphy and decorated pieces of art that may be framed and displayed in the home. The text may be written in the traditional Aramaic or include modern expressions.

The *ketubah* is designed to protect the woman. It delineates the obligations and responsibilities of the husband toward the wife in terms of helping her raise children, financial responsibility of the man for the woman in the event of divorce, and conditions of inheritance upon the death of the husband. By mutual agreement, additional provisions may be made to the contract.

The Wedding Ceremony

Wedding parties vary widely, depending on the couple's religious denomination, cultural traditions, and personal preferences—there is really no one Jewish way to celebrate a wedding. However, it is possible to discuss the traditional Jewish wedding ceremony that precedes the party.

Note that not all of the customs and observances are performed at every Jewish wedding. Often, the participants want a say in determining the contents of the ceremony, sometimes foregoing certain rituals and in other places embellishing the litany with original and personal thoughts. And as for the type of ceremony where only one of the key participants is Jewish—well, this is a different story altogether and will be discussed separately.

Before the Ceremony

In the basic wedding ceremony that is conducted in accordance with the principles of Judaism, custom dictates that the bride (*kalah* or *kallah*) and groom (*chatan*) are not allowed to see each other for one week prior to the wedding ceremony. Generally, on the *Shabbat* preceding the wedding, an *aliyah* is given to the groom or to the couple. This special *aliyah* is called an *aufruf*. The congregation blesses the couple and, in some synagogues, showers the couple with candy. In other synagogues, in lieu of an *aliyah,* the couple is called to the *bimah* for a prenuptial blessing.

On the day of the wedding, the bride and groom are expected to fast. Given that they may be nervous and have "butterflies" in their stomachs, this may not be a difficult tradition to follow. The reason behind this practice is that by fasting and repenting their sins, and being forgiven in the process, the new couple commences their life together with a clean slate.

Before the ceremony, the bride is veiled in remembrance of Rebecca who veiled her face when she was brought to Isaac to be his wife. In more traditional circles, it is common for the groom to wear a long white *kittel* similar to that worn on Yom Kippur and Passover.

The *Chupah*

Jewish wedding ceremonies can take place anywhere. A wedding held in a synagogue is no more sanctified than one held in a hotel ballroom or in a home or outdoors. What is required is that during the ceremony the couple be standing under the *chupah,* the central symbol of the wedding ceremony.

The *chupah* is symbolic of several things. Foremost, it depicts the roof of the new home, in which the bride and groom will live and raise their family. Second, the *chupah* suggests a royal canopy, for tradition holds it that on the wedding day, the bride and groom are like a king and queen. The *chupah* also represents a third element of creating a marriage (sexual relations).

FACTS

In Hebrew, *chupah* means "chamber" or "covering." The *chupah* can be made of a *tallit* supported by four poles, of fine fabric such as silk, or even a floral arrangement. Sometimes, the *chupah* is embroidered with a biblical quotation.

Kiddushin

With the *chupah* in place, the wedding ceremony can begin. The first part of the ceremony is known as *kiddushin* or "sanctified." While historically the *kiddushin* might have occurred as much as one year before the *nisuin* (full-fledged marriage), today they form two parts of the same event.

First, the wedding party comes to stand under the *chupah*. Practice in this regard varies. Sometimes, the bride is led to the *chupah* by her mother and mother-in-law or by any two women, and the groom is ushered by his father and father-in-law or by any two men. At other times, the parents escort the bride and groom, their respective children. In this case, the groom arrives to the *chupah* first and awaits the bride.

Jewish law does not require the presence of a rabbi at the wedding ceremony. In fact, it is incorrect to say that the rabbi "marries" the couple. In Judaism, two witnesses are sufficient; the rabbi's presence only helps ensure that the ceremony is properly performed. It is true, however, that a rabbi or public official must officiate the wedding in order to comply with modern civil law.

When the bride reaches the *chupah,* she is led seven times around the groom. There are many reasons for this practice. The Kabbalah, for instance, suggests that the bride symbolizes the earth; by encircling the groom seven times, she re-enacts the seven days of Creation. This is particularly significant since the married couple will soon become involved in the creation of new lives.

In Judaism, there is no such concept as "giving away" the bride. That is why the bride is escorted by two people and not just by her father. The bride's parents remain with her under the *chupah* during the ceremony, as do the groom's parents.

Blessings over the wine follow. First the rabbi drinks from the wine, and then the groom and the bride do likewise. The groom places the ring on the bride's right index finger, reciting, "You are hereby sanctified to me with this ring according to the Laws of Moses and Israel." This act of "sanctification" is *kiddushin*. If there is a double ring ceremony, the bride makes a similar vow. *Kiddushin* is now complete.

Nisuin

Without skipping a beat, the ceremony proceeds with the reading of the *ketubah* that serves to separate the two parts of the service. Then, the ceremony continues with *nisuin* ("elevation"). Seven blessings are recited, the first of which is the blessing over the wine. Again, the rabbi drinks from the goblet, and the groom and the bride follow.

The ceremony concludes with the breaking of the glass, probably the best-known feature of a Jewish wedding. A glass is wrapped in a cloth, and then the groom smashes it with his right foot. This action reminds the Jews that even on the most happy of occasions, they must remember the destruction of the Temple.

The new husband and wife are escorted to a private room, where they are secluded for a brief time. This custom, known as *yichud,* is symbolic of the husband bringing his wife to his home. Although they are left alone and no one knows what does or does not go on inside, the couple is not expected to actually consummate the marriage at that time.

As with any joyous event, it is customary to celebrate the wedding with music and dancing and fine food. However, this is not the focal point of the wedding day. Rather, the center of attention should be the ceremony where the bride and groom are joined as soul mates.

SSENTIALS

There are additional reasons offered for the custom of breaking the glass. One explanation is that it reminds the gathered that the world is broken and they must help repair it. Another rationale suggests that the love between bride and groom will last until the scattered shards of glass come back together.

Interfaith Marriages

In traditional Judaism, a marriage between Jew and Gentile is not an issue or open to question. It is forbidden, and that's that. There are many justifications for this stance. Some reasons are spiritual, such as the notion that a Jewish marriage reunites two parts of the same soul. How can it be possible for one of the halves to be non-Jewish?

This prohibition also stems from more practical considerations. For one thing, there is the matter of the viability of the Jewish people to remain a distinct religious and ethnic group despite widespread intermarriage. In the United States, where the intermarriage rate is 50 percent, only a quarter of children born in these marriages are raised as Jews. The Jewish population in the United States is actually decreasing.

Naturally, if the non-Jew converts, then the marriage ceremony is not an interfaith wedding at all, and the couple can hold a Jewish wedding.

A L E R T

Bear in mind that the conversion process selected determines the type of rabbi who will officiate and what branch of Judaism will recognize the marriage. The Orthodox will acknowledge a marriage and an Orthodox rabbi will officiate at the ceremony only if the conversion was consistent with Orthodox requirements.

Nonetheless, interfaith marriages have existed all through history and cannot be ignored. Although the Reform and Reconstructionist branches of Judaism do not encourage intermarriages, they have adopted a more accepting approach to the issue. If the non-Jewish bride or groom chooses not to convert, there is always the option of having a joint-faith ceremony with the presence of clergy of both faiths. However, under these circumstances, it is more difficult to secure the services of a rabbi.

An alternative option is to have a civil official such as a judge or justice of the peace preside at the wedding. In such instances, it is wise to take extra caution regarding what might prove offensive to some of the guests present.

SSENTIALS Options for interfaith marriages abound. A plethora of resource materials, including books, Web sites, outreach programs, and interfaith organizations, are available for the engaged couple.

Getting a Divorce

Judaism is pragmatic about marriage and has always been realistic about the fact that some marriages may end in divorce. As you already know, the marriage contract (the *ketubah)* makes provisions for what happens in the event of divorce. However, while the *ketubah* is designed to protect the woman, the rules of divorce are definitely lopsided in favor of the man.

Under Jewish law, a woman cannot commence divorce proceedings, yet a man can divorce his wife for any reason or no reason at all. (Though if the husband is unable to provide a rational reason, the rabbi will suggest counseling or reconsideration.) There are also cases in which a man must divorce his wife, regardless of whether he wants to, as, for example, if she has committed adultery. Though it may seem easy for a man to secure a divorce, the truth is that the process is far from simple.

Obtaining a Divorce

In the Torah, a divorce is accomplished by writing a bill of divorce that is called a *sefer k'ritut* ("scroll of cutting off"), delivering it to the wife, and sending her away. In fact, the Hebrew word for divorce is *gerushin,* a term that comes from the verb "to send away." Today, the Jewish divorce is known as a *get,* a "bill of divorce" in Hebrew.

Does Judaism recognize a civil divorce?
In order to be divorced after having been married according to the laws and customs of Judaism, the Orthodox and Conservative movements require that a *get* be obtained. Reform and Reconstructionist Judaism, on the other hand, generally recognize a civil decree.

The procedures involved in obtaining a *get* are complicated and demanding, and can be extremely frustrating. A *get* is procured from a rabbinical court. Although the woman must be provided for financially, the laws favor the husband. However, over the years, efforts have been made to bring a greater degree of equality into the process. For example, while only a man can initiate a divorce, it is now necessary for the wife to agree to it.

Judaism's particular attitude to divorce has led to another problem. If a man deserts his wife or disappears and no proof of his death exists, his wife technically remains married—since a woman cannot initiate a divorce. A woman in such a situation is referred to as *agunah* ("anchored"). She cannot remarry because in the event her husband is alive, the rabbis do not want to have condoned an adulterous marriage.

CHAPTER 19

Death, Mourning, and the Afterlife

Judaism sets a high value on human life, and it recognizes the need for a mourning process. The Jewish tradition has a great deal to impart about how to confront death, the way a person should be buried and grieved, and what is beyond the world as we know it, where the soul of the dead person will dwell.

The Soul

The idea of a "soul" (*neshamah* in Hebrew) is fundamental to Judaism, which sees the soul as eternal. Although clear references to the human soul do appear in the Bible, most of what the Jewish tradition teaches about the soul comes from rabbinical (post-Biblical) times. The soul comes from God, and it precedes the existence of a human body. As for where the soul is headed after this life, we are told in Ecclesiastes that the soul returns to God (thus, the idea of an afterlife): "The dust returns to the earth as it was, and the spirit returns to God who gave it" (12:7).

The Soul's Components

The Jewish conception of a soul is rather unique. In Judaism, the soul is not indivisible. Rather, it is more like an amalgamation of five basic elements that are in turn subdivided into even more elements. This is a very complicated subject that has a lot to do with Kabbalah (Jewish mysticism) and that will only be briefly summarized here.

The lowest constituent of the soul is *nefesh,* and it is the soul's most physical aspect. In ascending order, the soul's other, more spiritual elements are *ruach, neshamah, chayah,* and *yechidah.* To refer to all five of these components, you can use the term *narachai* (an acronym of the five terms). Since the *naranchai* is numinous, it seeks spirituality, which is why humans seek to pursue the spiritual.

After a person dies, that person's *naranchai* will desire to leave the physical body. If the person has led a spiritual life, this desire will be fulfilled. However, the *naranchai* of those who were focused on the material aspect of the world may remain rooted to the physical. (It gets even more complex than this, but the point is that there is a soul within each of us. To what extent it reaches its spiritual destination depends upon how we lived our lives.)

The Afterlife

Although Judaism focuses primarily on life in the here-and-now, the belief in an afterlife is well established, with references found in the Torah. In several places, there are indications that the righteous, but not the wicked, will be reunited with their loved ones. A number of Biblical luminaries (Abraham, Jacob, Moses, and others), are said to have been "gathered to their people" after their death.

While the idea of an afterlife is firmly established in traditional Judaism, little in the way of doctrine and tenets surrounds it. As a result, you will find different conceptions about the afterlife within Judaism, including some that consider the entire notion irrelevant.

FACTS

Many Hasidic sects believe in reincarnation, which is an element in Kabbalah. Some hold that the souls of the righteous are reborn to continue their good work, while other sources indicate that a soul is reincarnated only if there's a need to complete some unfinished business, such as repaying a loan.

Among the Orthodox, some are of the opinion that wicked souls will be tormented by demons of their own making or that they will cease to exist altogether. There are those who believe in reincarnation, while others think it is a matter of waiting for resurrection. In any event, reincarnation and resurrection are not incompatible, and one does not preclude the other. It's important to remember, however, that regardless of what ideas you choose to accept or reject about the soul and the afterlife, a Jew is still expected to live his or her life in accordance with the Jewish laws and principles.

Biblical Background

During biblical times, the Jews believed in *sheol,* a world of shadows wherein dwell the dead. Later, they came to believe in a paradise called *Gan Eden* (Garden of Eden), not to be confused with the famous garden inhabited by Adam and Eve. This concept is somewhat similar to the Christian idea of Heaven.

Only the righteous go directly to *Gan Eden.* Most souls descend to *Gehinnom,* the valley of Hinnom, which is a place of punishment or purification. Souls are not consigned to *Gehinnom* for eternity but only for a limited time. The idea of a soul's being damned forever is not consistent with Judaism. In fact, the Jewish tradition maintains that all souls will ultimately be resurrected.

ESSENTIALS

Gehinnom is named for a place that really existed in Biblical times. Located outside Jerusalem, the historical Gehinnom was a place inhabited by pagans who offered their children as sacrifices, thus earning a reputation as the most abominable place imaginable.

The Messianic Era

Although traditional Judaism does contain the basic belief that all souls will be resurrected, there is no complete agreement on the details—an account that follows is only one scenario. However, all ideas regarding resurrection have one point in common: resurrection cannot take place until the coming of the Messiah, who will usher in the Messianic Era.

FACTS

The notion of resurrection has never been universally accepted in Judaism. Initially, the Pharisees (the forerunners of Rabbinical Judaism) deduced the concept from certain verses in the Torah, but the Sadducees rejected the idea because it was not explicitly mentioned. Nonetheless, the belief in resurrection and an afterlife is fundamental in traditional Judaism.

Actually, it is believed there will be a succession of three messiahs. The word *messiah* means "anointed" and therefore does not rule out more than one messiah. The first messiah will be the first king who governs over a world that, while still physical, will be a wonderful place in which to live. People will still die, but they will lead long and healthy lives. Some believe that the righteous dead will be resurrected at this time to experience this perfect world. After the death of the first messiah, his son, and then grandson, will succeed him. Since the Messianic Era spans 2,000 years, these messiahs will live a very long time!

At the conclusion of the Messianic Era, the world as we know it, *Olam Ha-Zeh* ("this world"), will come to an end. A thousand-year interval known as the years of desolation will follow. Nothing will be alive and all souls will be in the Realm of Souls engaged in a state of spiritual growth while awaiting the World to Come.

The World to Come

When the World to Come, or *Olam Ha-Ba*, arrives, each soul will be reunited with its body (that is, each human being will be resurrected), and humans will live in the World to Come for eternity. The Talmud and Midrash provide much of what we know of *Olam Ha-Ba*.

Although some have suggested that the wicked will not have a share in the World to Come, it is more widely held that all souls will be gathered together there. However, any particular soul's place, or its share in *Olam Ha-Ba*, is largely based on how it lived and the *mitzvot* it performed as a human being.

Do not confuse the World to Come with the Messianic Era. Although sometimes the two terms are used interchangeably, this is incorrect. The Messianic Era that accompanies the appearance of the Messiah takes place in This World, which precedes the World to Come.

Is there a timetable for when the Messianic Era and the World to Come will finally arrive? The answer is yes, but like most schedules, it doesn't always quite work out. The original plan was for the world to last 6,000 years, including 2,000 years of "void" before Abraham. The Messiah was slated to appear 2,000 years after Abraham and then there would be the 2,000 years of the Messianic Age. However, people have failed to adequately pave the way for the coming of the Messiah, so things are a bit off schedule. Today, we are well beyond the 2,000-year interval between Abraham and the Messiah.

While we cannot be certain when the Messiah will arrive and set things in motion for the World to Come, we can be sure about one thing—that all of us will die in this world (*Olam Ha-Zeh*). The rest of this chapter examines how Judaism treats death, as well as the customs of burial and mourning.

QUESTIONS?

Can non-Jews enter the World to Come?
All humans will enter the *Olam Ha-Ba.* Furthermore, because one's position in *Olam Ha-Ba* is predicated upon righteousness and not just belief, the religion that any human being professed or followed is irrelevant. All the righteous, regardless of their religious beliefs or cultural backgrounds, share the World to Come.

Taking Care of the Dead

As you already know, souls of the dead eventually end up in the *Olam Ha-Ba,* where they will be reunited with their bodies, emerging as ultimately spiritual beings. In Judaism, the body is not merely some superfluous shell to be discarded but rather an indispensable part of that new ethereal being.

In general, Jewish burial customs derive from the concept of *Kevod Ha-Met* ("honor due to the dead"). The same concept also provides the Jews with explicit guidelines for how to behave toward the body of the deceased, which is treated with the utmost respect.

Care for the Body

Once a person dies, somebody needs to close the body's eyes and mouth, cover its face, and light candles. It is customary to lay the body in such a fashion that the feet point toward the door; the body may be laid on the floor.

Out of respect for the deceased, the dead body is never left alone from the moment of death until burial. Sometimes arrangements are made for someone to sit with the body. These sentinels are called *shomerim* (from the root *shin-mem-resh* that means "guards" or "keepers"). The *shomerim* recite Psalms and may not eat, drink, or perform *mitzvot* in the presence of the deceased because performing a commandment of God is a joyous action.

Don't forget to open a window in the room where the deceased is at rest! While not always followed, this custom has to do with the belief that the window should be open so the *neshamah* (soul) can escape as soon as possible.

Burial Customs

The Torah forbids leaving a body unburied overnight (Deuteronomy 21:23), so the burial process happens relatively fast (though in present times the internment actually occurs one or two days after death). The reason behind this haste to the cemetery, a tradition that is alien to most cultures and religions, has to do with reverence for the dead body and not a desire to get rid of it and move on.

If there is a local burial society, often known as *Chevra Kadisha* ("the holy society"), the relatives contact its representative in order that they may prepare the body. The alternative is for a Jewish funeral home to assume the responsibilities regarding the body. The deceased should be cleaned and wrapped in a simple shroud (*tashrichim*), usually made of white linen. The reason for the uniformity in attiring the deceased is that all people are alike, wealthy and poor, and nothing should distinguish one from the other at death. This is also one of the reasons each person is buried in a plain wooden coffin.

It should be noted that many Jewish families deviate from some of these procedures. For example, the body may be dressed in clothes and not a shroud, and the coffin may be made of a material more durable than wood. Though cremation and entombment are prohibited, some Jews nevertheless opt for these alternatives.

Jewish tradition discourages autopsies and organ transplants; the reason for that is the respect for the body. However, where required by law or to save a life, these prohibitions may be ignored. Traditionally, Jewish corpses do not undergo embalming or cosmetology, although, once again, it is not unusual for many Jewish families to select these procedures.

FACTS

Another explanation for the use of a wooden (frequently pine) casket is that wood decomposes at about the same rate as the body. Therefore, the body can return more rapidly to dust. In Israel, caskets are not used; the body is buried wrapped in a prayer shawl.

Funeral Preparations

As the family of the deceased arranges for the funeral and picks out the casket, they must also decide whether to have a service at the funeral parlor or at the graveside. Typically, the funeral director helps the family make their choices and prepares them for the funeral. Although a rabbi is generally invited to conduct the funeral service, his presence is not required. The rabbi is there to ensure that the service goes according to the Jewish tradition and to provide comfort and guidance for the relatives and friends of the deceased.

The Funeral Ceremony

One of the chief purposes of the funeral service is to pay reverence to the deceased. During the service, a rabbi reads selected prayers and psalms, including *El Malei Rachamim,* a prayer that asks for repose of the departed soul. Carrying on a tradition that began with Abraham, who eulogized his wife Sarah (Genesis 23:2), a eulogy is given to praise the departed one and express the grief felt by family and friends.

Before the chapel service or at the graveside service, the ritual of *Keriah* (tearing) is performed. This involves rending (tearing) one's garments as a display of separation. The practice has its origins in Genesis 37:34, where "Jacob rent his garments" when informed (erroneously) that his son, Joseph, was killed by a wild animal. The garments may also be torn immediately upon hearing of the death of a loved one. In lieu of tearing up their clothes, some Jews wear a black ribbon.

ESSENTIALS

All branches of Judaism agree that, out of respect for the body, the casket must remain closed. There should not be a public viewing. Although it's contrary to traditional practices, it is not unusual for members of the immediate family to conduct a private viewing before the funeral service.

Note that people tear their garments as an act of mourning for a parent, child, sibling, or spouse. Others tear their clothes in mourning for their parents but wear a black ribbon for all other relatives.

It is Jewish custom that the family and friends physically assist in the burial, throwing clumps of earth over the coffin. Those gathered at the grave then say the *Kaddish*, which marks the end of the burial service. Interestingly, this traditional prayer for the dead actually doesn't discuss death but exalts God and appeals for world peace.

From that point on, when the deceased has been given due respect and the body properly buried, the person who passed away is no longer the focus of attention. The concern now must focus on the mourners, whose sense of anguish at the loss of a loved one does not cease as the last shovel of earth is thrown over the grave. In recognition of the feelings of the mourners and to pay proper deference to the memory of the departed one, Judaism has specific procedures in place for the period of mourning.

The Mourning Period

Mourning customs in Judaism are comprehensive and serve two purposes: to demonstrate respect for the deceased and to provide solace for the mourners. There are four distinct stages of mourning:

1. *Aninut,* the time period between death and interment
2. *Shiva,* a seven-day mourning period that begins immediately after burial (note that for the first three days of *shiva,* guests are generally discouraged from visiting the bereaved family.)
3. *Shloshim,* a thirty-day period following burial (including *shiva*)
4. *Avelut,* a twelve-month period after interment (including *shloshim*)

Aninut

From the moment of death until the deceased is buried, known as the *aninut* period, the mourner's chief responsibility is to attend to the deceased and make the necessary funeral and burial preparations. Because these tasks take priority, mourners are exempt from all positive, time-honored *mitzvot.* Since Judaism requires a prompt interment, *aninut* lasts a day or two. During this time, it is inappropriate to make condolence calls.

Shiva

The next stage of mourning is *shiva,* a period that lasts for seven days (*shiva* is Hebrew for "seven"). The day of burial is included in the *shiva* period and counts as the first day. In some less traditional communities, *shiva* is observed for three days.

FACTS

"Sitting *shiva*" is the expression commonly used to refer to what mourners do during the period of *shiva.* The term is derived from the practice of not sitting in a comfortable chair but instead sitting on a low bench, stool, or even on the floor.

Parents, siblings, spouse, and children of the deceased sit *shiva* at the home of the deceased or at one of the mourner's homes. They go directly to the *shiva* house from the cemetery, wash their hands before entering (as does everyone who leaves a funeral), light a candle that will remain burning throughout the *shiva* period, and begin to sit *shiva*.

The meal of consolation, *Seudat Havra'a,* is the first meal served to mourners. It is often provided by friends. Traditionally, this meal consists of hard-boiled eggs, bagels, and dairy products. The circular shape of some of these foods is symbolic of the eternal nature of life.

There are a number of observances and prohibitions that should be followed during *shiva*. The following is a list of some of these interdictions and observances:

- Mourners should cover all the mirrors in the house.
- Mourners may not bathe, shave, or cut their hair or nails.
- Mourners may not wear leather shoes.
- Mourners may not wash their clothes or wear new clothes (except clothes to be worn on *Shabbat*).
- Sexual relations are forbidden.
- Conducting business is prohibited, except under extraordinary circumstances.
- Limitations are set on leaving the *shiva* house.
- Mourners must sit on a low stool, bench, or on the floor.

It is a *mitzvah* to comfort a mourner, so making a *shiva* call is encouraged. The first three days are generally reserved for visits from family and close friends. If you did not know the deceased well, try to hold off your visit until the first three days have passed. However, if you know that you won't be able to visit later, it is better to visit during the first three days than not at all. Naturally, if *shiva* is observed for only three days, any time during that period is appropriate.

Because the mourners say their prayers and the *Kaddish* at the *shiva* house, they must rely upon guests to make up the *minyan*. As for decorum, the basic guideline is just to be present, which, in and of itself, brings comfort to the mourner. It is more important to listen than to speak, and it is even customary not to say hello or good-bye, since the mourner is forbidden to extend greetings and salutations. However, upon leaving, it is traditional to say to the mourner, "May God comfort you among the other mourners of Zion and Jerusalem."

Shiva ends on the afternoon of the seventh day after the burial. At that time, it is customary for the mourners to leave the *shiva* house and take a walk, accompanied by friends and family. This excursion indicates that the mourners are ready to return to the external world from which they had withdrawn. At this time, the remaining stages of mourning begin.

Note that the *Shabbat* that falls within the shiva period is counted as a day even though it is not observed as a day of mourning. If a major festival (Rosh Hashanah, Yom Kippur, Passover, Shavuot, or Sukkot) falls during *shiva,* then *shiva* comes to an abrupt end. Should death occur on a major holiday, everything is delayed, including the burial, until the holiday is over.

Shloshim, Avelut, and Beyond

The third period of mourning is called *shloshim.* This period extends to the thirtieth day after burial (*shloshim* is Hebrew for "thirty"). During *shloshim,* some prohibitions that apply to *shiva* also remain valid, including the following:

- Cutting nails or hair
- Shaving
- Wearing new clothes
- Attending parties or listening to music

The final period of mourning, which only applies to those who have lost a parent, is *avelut,* a mourning period of twelve months. During this time, mourners abstain from parties, celebrations, and other venues of entertainment. However, the mourners should otherwise make it a point to begin their return to a normal life.

Other practices are observed in memory of the departed. Throughout the year of mourning, at the end of every prayer service, each mourner should recite the *Kaddish.* While commonly known as the mourner's prayer, *Kaddish* is really a prayer of praise to God and has nothing to do with death or mourning. The importance of reciting the *Kaddish* lies in the fact that it is performed standing up at public prayer. Through this public exaltation of God, the mourner demonstrates a reaffirmation of faith even after the death of a loved one.

A L E R T

Keep in mind that the final period of mourning, *avelut,* lasts for twelve months and is based upon the Hebrew calendar, which sometimes has a "leap" month, the second month of *Adar.* During a leap year, when a thirteenth month is added, you observe *avelut* for only twelve months and not the entire year.

At specific times of the year (Yom Kippur, Passover, Shavuot, and Sukkot), the mourners also need to recite the *Yizkor* prayer. *Yizkor* (Hebrew for "may [God] remember") is the abridged popular name for the memorial service, *Ha-Zkarat Neshamot* (Remembrance of the Souls). At this service, congregants remember their loved ones who have passed on but also commemorate all those who died sanctifying God's name—for instance, the fighters of Israel's War of Independence. Some congregations make this an occasion to remember the six million Jews murdered by the Nazis. It is suitable to begin saying *Yizkor* either at the first holiday after the death of a loved one or at the first opportunity that takes place at the end of the twelve-month mourning period.

The *Yahrzeit* memorial lamp

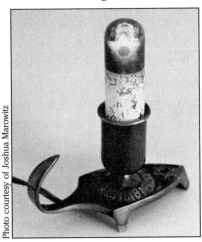

Photo courtesy of Joshua Marowitz

Another practice that continues to be observed past mourning is the lighting of a *Yahrzeit* candle. *Yahrzeit* occurs on the annual anniversary of the date of death, as set by the Hebrew calendar. At this time, in addition to reciting the *Kaddish,* a twenty-four-hour candle is lit in the home and, often, in the synagogue in memory of the departed person. This burning light of the *Yahrzeit* candle is symbolic of the immortal soul.

Yahrzeit is actually a German word that means "year's time" or "anniversary." Sometimes, the Yiddish word, *Yortzeit,* is used in its place. In any event, this ritual to honor the dead may be the only Jewish ceremony that does not have a Hebrew name!

The Unveiling

Jewish law requires a tombstone to mark the grave of the deceased so that the departed one will not be forgotten and the grave will not be desecrated. While the tombstone can be erected anytime after *shloshim* (the thirty-day period of mourning), in many communities it is customary either to refrain from setting up the tombstone or to keep it veiled until the end of the twelve-month mourning period.

However, some time before the end of the year of mourning (usually around eleven months), the mourners hold a ceremony to dedicate the grave marker. This ceremony is generally referred to as an "unveiling" (*Ha-Kamat Matzeyvah*).

There are no specific requirements concerning how the tombstone must be inscribed. In some communities, it is customary to place small stones on the grave site when visiting. The origin of this practice is uncertain. A popular explanation states that in the desert environment of ancient Israel, mourners piled stones and rocks to prevent the sandy soil from blowing away and exposing the corpse.

In any event, for some Jews, the placement of a small stone at a grave marker is something that absolutely must be done. Why? Not for religious reasons but for cultural reasons. As you shall see in the following chapter, Jewish culture has always had a major impact on the way Jewish people think and behave.

CHAPTER 20

The Jewish Culture

It is impossible in these pages to do the subject of Jewish culture much justice. Nevertheless, this chapter briefly examines what Jewish culture embodies and what it has to offer, from *Fiddler on the Roof* and gefilte fish to klezmer music and Jewish humor.

Is There a Jewish Culture?

This book's primary focus has been Judaism, but quite often it also refers to the "Jewish people." Jews share more than Judaism, their religion. They also have a common culture, though this may not always be apparent at first glance.

Culture may be defined as a common set of beliefs and practices that a group of people adopt over time. Different communities of Jews living at different times and in different societies have sometimes appeared to have little in common beside Judaism. Over time, however, each group of Jews has contributed to the mix that we have come to know as "Jewish culture."

Given a history of almost 4,000 years and the geographic dispersal that forced the Jews to confront and sometimes assimilate other world cultures, Jewish culture has always been heterogeneous. Yet somehow all the diverse customs and practices have managed to come together, much like Joseph's coat of many colors. And like the variegated hues of Joseph's coat, the result has been a truly wondrous and remarkable synthesis.

Jewish Literature

Jewish literature, both religious and secular, could easily fill voluminous anthologies, divided by language, subject, or time period when a particular work was authored. In this book, you'll have to be satisfied with just a few words on this topic.

Recall that Chapter 4 reviewed Yiddish literature, drawing attention to how the tales, stories, and novels had affected Ashkenazic Jews in Europe for hundreds of years, and how they continued to affect the Jews who emigrated to the United States from Europe at the turn of the twentieth century. Today, however, Yiddish is in decline, and despite renewed interest in Yiddish literature, little new work is forthcoming.

Wherever Jews live in respectable numbers, there is a presence of Jewish literature that augments a sense of oneness as a people. In the last fifty years, American Jewish literature has flourished (if, that is, you count all types of work written by Jewish writers as Jewish literature).

In Israel, not only have Israeli novelists had a great impact on Israelis, but much of their work has been translated from Hebrew, making them accessible to Jewish communities around the globe. We have been fortunate to witness the likes of Aharon Appelfeld, S. Y. Agnon, A. B. Yehoshua, and Amos Oz, as well as the emergence of a new generation of gifted Israeli writers such as David Grossman and Etgar Keret.

FACTS

A variety of well-established Jewish American writers have achieved critical acclaim, including Saul Bellow, Henry Roth, Bernard Malamud, Philip Roth, Joseph Heller, Elie Wiesel, Chaim Potok, Cynthia Ozick, and Leon Uris. With young writers of fiction such as Michael Chabon, Myla Goldberg, Thane Rosenbaum, and Allegra Goodman, the future of Jewish literature in twenty-first century America is secure.

Although this brief review does not even scratch the surface of Jewish literature, an appendix at the end of this book is devoted to both Jewish literature and works of nonfiction, as well as other reading material of Jewish interest. Just think, after you finally get to put this book down, you can spend all your waking hours just trying to make a dent in the thousands of books that comprise Jewish literature!

Jewish Music

Jewish music is another mammoth topic that can never be fully summarized in a book such as this one. Some say that music soothes the savage beast. But music also manages to pluck the strings of the heart and stir the emotions in ways that words cannot describe. Just listening to the chanting of *Kol Nidre* on Yom Kippur, you cannot help but feel connected to the Jews who have joined in this plaintive prayer for hundreds of years in thousands of communities.

How can you not sense the bond with Jews living in Israel when the resonance of *Ha-Tikvah* (the Israeli anthem) fills your ears? And when hearing *Jerusalem of Gold,* do you not find yourself closing your eyes and seeing before you the hills of Jerusalem? Nor do you need to understand a word of Yiddish in order to perceive a kinship with all the sons and daughters who ever sang "My Yiddish Momme."

Today there is a resurgence of Jewish music called klezmer music, reminiscent of the times when groups of itinerant musicians went from village to village in Eastern Europe, entertaining the local Jewish populace with folk songs and folk dance as well as traditional music. Another branch of Jewish music is comprised of traditional and contemporary songs in Hebrew that originate from Israel.

Like Jewish literature, Jewish music has played a large part in what has bound the Jewish people together, particularly during the Diaspora. Yet not every Jew appreciated nor paid attention to Jewish music or Jewish literature—but every Jew had to eat. So, it might not be so unlikely that more than any other aspect of Jewish culture, it is Jewish food that has held the Jews together all these years!

Jewish Food

If you've read the preceding pages, you must have already noticed that all Jewish holidays and festivals, no matter how major or minor, have at least one thing in common—there is always a feast (*seudah*). Food plays an important part in many cultures, and the Jews are no exception in this regard. In fact, food has probably had a greater role in keeping the Jews together as a people than it has for most other groups because food frequently serves both ethnic and religious functions.

What Is Jewish Food?

Technically, there probably is no such thing as "Jewish" food. There is, however, food that is not Jewish because it is not kosher and no amount of preparation will change that. (For more specifics on the laws of *kashrut,* see Chapter 6.)

Obviously, food that complies with the laws of *kashrut* or is prepared accordingly is Jewish food. That's pretty much a no-brainer. Just as clearly, *kashrut* has helped keep the Jews together during the Diaspora. For example, if a Jew found himself in a strange town and he wanted to eat, he sought out a Jewish family or Jewish restaurant where he could have his meals. Even today, you will find sites on the Internet informing you where you can have a kosher meal in various towns and cities.

Jewish Cuisine as a Synthesis

Jewish food as a concept is really an amalgamation of many cultures. It reflects the numerous places the Jews have lived over the centuries. Therefore, you will find the influence of Middle-Eastern, Spanish, German, Mediterranean, and Eastern European styles of cooking in Jewish cuisine.

FACTS

Many foods that you might consider "Jewish" are not exclusive to Jewish cuisine. For example, hummus and falafel are common in much of the Middle East; stuffed cabbage is not just a Jewish food but is prevalent in Eastern Europe; and knishes are familiar to Germans as well as to Jews.

Nonetheless, in part because the style of preparation and cooking had to conform with *kashrut* and in part out of a desire to be original, a Jewish flair and distinct touch was often applied to the foods and cooking techniques extracted from the lands in which Jews resided. Added to this was the economic factor. Where Jews were poor, particularly in the shtetls of Eastern Europe, it was necessary to make a few inexpensive ingredients go a long way, and this affected the manner of cooking.

As you might remember from Chapter 2, Sephardic and Ashkenazic Jews differ culturally (and sometimes even in minor matters of religion) as a result of having lived for centuries in different areas of the world. Just as they have their own respective dialects, ways of speaking Hebrew, particular religious practices, and cultural customs, they also have different ideas of what Jewish cuisine is. Sephardic Jewish cuisine, subject to Mediterranean influences, is characterized by the use of spices, olive oil, rice, and lamb. Ashkenazic Jewish cooking reflects the Central, Northern, and Eastern European countries in which Ashkenazim lived.

Do not take *matzah* meal off your shopping list after Passover! You will find that in many recipes for Jewish dishes, *matzah* meal is a common ingredient. You should be able to purchase *matzah* meal in the kosher section of your food market all year round.

For the most part, the food considered to be "Jewish" by Jews living in the United States corresponds more with the Ashkenazic style of cooking. This is generally true of the fare mentioned below. In some cases, there is an American touch and there are a few dishes that are entirely in the American Jewish tradition. In other words, it's a real mix. You might find some of your own favorites in here, or be introduced to new delectable dishes you'll just have to try soon.

Foods Associated with Holidays

Certain Jewish foods are associated with particular holidays because they are generally served on specific occasions. Of course, there is nothing wrong in having these dishes served throughout the year, which many people choose to do. For instance, Jews serve *challah* as part of the *Shabbat* dinner, as well as at most other festive meals. *Challah* is a soft, sweet, eggy bread glazed with egg white. Sabbath *challah* is usually braided, but at other times it may be round or in the form of a ladder.

The word *challah* refers to the portion of dough that was set aside as "the priest's [*kohein's*] share" (Numbers 15:20 and Ezekiel 44:30). When *challah* is baked, a small piece is customarily tossed into the oven or fire as a token and remembrance of this practice.

In Chapter 14, you learned that *matzah* is a flat bread made of a simple mix of flour and water (without any eggs). While *matzah* doesn't really have a flavor and is rather bland, some people with Herculean digestive systems do enjoy *matzah* all year round, eating it instead of crackers or bread. Food dishes made with *matzah* abound. One good example is *matzah* ball soup, which is made of chicken broth and vegetables, like celery and carrots, with *matzah* balls floating in it. These *matzah* balls are known as *knaydelach* (Yiddish for "dumplings").

Some people like *matzah* soaked in water and egg and then fried. There is even a Passover variation of latkes (which, by the way, are served on Chanukah) that are made out of *matzah* meal.

Recall that cooking is forbidden on *Shabbat.* To solve the problem of having to eat cold food, the Jews of Eastern Europe invented *cholent,* a slowly cooked stew of beans, barley, potatoes, and beef that can be started before *Shabbat* begins and then left to simmer. Another stew, though a sweet one, is *tzimmes;* it consists of carrots, sweet potatoes, and/or prunes. *Tzimmes* is traditionally served on Rosh Hashanah and Passover.

Common Jewish Food Dishes

Arguably the most quintessentially Jewish food item is the bagel, a donut-shaped piece of bread that is boiled and then baked. Bagels are often topped with sesame seeds or poppy seeds or given a touch of flavor with other ingredients. The word *bagel* is derived from the German *beugel,* which means "a round loaf of bread." The addition of cream cheese and lox is a custom born in America.

ESSENTIALS

The first printed reference to the bagel can be found in the Community Regulations of Cracow, Poland in 1610. At that time, it was the custom to give bagels as a gift to pregnant women shortly before childbirth.

Another popular food item is the blintz. The word *blintz* is really what might be called "Yinglish." You may remember that after Yiddish

From top left, clockwise: *matzah*, gefilte fish, *hamentaschen*, cheese blintzes, and potato latkes.

Photo courtesy of Joshua Marowitz

made its way to the United States, some English was incorporated into the language. The Yiddish word is *blintzeh* (from the Ukrainian for "pancake"), but blintzes bear a closer resemblance to crêpes than pancakes. Looking a bit like an egg roll, a blintz is a flat pancake rolled around sweetened cottage cheese, mashed potatoes, jam, or fresh fruit. Blintzes are frequently accompanied with sour cream or applesauce.

Other common Jewish food items include the following:

Borscht. Borscht is beet soup, served either hot or cold. Eastern European Jews borrowed the *borscht* recipe from their Gentile neighbors. This dish became especially popular with the poor, who could afford the easily available beets. When eating borscht, people often add sour cream as a condiment.

Knishes. A knish is a potato and flour dumpling normally stuffed with mashed potato and onion, chopped liver, or cheese. In fact, the word *knish* is Ukrainian for "dumpling." Another type of dumpling is *kreplach* (from the German *kreppel*). *Kreplach* are triangular or square dumplings, similar to ravioli, and contain cheese or meat and are usually served in soup.

Kasha. *Kasha* or *kasha varnishkes* is a mixture of buckwheat and bow-tie macaroni noodles. The term *kasha* comes from the Russian word for "porridge."

Kugel. The term *kugel* comes from the German word for "pudding." The name is derived from the pan in which the pudding was baked and where it remained to be enjoyed throughout the Sabbath day. Kugel is either served as a casserole of potatoes, eggs, and onions or as a desert made with noodles, fruits, and nuts in an egg-based pudding.

Kishkas. You may have heard the expression, "I laughed so hard until my *kishkas* were sore!" The word *kishka* is derived from Russian and means "intestines" or "entrails." So what are intestines doing here in a list of Jewish cuisine? Good question. Originally, *kishka* was just that—entrails stuffed with meat, flour, and spices. Today, the intestines are normally dispensed with and have been replaced with parchment paper or plastic filled with either meat or celery and carrots, onions, flour, and spices.

Gefilte fish. No, gefilte fish is not a species of fish. The word *gefilte* comes from German and it means "stuffed." Originally, gefilte fish was stuffed fish, but today it looks more like fish cakes or fish loaf. Gefilte fish may be made from a variety of fish, though it's most often made of carp. The fish is chopped or ground, then mixed with eggs, salt, onions, and pepper, or a vegetable mix. Traditionally, gefilte fish is served with horseradish, a popular Eastern European condiment.

Stuffed cabbage. Also known as *holishke, praakes,* or *galuptzi,* stuffed cabbage is a popular Jewish food item. You can prepare stuffed cabbage in a number of ways, one of which is to fill it with beef and then serve in a sweet-and-sour sauce.

QUESTIONS?

Is the "Borscht Belt" something a man wears around his trousers? Not quite. The term "Borscht Belt" refers to the resorts in New York's Catskill Mountains that catered to and were used almost exclusively by Jews until the last decades of the twentieth century. Many famous entertainers, particularly comedians, launched their careers in these vacation spots.

There is a good reason that numerous cookbooks are devoted to Jewish cuisine. With so many Jewish dishes from which to choose, the previous list has just barely scratched the surface.

A few of the typical Jewish dishes, like chicken soup, are known for their medicinal value. At the other extreme, however, there is *schmaltz* (chicken fat, fried with onion and garlic), which probably clogged more arteries than any other food consumed by humans! Not far behind *schmaltz* on the list of foods guaranteed to raise your cholesterol count and fat levels are corned beef, pastrami, tongue, and chopped liver—all of which have been part of the American Jewish diet.

But times are changing and people have become more health-conscious in their dietary habits. What is more, there is also an increasing awareness of moral issues when it comes to eating animal products. Consequently, you can find a number of Jewish vegetarian cookbooks containing recipes of some traditional Jewish offerings without meat, fish, or fowl. How can a vegetarian dish be Jewish? Maybe not now, but in a hundred years or so, why not? What is and is not Jewish food has always been relative and probably always will be subject to change.

Jewish Humor

Despite all the hardships of exile and persecution over the centuries, the Jews never lost their particular sense of humor. In fact, laughing at themselves often helped them survive and flourish. Humor does not become "Jewish" because it is about Jews. Nor, for that matter, are jokes considered "Jewish" because they were told or created by someone who happens to be Jewish. And yet it is not hard to tell when a joke or funny story or tale fits into this category. Jewish humor has different themes, but, as you shall see, it always speaks to the existential condition of the Jewish people.

Themes in Jewish Humor

To a large extent, Jewish humor is the result of the 2,000-year Diaspora when the Jews lived without a "home" (country) of their own. This perpetual exile was a source of both physical and emotional insecurity. While it is true there were shining moments in history, such as the Golden Age in Spain, they often ended in a period of Jewish persecution. In Spain, the Golden Age came to an end in 1492 when the Jews were told to convert to Christianity or promptly depart.

In the face of misfortune and calamities, Jewish humor evolved to become an affirmation of life. Gaiety and laughter were necessary to offset harsh and despairing conditions. In a way, the laughter generated by their humor was a form of therapy to assuage the pain from persecutions, grief, and poverty.

FACTS

When God told Abraham that he and Sarah would have a son, Sarah's first reaction was to laugh in disbelief. Perhaps it was not a coincidence that the name they bestowed upon their son, Isaac (*Yitzchak* in Hebrew), who would become one of the patriarchs, means "laughter." (The Hebrew word for laughter is *tzechak*.)

Jewish humor is more than a confirmation of life. It is a defiant answer to the question of why and how to go on. How else, when confronted by a hostile world for thousands of years, could this small band of people so audaciously cling to their beliefs and to Torah?

A number of motifs are woven through Jewish humor. Some of these motifs are apparent in the tales and jokes included here. You will see for yourself how Jews have a way of poking fun at themselves, as if to say to the world, "Hey, you can't malign us, we'll do it to ourselves!" Jewish humor is often incisive and succinct. Henny Youngman's one-liners have their source in hundreds of years of Jewish jokes.

Jewish jokes also deal with the world in which the Jews live. And if the things they see about themselves aren't to their liking, criticism is freely dispersed. Some Jewish humorists, perhaps epitomized by Lenny Bruce, became critics of the societies in which they lived. At other times, Jewish humor conveyed a message and even encouraged certain types of moral conduct. It also had a way of deflecting the trauma endured by anti-Semitism.

Jewish humor is so vast it deserves a book by itself. In fact, there are many such books available, and Web sites with Jewish humor abound online. As a simple and entertaining introduction to Jewish humor, the rest of this chapter will illustrate some Jewish humor, organized by some of its most common themes.

Poverty, Justice, and Iconoclasm

The rabbi was walking along a street in the Bronx when he met an obese man attired in the finest clothing. The obese man was smoking.

"Why do you smoke? It's an awful vice!" the rabbi rebuked the man.

"I smoke to help me digest my dinner and, to tell the truth, I overate," retorted the man.

A little further on, the rabbi came upon a skinny fellow wearing rags for clothes. The skinny fellow was also smoking.

"Why do you smoke?" the rabbi said severely. "Don't you know it is a terrible vice?"

"I smoke to drive away the pangs of hunger," murmured the poor man apologetically.

"Lord of the world!" cried the rabbi, lifting his eyes to the heavens. "Where is your justice? If only the fat rich man would give the poor skinny man some of his dinner, both of them would be healthier and happier and neither of them would ever smoke again!"

This joke illustrates more than one motif in Jewish humor. It reminds the Jews of the suffering of those who are less fortunate and of the *mitzvah* to give to the poor, which is what the rich fat man should have done.

Yet, does the rabbi chastise the wealthy man? No, he does not. Instead, the rabbi, without any hesitation whatsoever, dares to hold God accountable for the failure to dispense justice. Thus, this joke also exemplifies the audacity of the Jews, who have never refrained from questioning God. Can it be any wonder, then, that throughout the centuries, this race of iconoclasts has never winced from challenging all forms of authority when justice was at stake?

Seeing the Glass as Half Full

One night, in the city of Chelm, a fire broke out. All the inhabitants rushed to the burning building to extinguish the blaze. When the conflagration had been put out, the rabbi mounted a table and addressed the citizens of Chelm.

"My friends, this fire was a miracle sent from heaven above."

There were murmurs of surprise in the crowd and the rabbi hastened to explain. "Look at it this way," he said, "If it were not for the bright flames, how would we have been able to see how to put out the fire on such a dark night?"

This particular joke exemplifies the motif in Jewish humor of looking on the bright side of things—a disposition so important in surviving the trials and tribulations Jews often faced. In fact, in this tale of Chelm, looking on the "bright" side of things is literal, because the rabbi says the citizens should be grateful for the "bright" flames. Even in a fire, there is always a bright side!

There are numerous jokes and tales about the people who populate the town of Chelm. They are consistently portrayed as being silly and having below-average intelligence—to put it mildly. Poking fun at the Jewish citizens of Chelm is a form of self-effacing humor, since they too were Jews, but it also distances the jokers from the characters of the joke—unless, of course, they are from Chelm!

How to Succeed in the World

Bella was the only Jewish girl in her class at an exclusive school in Scarsdale. Quite rightly, she considered herself very lucky. Bella's closest friend was Cynthia, a Greek Catholic. When the girls took their final examinations, Bella passed with straight A's, but Cynthia failed.

"I just can't understand it," complained Cynthia. "Just before the tests, I lit candles to Saint Peter, Saint Barnabas, and several other saints. And look what happened!"

"I lit a candle, too," said Bella.

"What! You, a Jewess, lit a candle? To whom?"

"To nobody," answered Bella. "I lit the candle and stayed up all night studying!"

The Jews frequently faced discrimination that sometimes made access to higher education difficult. In such cases, the general response—illustrated by this joke—was to work twice as hard. Sitting back and complaining and hoping things would be made easier is not how the Jews have made their way up the ranks of the societies in which they lived. This joke conveys a moral and a message, albeit a realistic and hard one, that you must work for whatever success you would like to achieve.

Anti-Semitism and Survival

While riding through a forest, a collector for a Jewish institution in Russia was held up by an armed Cossack who robbed him of all his money.

"Let me ask a favor of you," said the collector to the Cossack. "The money you have taken from me belongs to an institution in the next city. When I get there and tell the people I have been robbed, they will refuse to listen to me."

"There is nothing I can do about that," growled the Cossack.

"Oh, but you can," replied the Jewish collector. "I will hang my hat on a branch of this tree and you will kindly shoot a hole through it so that they may believe I was actually held up."

The Cossack consented and shot two holes through the hat. The collector took off his coat and begged the robber to shoot two holes through each of his sleeves. Again, the thief did as he was asked. Finally, the Jew took off his vest and asked the Cossack to make another hole but the robber said, "No more holes for you, *Zhid*. All my bullets are gone."

"That's all I wanted to know," retorted the collector, who then leaped upon the Cossack, knocking him down and bloodying his nose. The Jew recovered the money and then tied the Cossack up hand and foot.

Watching his intended victim depart and struggling with his bonds, the Cossack snarled to himself, "Well, this proves it. You just can't trust a damned Jew!"

This tale typifies the utter absurdity of anti-Semitism and how it is impossible to try and convince those who harbor such ill will how ludicrous their feelings are. After all, here a thief blames a poor Jew for defending himself! This joke also depicts how Jews survived by their wits in societies where they had little else with which to defend themselves.

And the Jews did indeed survive. Over a span of four millennia, in hostile environs and under harsh conditions, subject to persecution and oppression, strengthened by their culture, shared history, and ethnic practices, the Jewish people endured. They also persisted because of shared beliefs, which, despite disparities and divergent opinions over the centuries, can nonetheless properly be called what we have come to know as Judaism.

APPENDIX A
Glossary

The following glossary contains all the terms you might need to know to be literate in Judaism and Jewish culture. In here, you will find names of biblical heroes, religious terms and phrases, and *Yiddishkeit* (Yiddish terms).

Aaron: Older brother of Moses and the founder of the priesthood (*Kohanim*).

Abraham: The first Jew and the first of the three patriarchs.

Adar: The twelfth month of the Hebrew calendar.

Adosham: One of the words used to refer to God, an amalgam of *Adonai* (my Lord) and *Ha-Shem* (the Name).

Afikoman: The larger half of a piece of *matzah,* set aside during the Passover *seder* and hidden to later be found by the children who ransom it so the *seder* can continue. The word *afikoman* is derived from the Greek for "dessert." Jews eat the *afikoman* at the end of the *seder* meal, and it serves as a reminder of the paschal lamb that had been eaten at the end of the first *seder.*

Agunah: A woman who cannot remarry because her husband disappeared and she is unable to get a divorce. Appropriately enough, this Hebrew word means "anchored."

Akiba: One of the greatest of Jewish scholars and rabbis (50–135 C.E.).

Alav ha-shalom: The Hebrew phrase that means "peace be upon him" and is said after mentioning the name of a departed loved one. Note that the feminine version of *alav ha-shalom* is *aleha ha-shalom.*

Al Chet: A Yom Kippur formulaic prayer that lists sins for which the praying person seeks forgiveness.

Alefbet: The Hebrew alphabet (*alef* and *bet* are the first two letters of the Hebrew alphabet).

Aliyah: The honor of reading from the Torah or reciting a blessing over the Torah reading that is held during services. *Aliyah* is Hebrew for "going up"; the phrase "to make *aliyah*" refers to emigrating to Israel.

Amidah: A central prayer during the daily and Sabbath services.

Ani Ma'amin: A song of faith often sung at the *seder* and during *Yom Ha-Shoah* observances in memory of the Holocaust victims. The title of this song, written by Maimonides, may be translated as "I believe."

Aninut: The mourning period between the time of death of a loved one and the burial.

Apikoros: An unbeliever or agnostic (from the Greek for "heretic").

Arba Minim: The Four Species of plants used in the religious rituals during Sukkot: *etrog* (a member of the citrus family native to Israel that resembles a lemon), a *lulav* (a dried palm branch), *aravot* (two willow branches), and *hadasim* (three myrtle branches).

Aron Kodesh: The Holy Ark, the special cabinet that stores the Torah scrolls in the synagogue. Sephardim also refer to the *Aron Kodesh* as *Heichal.*

Ashkenazic Jews, Ashkenazim: Jews who lived in France, Germany, and Eastern Europe, as well as their descendants (from the Hebrew *Ashkenaz,* Germany).

Aufruf: The *aliyah* given to the groom (and sometimes to the bride as well) on the *Shabbat* before the wedding.

Av: The fifth month of the Hebrew calendar.

Avelut: The year of mourning following the loss of a parent.

Avinu Malkeinu: A prayer of supplication recited on Rosh Hashanah, Yom Kippur, and most fast days.

Ba'al Shem Tov: Rabbi Israel ben Eliezer (c. 1700–1760), the founder of Hasidism. Rabbi ben Eliezer's title may be translated as "Master of the Good Name." (The acronym of Ba'al Shem Tov, *Besht,* is also commonly used.)

Badeken: The traditional veiling of the bride by the groom preceding the wedding ceremony.

Bagel: Doughnut-shaped bread that is boiled before it is baked.

Bar Kokhba: The military leader of the final rebellion against Rome in the second century C.E.

Bar Mitzvah: Upon reaching the age of thirteen, a boy becomes a bar mitzvah ("son of the commandment"). Traditionally, a bar mitzvah ceremony accompanies this rite of passage.

Bashert: Yiddish word for "fate" or "destiny," *bashert* also represents the idea that each person has a soul mate.

Bat Mitzvah: Upon reaching the age of twelve, a girl becomes a bat mitzvah ("daughter of the commandment"). This transition is often accompanied by a ceremony, usually when the girl is twelve.

B.C.E.: Before the common era or before the beginning of the Christian calendar.

Bentsch: The Yiddish word "to bless" or "to make a blessing."

Berakhah: A blessing (from Hebrew).

Berit Ha-Bat: The covenant for a newborn daughter that usually refers to the naming ceremony.

Bet Din: A rabbinical court that resolves disputes under Jewish law and deals with issues such as divorce and conversion.

Bimah: The raised platform upon which the Torah scrolls are set when they are read. In Sephardic synagogues, this is called a *tevah.*

Birkhat Ha-Mazon: The grace that is recited after meals.

Blintzes: Folded pancakes that are similar to French crêpes. Usually, blintzes are filled with cheese or fruit. Traditionally, Jews eat blintzes on Shavuot (as well as throughout the year).

Bobbe-myseh: Yiddish expression for an old wives' tale.

Brit Milah: The covenant of circumcision made between God and Abraham (and his descendants). Ashkenazic Jews commonly refer to circumcision as the *bris.*

Bubeleh, Bubbe: Yiddish term of endearment for grandmothers that means "little grandma."

C.E.: Common Era, the date corresponding to the current Christian calendar.

Chag Sameach: "Happy holiday!" (from Hebrew).

Chai: The Hebrew word for "living" or "life."

Challah: A sweet, eggy bread that is usually braided and served on *Shabbat* and other holiday meals. On Rosh Hashanah, in order to signify the beginning of the cycle of a new year, the *challah* is round and is distinguishable from the shape of the *Shabbat challah.*

Chametz: Leavened grain products that may not be eaten or even owned during Passover.

Chanukah: The eight-day festival that commemorates the rededication of the Temple after the successful Jewish rebellion against the Syrians in 165 B.C.E.

Chanukkiah: A Chanukah menorah.

Charoset: A blend of fruit, wine, and nuts that is one of the symbolic dishes on the Passover *seder* table because it represents the mortar that the Hebrew slaves worked with in Egypt. It is customary to eat *charoset* with *matzah.*

Chatan: "Bridegroom" (from Hebrew).

Chatan Bereshit: The man called to chant or recite the first blessings over the first section of the Torah on Simchat Torah.

Chatan Torah: The man called to recite or chant the blessings over the final section of the Torah on Simchat Torah.

Chavurah: An informal study or prayer group.

Chazzan: A cantor who leads prayers in synagogue services.

Cheder: This Hebrew word literally means "room" and refers to a school.

Chevra Kaddisha: The Holy Society, an organization that cares for the dead.

Cholent: A stew of beef, beans, and barley that is slowly cooked so it can be served on *Shabbat.*

Chukkim: Those laws *(halakhot)* that do not receive an explanation in the Torah.

Chumash: Literally, this term refers to the first five books of the Bible (the Pentateuch). In its common usage, *chumash* has come to include selections from the Prophets.

Chuppah: The wedding canopy that can be made of a *tallit,* fine linen, or a floral arrangement.

Confirmation: A ceremony conducted to mark the completion of additional study about three years after bar or bat mitzvah; Confirmation ceremonies are generally held on Shavuot.

Consecration: The ceremony marking the beginning of a child's formal Jewish education, conducted by some branches of Judaism on Simchat Torah.

Conservative: One of the branches of Judaism. While accepting the binding nature of Jewish laws, the Conservative movement believes they are subject to reinterpretation and change because, although divinely inspired, *mitzvot* did not come directly from God.

Counting of the Omer: The counting of the days between Passover and Shavuot.

Cup of Elijah: The wine goblet set aside on the Passover *seder* table for the prophet Elijah.

Daven: "To pray" (from Yiddish).

Days of Awe: The ten days from Rosh Hashanah to Yom Kippur.

Diaspora: Any place other than Israel where Jews live. Often refers to the time period following the destruction of the Second Temple in 70 C.E. until the establishment of the modern State of Israel in 1948.

Dreidel: A four-sided top used to play a traditional game during Chanukah.

Dybbuk: An evil spirit, demon, or mischievous sprite (from Yiddish).

Ein Sof: A term that means "without end." It is used in Jewish mysticism to refer to the nature of God.

Elohaynu: "Our God" (from Hebrew).

Elul: The sixth month of the Hebrew calendar.

Essenes: A mystical and ascetic movement in Judaism that commenced around 200 B.C.E. but vanished after the destruction of the Second Temple.

Esther: The heroine of the Purim story.

Etrog: A citrus fruit used in religious rituals during Sukkot.

Fleishig: Foods derived from meat or meat products, not to be mixed with dairy under Jewish dietary laws (from Yiddish).

Four Questions: Four questions that are asked by the youngest person present at the Passover *seder*. In responding to these questions, the *seder* leader recounts the Passover narrative.

Four Species: See *Arba Minim*.

Frum: Yiddish word for "pious."

Gan Eden: Though literally meaning "Garden of Eden," the term refers to a place of spiritual reward for the righteous dead.

Gefilte Fish: Yiddish for "stuffed fish." A traditional Ashkenazic Jewish dish that looks like fish cake, served cold, often with horseradish.

Gehinnom: A place where the less righteous go after death for spiritual purification over a period that may last as long as twelve months. The Yiddish version of this term, *gehenna,* is "hell."

Gelt: Yiddish for "money." *Gelt* also refers to the money given as gifts on Chanukah (Chanukah *gelt*).

Gemara: Collection of commentaries on the Mishna made by the rabbis of the third through the fifth centuries C.E. Taken together, the Gemara and Mishna comprise the Talmud.

Gerut: The conversion process (from Hebrew).

Get: A written bill of divorce.

Gevalt: Yiddish expression for a cry of astonishment or help.

Gezeirah: Any law promulgated by the rabbis so that people will not unintentionally violate *mitzvot*.

Glatt Kosher: A law of *kashrut* that requires abstaining from consumption of cattle with lung lesions; the practice of this law.

Gonif: A thief or crook (from Yiddish).

Grogger: A noisemaker used during the reading of the Megillah on Purim; *groggers* are sounded to drown out Haman's name each time it appears in the narrative (from Yiddish).

Gut Shabbes: The Yiddish expression used for wishing a good Sabbath.

Gut Yontiff: The Yiddish expression used for wishing a good holiday.

Haftorah: A reading from the Prophets that concludes the weekly Torah portion.

Haggadah: The book read during the Passover *seder;* the *Haggadah* includes the Exodus narrative and traditional prayers and ceremonies performed during the *seder.*

Haimish: Yiddish description of someone who is warm and friendly.

Hakafah: The carrying of the Torah scrolls in a procession around the synagogue.

Halakhah: The laws and rules that Jews are obligated to follow.

Hallel: Psalms 113–118 that praise God, recited at certain festivals.

Hamentaschen: Triangular fruit-filled pastries that are eaten during Purim.

Hamesh Hand: Also known as the *hamsa* (from Arabic), this is an inverted hand with the thumb and pinkie pointed downward that is the design for certain ornaments found in Judaica shops.

Hashanot: Medieval poems and prayers that are chanted when carrying the Torah scrolls in a procession on Sukkot.

Ha-Shem: Literally "The Name" (from Hebrew), *Ha-Shem* refers to The Name of God, one of the alternate names that are used to address or refer to God.

Hasidism: A sect of Orthodox Jews with its own distinctive lifestyle. Hasidism was founded in eighteenth-century Eastern Europe by the Ba'al Shem Tov (the Besht).

Hatafat Dam Berit: The taking of a drop of blood from the penis as a sign of the covenant during the conversion process of a male already circumcised. (This practice is generally performed during the *Berit Milah* ceremony of babies previously circumcised at the hospital.)

Ha-Tikvah: The anthem of the Zionist movement and of the State of Israel.

Havdalah: The word means "separation." *Havdalah* is the ritual that marks the end of *Shabbat* or a holiday.

Hebrew: The language of the Torah and Jewish prayers. Hebrew is also the official language of the State of Israel.

High Holidays, High Holy Days: The period that comprises Rosh Hashanah, the Days of Awe, and Yom Kippur.

Hillel: A great rabbi and sage (30 B.C.E.–10 C.E.) whose more liberal interpretations contrasted with those of Shammai.

Holishkes: Stuffed cabbage served in a sweet tomato sauce (from Yiddish).

Hoshanah Rabba: The seventh day of Sukkot, known as the "great hosanna," during which the congregation makes seven circuits around the synagogue and recites special prayers.

Isaac: The son of Abraham and second of the three patriarchs.

Iyar: The second month of the Hebrew calendar.

Jacob: The son of Isaac and the third of the three patriarchs, who took on the name of Israel ("one who wrestled with God"). The twelve tribes of Israel are descended from twelve of his sons.

Jewish star: The six-pointed star emblematic of Judaism, the Jewish people, Zionism, and the modern State of Israel. The Jewish star is also known as the *magen david* or the Star of David.

Joseph: The son of Jacob, the third patriarch. Joseph was responsible for the Israelites' settling in Egypt.

Judah Ha-Nasi: The compiler of the Mishna.

Kabbalah: Jewish mysticism.

Kaddish: A prayer in Aramaic that praises God and is commonly associated with mourning rituals.

Kalah, kallah: Bride (Hebrew).

Kalat Bereshit: The woman called to recite or chant the blessings over the first section of the Torah on Simchat Torah.

Kalat Torah: The woman called to recite or chant the blessings over the last section of the Torah on Simchat Torah.

Kallah: Enclave or retreat.

Karpas: One of the food dishes on the *seder* plate at Passover. The *karpas* is a green herb (often parsley), green vegetable, or potato that symbolizes spring.

Kashrut: Jewish dietary laws. The English word describing foods that comply with the laws of *kashrut* is "kosher."

Kavanah: The word means "intent" (Hebrew) and describes the proper state of spiritual concentration during prayer.

Kayn aynhoreh, kine-ahora: Yiddish expressions to ward off the evil eye.

Keriah: The word means "tearing" (Hebrew) and refers to the custom of tearing one's clothes upon hearing of the death of a loved one. Sometimes, a black ribbon is worn in place of rending the garment.

Ketubah: The Jewish marriage contract (Hebrew).

Kevod Ha-Met: Honor due the dead (Hebrew).

Kibbutz: A collective settlement in Israel. Most *kibbutzim* are involved in agriculture.

Kiddush: A blessing recited over wine sanctifying the Sabbath and other holidays.

Kiddush cup: The ceremonial wine cup used for *Kiddush*.

Kiddushin: The first of the two-part process of consummating a Jewish marriage. The word means "holiness" (Hebrew) and also refers to the state of matrimony.

Kippah: The Hebrew word for the skullcap worn during services or by more observant Jews at all times. In Yiddish, the word is *yarmulke*.

Kishka: Literally meaning "intestine," *kishka* is a type of Jewish food consisting of intestines or parchment paper stuffed with meat, flour, and spices.

Kislev: The ninth month of the Hebrew calendar.

Kitniyot: Additional foods that Ashkenazic Jews do not eat on Passover, including rice, corn, beans, and peanuts.

Kittel: A white robe worn by more observant Jews during Yom Kippur services and at the Passover *seder*. Some grooms wear a *kittel* during the wedding ceremony.

Klezmer: Informal group of Yiddish musicians; the type of music generally played by such a group.

Knaydelach: The Yiddish word for "dumplings."

Knish: The Yiddish word for a dumpling that is stuffed with potato and onion, cheese, or chopped liver.

Kodesh: Holy (from Hebrew).

Kohanim: The priestly sect descended from Aaron.

Kol Nidre: The prayer that begins the evening service of Yom Kippur, for which the service is named.

Kreplach: Triangular dumplings stuffed with meat or cheese and served in soup (from Yiddish).

Kugel: The Yiddish word for pudding that is a casserole of potatoes, eggs, and onion or, if served as dessert, a mix of noodles, fruits, and nuts.

Kvell: Yiddish expression meaning "to beam with pride."

Kvetch: Yiddish term for complaining; also, a noun that describes those who like to complain.

Ladino: The language of Sephardic Jews that is a mix of Spanish, Arabic, Hebrew, and other languages. Ladino (also known as Judezmo) uses Hebrew script.

Lag B'Omer: A minor holiday that occurs on the thirty-third day of the Counting of the Omer, between Passover and Shavuot.

Landsman: Yiddish word for someone who comes from the same town. In some cases, a Jew may use the term *landsman* to refer to another Jew.

Lashon ha-ra: Literally "evil speech" (from Hebrew), *lashon ha-ra* refers to the *mitzvah* forbidding people to harm others by inflammatory speech such as slander and gossip.

Latkes: A Yiddish term for potato pancakes fried in oil and customarily eaten during Chanukah (or *matzah* meal pancakes served during Passover).

L'Chayim: A traditional Jewish toast that means "to life" (from Hebrew).

Leah: Jacob's wife and one of the matriarchs.

Leap year: In order to adjust the Hebrew calendar, which is lunar, an extra thirteenth month (second *Adar*) is added during leap years. It is because the Hebrew calendar is based on the moon rather than on the sun that each year holidays fall on different days of the Gregorian calendar used in the Western world.

Lehitpalel: The Hebrew word meaning "to pray."

Levite: Descendants from Levi, one of the sons of Jacob (Israel), whom God had charged with performing certain duties at the Temple.

L'Shanah Tovah: "For a good year," an abbreviated version of the traditional greeting made during Rosh Hashanah and throughout the Days of Awe.

L'Shanah Tovah Tikatevu: "May you be inscribed [in The Book of Life] for a good year," a traditional greeting on Rosh Hashanah.

Liturgy: The prayers and blessings that constitute worship services.

Lubavitch: A sect of Hasidic Jews noted for conducting outreach programs to other Jews.

Lulav: A collection of palm, myrtle, and willow branches used in religious rituals during Sukkot.

Ma'ariv: Evening prayer services.

Machzor: A prayer book unique to the High Holidays of Rosh Hashanah and Yom Kippur. There are also *machzorim* for Passover, Shavuot, and Sukkot.

Maftir: The person who reads or blesses the last part of the Torah and entire *Haftorah* reading.

Maimonides: One of the foremost medieval Jewish scholars, also known as Rambam (an acronym of his full name).

Mame Loshen: Yiddish for "mother language," an endearing reference to the status of Yiddish in Ashkenazic culture.

Ma'oz Tzur: A well-known Chanukah song (its English version is "Rock of Ages").

Maror: A bitter herb, often horseradish, served on the Passover plate as one of the symbolic food dishes of the Passover *seder*.

Marranos: Spanish and Portuguese Jews who publicly converted to Christianity but continued to practice Judaism in secret.

Mashgiach: An official who certifies that food is kosher.

Matzah: Unleavened bread that replaces regular bread (which is considered *chametz*) during Passover.

Matzah ball soup: Chicken soup with *matzah* dumplings.

Matzah meal: *Matzah* crumbs used in lieu of flour or bread crumbs.

Mavin: Yiddish word for a person who is an expert or very knowledgeable about a subject.

Mazel tov: While literally meaning "good luck," this phrase is used to offer congratulations.

Megillah: Literally "scroll" (in Hebrew), a *megillah* is any of the following five books of the Bible: Esther, Ruth, Song of Songs, Lamentations, or Ecclesiastes. Most frequently, this term is used to refer to the Book of Esther. In Yiddish, the word *megillah* connotes something that is long and convoluted.

Menorah: Generally a nine-branched candelabrum used to light the Chanukah candles, this term also refers to the seven-branched candelabrum that was used in the Temple.

Mensh: A Yiddish word for "human being," used when referring to someone who is a caring and honest person.

Meshugge: Yiddish word for one who is crazy, nuts, or extravagant.

Messiah: The English word for *moshiach*, which is Hebrew for "anointed" and refers to the messianic king who will usher in the

Messianic Age by ending all the world's evil and commencing 2,000 years of justice and peace.

Mezuzah: A scroll of passages of scripture, housed in a case that is affixed to the doorposts of houses and of some rooms.

Midrash: The collection of *midrashim* ("interpretations," from Hebrew) that expand on incidents in the Bible in order to derive explanations, principles, and moral lessons.

Mikdash Me'at: This Hebrew phrase, literally translated as "a small sanctuary," is used to refer to the home.

Mikvah: A ritual bath used for spiritual purification in the conversion process, after the period of sexual separation following a woman's menstrual cycle, and during other ceremonies related to purity.

Milchig: Dairy foods or dairy products (from Yiddish).

Mincha: Afternoon prayer services.

Minhag: A custom that evolved into a binding religious practice.

Minyan: The quorum consisting of ten adults that is required to recite specific prayers. In Orthodox and some Conservative congregations, only men are counted for a *minyan*.

Mishegoss: Yiddish for "insanity" or "madness," this term is just as likely to be used when referring to irrational beliefs.

Mishloach Manot: A tradition of sending food packages to friends during Purim (in Hebrew, *mishloach manot* literally means "sending out portions").

Mishpachah: Hebrew word for "family"; in Yiddish, the term *mishpochah* (pronounced with accent on the second syllable) is used to refer to one's extended family.

Mishna: Code of Jewish law, edited by Rabbi Judah Ha-Nasi around 200 C.E., that is based upon oral tradition and together with the Gemara constitutes the Talmud.

Mitnagdim: Orthodox Jews who opposed the Hasidim.

Mitzvah: Any one of the 613 *mitzvot* (commandments) that Jews are required to obey. This word is sometimes used to refer to any Jewish obligation.

Mohel: A person who is trained in performing the ritual circumcision.

Moses: The great prophet who led the Jews out of Egypt and who received the Commandments from God at Mount Sinai.

Musaf: An additional prayer service held on *Shabbat* and other holidays.

Naches: Yiddish term for "joy" or "pleasure."

Neilah: The concluding service on Yom Kippur.

Ner Tamid: A candelabrum or lamp over the Holy Ark in the synagogue. The *ner tamid* is the "eternal flame" because it is kept burning or lit at all times.

Neshoma: Derived from the Hebrew *neshamah*, this is the Yiddish word for "soul."

Niddah: The separation of a husband and wife during the wife's menstrual period.

Nikkud: A dot or dash used to represent vowels and other pronunciation guidelines in Hebrew script.

Nisan: The first month of the Hebrew calendar.

Nisuin: The second and final part of the Jewish marriage process.

Olam Ha-Ba: The World to Come that will follow the Messianic Age. All souls will be resurrected to live in the World to Come for all eternity.

Oneg Shabbat: Reception after *Shabbat* services, where refreshments and fellowship are enjoyed.

Oral Torah: Jewish teachings and elucidations about the written Torah, handed down by word of mouth through the second century C.E.

Orthodox: The Orthodox branch of Judaism adheres to the belief that Jewish law comes from God and is not subject to change. The Orthodox branch may be subdivided into the ultra-Orthodox and the modern Orthodox movements.

Pareve: Kosher foods that are neither meat nor dairy and may be eaten with either.

Parokhet: The curtain inside the Holy Ark, which stores the Torah scrolls.

Parshah: A weekly Torah portion that is read in synagogue during services.

Passover, Pesach: A holiday that commemorates the Exodus from Egypt and is one of the three pilgrimage festivals. *Pesach* is Hebrew for "passed over," a phrase that refers to the Angel of Death's passing over the homes of the Jews as he carried out the tenth plague (killing the firstborn of the Egyptians).

Patriarchs: Abraham, Isaac, and Jacob (Israel).

Payees: Side earlocks or curls worn by ultra-Orthodox males.

Pharisees: A movement in Judaism that began around the third century B.C.E. The Pharisees saw the written and oral Torah as equally important and are considered to be the forerunners of rabbinic (post-Temple) Judaism.

Pidyon Ha-Ben: The ritual of redeeming the firstborn son.

Pilgrimage festivals: The three harvest festivals of Passover, Shavuot, and Sukkot. During each of these holidays, Jews made pilgrimages to the Temple in Jerusalem (until its second destruction in the first century C.E.).

Pirkei Avot: The Ethics of the Fathers, a tractate of the Mishna.

Pogrom: An organized attack on a Jewish community (from a Russian word *pogromit*, "to wreak havoc").

Purim: A holiday celebrating the deliverance of the Jewish population in Persia from annihilation, as recounted in the Book of Esther.

Purimspiel: A Yiddish term for a humorous skit or play performed on Purim.

Pushke: A container kept in homes and synagogues to collect money for charities (from Yiddish).

Rabbi: A religious teacher who often interprets the application of Jewish law and may be called upon to settle disputes. Today, the rabbi's duties are similar to the clergy in most other religions.

Rabbinical Judaism: A term that includes virtually all branches of Judaism that descended from the Pharisees.

Rachel: A matriarch and one of the wives of Jacob.

Rashi: Rabbi Shlomo Yitzchaki, a great medieval scholar.

Rashi script: A style of writing that is distinguishable from the text proper and was introduced by Rashi to write commentary.

Rebbe: A term used for any leader of a Hasidic community.

Rebbetzin: A rabbi's wife (from Yiddish).

Rebecca: Wife of Isaac and one of the matriarchs.

Reconstructionism: One of the branches of Judaism, the Reconstructionist movement believes Jewish law was created by people and can be changed to meet new conditions; it emphasizes Judaism's cultural components versus strict adherence to all laws and regulations.

Reform: A branch of Judaism that emphasizes ethical teachings. The Reform movement believes that Jewish law was inspired by God and is therefore dynamic; each individual has the freedom to determine which laws to practice.

Responsa: Written answers from respected rabbis to questions of Jewish law.

Rosh Hashanah: The Jewish New Year and one of the High Holy Days.

Sabbath, Shabbat: Sabbath (in English) and *Shabbat* (in Hebrew) is the day of rest, prayer, and study as well as a time to pursue spiritual and nonworldly matters.

Sadducees: An oppositional movement to the Pharisees that did not embrace the oral Torah and narrowly interpreted the written Torah.

Sandek: A person, sometimes called the "godfather," who holds the baby during the ritual circumcision.

Sarah: Abraham's wife and the first of the matriarchs.

Seder: The term *seder* is Hebrew for "order"; this term often refers to the Passover home ritual that includes the reading of the *Haggadah* and the festive meal.

Sefer K'ritut: The writ of divorce that comes from the Hebrew for "cutting off"; commonly, *Sefer K'ritut* is called a *get*.

Sefer Torah: Torah scrolls (Hebrew).

Sefirot: In Kabbalistic thought, this term refers to the emanations from God's essence.

Sekhakh: From the Hebrew for "covering," *sekhakh* refers to the material used to construct the roof of a *sukkah* during the holiday of Sukkot.

Selichot: Prayers for forgiveness that are added to the liturgy at certain times.

Sephardic Jews, Sephardim: Jews who had lived in Spain, Portugal, North Africa, and the Middle East, as well as their descendants (from the Hebrew *Sepharad*, Spain).

Seudah: Feast, from Hebrew.

Seudah Shelishit: The third meal, generally light, that is eaten late on *Shabbat* afternoon.

Seudat Havra'ah: The meal of condolence usually prepared by friends of the mourners and eaten immediately following the funeral.

Shabbat Shalom: The Hebrew expression for wishing a peaceful Sabbath.

Shacharit: The morning prayer service.

Shadchen: A matchmaker, from Hebrew.

Shalom: Hebrew word for "peace" that is also used to say "hello" and "good-bye."

Shammai: One of the great rabbis of the Talmud whose strict views contrasted with those of Hillel.

Shammash: Hebrew word for "servant" that refers to the caretaker of a synagogue. *Shammash* is also the candle on the Chanukah menorah that lights the other candles. (The Yiddish equivalent of *shammash* is *shammes*.)

Shavua Tov: Hebrew phrase for wishing a good week.

Shavuot: The harvest festival that also commemorates the giving of the Torah at Mount Sinai.

Shechinah: The Divine Presence of God, often considered to be God's feminine component.

Shehecheyanu: A blessing said for beginnings and joyful events in people's lives as well as other specific times and holiday observances.

Shekel: A popular silver coin used in Biblical times. Today, Israeli currency is based on the new shekel.

Shema: Perhaps the foremost Jewish prayer that embodies the primary statement of Jewish belief.

Shemini Atzeret: The last day (or two days) of Sukkot.

Shemoneh Esrei: "Eighteen" in Hebrew, *Shemoneh Esrei* is one of the major prayers in the weekday service.

Sheol: Biblical word that refers to hell or to the grave.

Shevat: The eleventh month of the Hebrew calendar.

Shidukh: Hebrew term for a marital match. (The Yiddish equivalent of *shidukh* is *shiddach*.)

Shiva: The seven-day mourning period that begins immediately following the burial.

Shlemiel: Yiddish word for a foolish person or simpleton.

Shloshim: The thirty-day mourning period following a burial.

Shnorrer: Yiddish term for a beggar or moocher.

Shochet: A ritual slaughterer who exercises his duties in accordance with the laws of *kashrut*.

Shofar: A ram's horn that is blown to emit specific sounds, particularly at synagogue services during the High Holidays.

Shomerim: The term used to describe those who remain with a dead body until the time of burial.

Shtetl: A small Jewish village in Eastern Europe.

Shuckle: A Yiddish term that describes the traditional act of swaying during prayer.

Shul: The Yiddish word referring to a house of worship or synagogue.

Shulchan Arukh: A code of Jewish law written in the sixteenth century.

Siddur: Prayer book.

Sidrah: The weekly Torah portion that is read in synagogue. *(Sidrah* shares a common root with *seder,* Hebrew for "order.")

Simchah: A joyous or happy event.

Simchat Torah: The holiday that celebrates the end and beginning of a new cycle in the public reading of the Torah.

Sivan: The third month of the Hebrew calendar.

Sofer: A trained scribe, from Hebrew.

STA'M: A type of style in writing Hebrew that is noted for its use of crowns on the letters and which is employed primarily in Torah scrolls, *tefillin,* and *mezuzot.*

Sukkah: The temporary dwelling (booth, hut, or tabernacle) erected and covered with branches that Jews live in or visit during the holiday of Sukkot.

Sukkot: The festival of booths that commemorates the Jews' wandering in the desert for forty years after departing Egypt before they entered the Promised Land. Sukkot is one of the three pilgrimage festivals (the other two being Passover and Shavuot).

Synagogue: The common term for a house of worship.

Tachrichin: Garments made out of linen that are used to drape the dead.

Taharah: Ritual purification of the deceased in preparation for burial.

Takkanah: Any law that is promulgated by rabbis but is not found in the Bible.

Tallit: A prayer shawl with *tzitzit* (fringes at the corners) that is worn during morning services.

Tallit katan: A small *tallit* worn under a shirt by more observant Jewish men to fulfill the *mitzvah* of wearing *tzitzit.*

Talmud: Collection of the Jewish oral tradition that interpret the Torah; the Talmud consists of the Mishna and Gemara and was edited around 500 C.E.

Tammuz: The fourth month of the Hebrew calendar.

Tanakh: An acronym of Torah (Law), *Nevi'im* (Prophets), and *Ketuvim* (Writings), the three sections of the Bible.

Tashlikh: The tradition of symbolically casting off sins at a river during Rosh Hashanah.

Tefilah: A Hebrew word for "prayer," this term specifically refers to the central group of prayers in each service, alternatively called the *Amidah* or *Shemoneh Esrei.*

Tefillin: Also known as phylacteries, *tefillin* are the leather boxes that contain scrolls with passages of scripture and are bound to the arm and forehead during morning prayers.

Temple: Refers to the First and Second Temple, places of worship in ancient Jerusalem. The word "temple" is also generally used in the Reform movement in lieu of the word "synagogue."

Teshuva: A Hebrew word for "turning" or "returning," *teshuva* refers to an act of repentance.

Tevet: The tenth month of the Hebrew calendar.

Tevilah: Immersion in the *mikvah,* the ritual bath used for spiritual purification.

Tikkun Olam: The concept of repairing the broken world.

Tisha B'Av: The ninth of *Av,* this day commemorates the destruction of both the First and Second Temples, as well as other tragedies in Jewish history.

Tishrei: The seventh month of the Hebrew calendar.

Torah: The five books of the Bible (Genesis, Exodus, Leviticus, Numbers, and Deuteronomy), also known as the Pentateuch and the Five Books of Moses.

Torah Scroll: Scrolls made of parchment on which the Torah is written and from which the Torah portions are read in synagogue.

Tractate: A subdivision of the Mishna and Talmud.

Transliteration: The method by which Hebrew words are written in the English language.

Treyf: Literally "torn apart" (from Hebrew), this term usually refers to food that is not kosher.

Tsuris: Yiddish word that means "troubles" or "suffering."

Tu B'Shevat: The fifteenth day of *Shevat* that is the new year for counting the age of trees.

Tzaddik: A righteous person. Some Hasidim believe that a *tzaddik* is a person who has mystical powers.

Tzedakah: Literally "justice" or "righteousness," this Hebrew term refers to acts of charity and kindness. (Remember, it's a *mitzvah* to practice *tzedakah.)*

Tzimmes: The Yiddish word for a sweet stew consisting of ingredients such as carrots, potatoes, prunes, and beef.

Tzitzit: The ritual fringes on the corners of a *tallit.*

Ulpan: An intensive course that teaches students (usually *olim,* or immigrants to Israel) modern Hebrew.

Unveiling: Dedication ceremony of a grave marker.

Western Wall: The only remaining wall of the Temple in Jerusalem, also known as the Wailing Wall. The site at the Western Wall is the holiest place in Judaism and is in custody of the Orthodox Jews.

Written Torah: The Hebrew Bible, which the Christians know as the Old Testament.

Yad: The hand-shaped pointer used by the readers to keep their place when reading from the Torah scrolls.

Yahrzeit: A Yiddish term that refers to the anniversary of the death of a close relative.

Yahrzeit candle: A memorial candle that burns for twenty-four hours and is lit on the *yahrzeit* of a loved one and on those days when mourners recite the *Yizkor.*

Yarmulke: The Yiddish word for the skullcap worn by most Jews during services and more observant Jews at all times. (The Hebrew word for *yarmulke* is *kippah.)*

Yetzer ra: The "evil impulse" of seeking gratification of personal and physical needs and desires.

Yetzer tov: The "good impulse" to follow God's commandments.

Yichud: The interval when the bride and groom spend time alone following the wedding ceremony.

Yiddish: The vernacular of Ashkenazic Jews that is a mix of Old German, Hebrew, and Slavic languages and which employs the Hebrew script.

Yizkor: Prayers said on specific holidays (Yom Kippur, Shemini Atzeret, Pesach, and Shavuot) to honor the memory of departed loved ones.

Yom Ha-Atzmaut: Israeli Independence Day.

Yom Ha-Shoah: Holocaust Remembrance Day.

Yom Ha-Zikkaron: Israeli Memorial Day.

Yom Kippur: The Day of Atonement set aside for fasting, prayer, and introspection. Yom Kippur is one of the High Holy Days.

Yom Tov: Hebrew phrase for "holiday" (literally, "good day").

Yom Yerushalayim: Jerusalem Day, a holiday that commemorates the reunification of Jerusalem in 1967.

Yontif: Holiday, in Yiddish.

Zayde: Grandfather, in Yiddish.

Zeman Matan Toratenu: Another term for Shavuot that literally means "the Season of the Giving of our Torah."

Zionism: The political movement that strove for the establishment of a Jewish homeland in the Land of Israel; support for the modern State of Israel.

Zohar: The primary written work of the Kabbalah (Jewish mysticism).

Common Prayers and Blessings

Translation and transliteration of prayers and blessings from the Hebrew lead to questions, inconsistency, and even controversy. At best, the process is an art and clearly not a science. Please keep this in mind as you consider the following prayers and, if you can, refer to the original Hebrew texts.

The *Shema*

Sh'ma Yisrael Adonai Elohaynu Adonai Echod.
Barukh Shem k'vod malkhuto l'olam va-ed.
V-ahavta et Adonai Elochecha b-chol l'vavcha
    u-v-chol naf'sh'cha u-v-chol m'odecha.
V-hayu ha-d'varim ha-ayleh asher anochi
    m'tzav'cha ha-yom al l'vavecha.
V-shinantam l-vanecha, v-dibarta bam
    b-shivt'cha b-vaytecha, u-v-lecht'cha
    va-derech, u-v-shachb'cha u-v-kumecha.
U-k'shartam l'ot al yadecha, v-hayu l-totafot
    bayn aynecha.
U-chtavtam al m'zuzot baytecha u-vi-sharecha.

Hear, O Israel, the Lord is our God, the Lord is
    One.
Blessed be the Name of His glorious kingdom
    for ever and ever.
And you shall love the Lord your God with all
    your heart and with all your soul and with
    all your might.
And these words that I command you this day
    shall be upon your heart.
And you shall teach them diligently to your
    children, speaking of them when you sit in
    your house, when you walk by the way,
    when you lie down and when you rise up.
And you shall bind them as a sign upon your
    hand, and they shall be for frontlets
    between your eyes.
And you shall write them on the doorposts of
    your house and upon your gates.

Blessing for Affixing the *Mezuzah*

Barukh atah Adonai, Elohaynu, melekh
    ha-olam, asher ke'edishanu b'me'etzvotav
    v'tze'evanu le'ekboa mezuzah.

Blessed art Thou, Lord, our God, King of the
Universe, who has sanctified us with His
commandments and commanded us to affix
a *mezuzah*.

Blessing over Bread

Barukh atah Adonai, Elohaynu melekh
    ha-olam, ha-motzi lechem min ha-aretz.

Blessed art Thou, Lord, our God, King of the
Universe, who brings forth bread from the
earth.

Blessing over Wine

Barukh atah Adonai, Elohaynu melekh ha-olam,
    borei p'riy ha-gafen.

Blessed art Thou, Lord, our God, King of the
Universe, who creates the fruit of the vine.

Blessing for Lighting *Shabbat* Candles

Barukh atah Adonai, Elohaynu melekh
    ha-olam, asher kidushanu b'mitzvotav,
    v'tzivanu l'hadlik ne'ir shel shabbat.

Blessed art Thou, Lord, our God, King of the
Universe, who sanctifies us with His
commandments, and commands us to light
the candles of *Shabbat*.

Erev Shabbat Kiddush (Holding Wine)

Va-ihi erev va-ihi boker yom ha-shishi.

Va-ikhulu ha-shamayim v'ha'aretz v'khol tzva'am.

Va-ikhal Elohim ba-yom ha-shvi'i melakhto asher asah va-ishbot ba-yom ha-shvi'i melakhto asher asah.

Va-ivarekh Elohim et yom ha-shvi'i va-ikadeish oto ki vo shavat mikol melakhto asher bara Elohim la'asot.

Barukh atah Adonai Elohaynu melekh ha-olam, borei p'riy ha-gafen.

Barukh atah Adonai Elohaynu melekh ha-olam, asher kidushanu b'mitzvotav v'ratzah vanu.

V'Shabbat kadasho b'ahavah u'v'ratzon hinchilanu, zikaron l'ma'aseh v'reishit.

Ki hu yom t'chilah l'mikra'ey kodesh, zeikher liytziyat mitzraim.

Ki vanu vacharta v'otanu kidashta mikol ha'amim v'shabbat kadish'kha b'ahavah u'v'ratzon hinchaltanu.

Barukh atah Adonai, m'kadesh ha-shabbat.

And there was evening and there was morning, a sixth day.

The heavens and the earth were finished, the whole host of them.

And on the seventh day God ended His work, which He had made, and He rested on the seventh day from all his work, which He had made.

And God blessed the seventh day, and sanctified it because in it He had rested from all His work, which God created and had done.

Blessed art Thou, Lord, our God, King of the Universe, who creates fruit of the vine.

Blessed art Thou, Lord, our God, King of the Universe, who sanctifies us with His commandments, and has been pleased with us.

You have lovingly and willingly given us Your holy *Shabbat* as an inheritance, in memory of creation.

The *Shabbat* is the first among our holy days, and a remembrance of our Exodus from Egypt.

Indeed, You have chosen us and made us holy among all peoples and have willingly and lovingly given us Your holy *Shabbat* for an inheritance.

Blessed art Thou, who sanctifies the *Shabbat*.

Blessing for Washing Hands

Barukh atah Adonai, Elohaynu, melekh ha-olam, asher kidUshanu b'mitzvotav, v'tzivanu al n'tilat yada'im.

Blessed art Thou, Lord, our God, King of the Universe, who sanctifies us with His commandments, and commands us concerning washing of hands.

Shehecheyanu

This prayer welcomes many holidays and festivals.

Barukh atah Adonai, Elohaynu, melekh ha-olam, she-hecheyanu, v'ke'eymanu, v'he'ege'eyanu la-z'man ha-zeh.

Blessed art Thou, Lord our God, King of the Universe, who has kept us alive, sustained us, and enabled us to reach this season.

Havdalah Home Ceremony and Blessings

The introductory verses of the *Havdalah* ceremony come from the books of Isaiah, Psalms, and Esther, and are usually chanted or read by the leader of the ceremony. At the appropriate place, however, everyone should join in the following:

La'yehudim hayta ora v'simchah v'sason vikar, ken tih'yeh lanu.

There was light and joy, gladness and honor for the Jewish people. So may we be blessed. (Esther 8:16)

Blessings

Barukh atah Adonai, Elohaynu, melekh ha-olam, borei p'riy ha-gafen.

Blessed art Thou, Lord, our God, King of the Universe, who creates the fruit of the vine.

Barukh atah Adonai, Elohaynu, melekh ha-olam, she-ha-kol nih'yeh bidvaro.

Blessed art Thou, Lord, our God, King of the Universe, by Whose will all things exist. (Recited only if blessing is made over a liquid other than wine.)

Barukh atah Adonai, Elohaynu, melekh ha-olam, borei minei v'samim.

Blessed art Thou, Lord, our God, King of the Universe, who creates varieties of spices.

Barukh atah Adonai, Elohaynu, melekh ha-olam, borei m'orei ha-eish.

Blessed art Thou, Lord, our God, King of the Universe, who creates the lights of fire.

Barukh atah Adonai, Elohaynu, melekh ha-olam, ha-mavdil bayn kodesh l'chol, bayn or l'choshekh, bayn yisrael la-amim, bayn yom ha-shvi'i l'shayshet y'may ha-ma'aseh.

Blessed art Thou, Lord, our God, King of the Universe, who distinguishes between the sacred and the secular, between light and dark, between Israel and the nations, between the seventh day and the six days of labor.

Barukh atah Adonai, ha-mavdil bayn kodesh l'chol.

Blessed art Thou, who distinguished between the sacred and the secular.

Blessings over Chanukah Candles

Barukh atah Adonai, Elohaynu, melekh ha-olam, asher ke'edshanu b'me'etzvotav v'tze'evanu l'hadlik ne'ir shel Chanukah.

Blessed art Thou, Lord, our God, King of the Universe, who has sanctified us with His commandments and commanded us to light the candles of Chanukah.

Barukh atah Adonai, Elohaynu, melekh ha-olam, she-asah ne'ese'em la-avotaynu ba-yame'em ha-he'im ba-z'man ha-zeh.

Blessed art Thou, Lord, our God, King of the Universe, who performed miracles for our ancestors in those days at this time.

For first night only, add Shehecheyanu (see p. 260).

Rosh Hashanah *Kiddush* (Holding Wine)

If Rosh Hashanah falls on a Friday night, also add the words in brackets.

Barukh atah Adonai, Elohaynu, melekh ha-olam, borei p'ryi ha-gafen.
Barukh atah Adonai, Elohaynu, melekh ha-olam, asher bachar banu me'ekol am, v'romemanu me'ekol lashon v'ke'edshanu b'me'etzvotav, va-te'eten lanu, Adonai Elohaynu, et yom [ha-shabbat ha-zeh v'et yom] ha-zikkaron ha-zeh, yom [zikhron] t'ruah b'b'ahavah me'ekra kodesh, zeicher le'etze'eyat me'etzrayim.

Ki vanu vacharta v'otanu kidashta mikol ha'amim u'dvar'kha emet v'kayam la'ad.

Barukh atah Adonai, melekh al kol ha-aretz, m'kadesh [ha-shabbat v'] Yisra'el v'yom ha-zikkaron.

Blessed art Thou, Lord, our God, King of the Universe, who creates the fruit of the vine.

Blessed art Thou, Lord, our God, King of the Universe, who has chosen us from among all people, and exalted us above every tongue and sanctified us with His commandments, and You gave us, Lord our God, with love this day of [Sabbath and this day of] remembrance, a day of [remembrance of] *shofar* blowing [with love] a holy convocation, a memorial of the Exodus from Egypt.

Indeed, You have chosen us and made us holy from all peoples and Your word is true and established forever.

Blessed art Thou, Lord, our God, King over all the land, who sanctifies [the Sabbath] and Israel and the Day of Remembrance.

Blessings for Apple and Honey on Rosh Hashanah

Before dipping the apple in honey, say the following:

Barukh atah Adonai, Elohaynu, melekh ha-olam, borei p'riy ha-eitz.

Blessed art Thou, Lord, our God, King of the Universe, who creates the fruit of the tree.

After eating the apple dipped in honey, say the following:

Y'hi ratzon me'elfanekha, Adonai Elohaynu v'elohey avoteynu sh'tichadesh aleinu shanah tovah u-m'tukah.

May it be Your will, Lord our God and God of our ancestors that You renew for us a good and sweet year.

Mourner's *Kaddish*

Yitgadal v'yitkadash sh'me rabbah [All say: *Amen*], *b'almah di-v'rah khir'utey.*

V'yamlikh malkhutei, b'chayechon, uv'yomeychon, uv'chayei d'chal bet yisra'el, ba'agalah u'viz'man kariv, v'imru: Amen.

[All say: *Y'hey sh'mei rabbah m'varach l'alam u'l'almei alma'yah.*]

Yit'barakh, v'yishtabach, v'yitpa'ar, v'yitromam, v'yitnasei, v'yithadar, v'yit'aleh, v'yit'halal sh'meh d'kudshah b'rikh hu.

[All say: *B'rikh hu.*]

L'eylah min kol birkhatah v'shiratah, tush'b'chatah v'nechematah, da'amiran b'almah, v'imru: Amen.

[All say: *Amen.*]

Y'hei shlamah rabbah min sh'ma'yah, v'cha'im aleynu v'al kol yisra'el, v'imru: Amen.

[All say: *Amen.*]

Oseh shalom bimromav, hu ya'aseh shalom, aleynu v'al kohl yisra'el v'imru: Amen.

[All say: *Amen.*]

May His great Name grow exalted and sanctified [All say: Amen], in the world that God created as God willed.

May God complete the holy realm in your lifetime, in your days, and in the days of the entire house of Israel, quickly and soon. Amen.

[All say: May God's great Name be blessed, forever and ever.]

Blessed, praised, glorified, exalted, extolled, mighty, upraised, and lauded be the Name of the Holy One, Blessed is He.

[All say: Blessed is He.]

Beyond any blessing and song, praise and consolation that we utter in this world. Amen.

[All say: Amen.]

May there be abundant peace, and life for us, and for all Israel. Amen.

[All say: Amen.]

May the One who created harmony above, make peace for us and for all Israel. Amen.

[All say: Amen.]

Appendix C

Books, Periodicals, and Web Sites

The following lists of resources represent only a fragment of what is readily available to you from shops in your synagogue, independent booksellers (both large and small), newsstands, and Web sites on the Internet. All of these media—books, Web sites, and periodicals—are excellent means for you to keep up with what is going on with the Jewish people and Judaism.

Books of Jewish Interest

Aaron, Rabbi David. *Seeing God: The Life-Changing Lessons of the Kabbalah.* (JP Tarcher, 2001)

Agnon, S. Y. *The Bridal Canopy.* (Syracuse University Press, 2000)

—. *Only Yesterday.* (Princeton University Press, 2002)

—. *A Guest for the Night.* (Schocken Books, 1968)

Aiken, Lisa. *To Be a Jewish Woman.* (Jason Aronson, 1992)

Aleichem, Sholom. *Tevye the Dairyman.* (Schocken Books, 1996)

—. *Old Country Tales.* (Putnam Publishing Group, 1966)

Appelfeld, Aharon. *Badenheim 1939.* (David R. Goden, 1998)

—. *The Age of Wonders.* (Texas Bookman, 1996)

Arendt, Hannah. *Eichmann in Jerusalem: A Report on the Banality of Evil.* (Penguin USA, 1994)

Babel, Isaac. *Collected Stories.* (Penguin USA, 1995)

Bacon, Josephine Levy. *Jewish Cooking from Around the World.* (Barrons Educational Series, 1986)

Baeck, Leo. *The Essence of Judaism.* (Schocken Books, 1980)

Baker, Kevin. *Dreamland.* (Harper Mass Market Paperbacks, 2000)

Barnavi, Eli and Miriam Eliav-Feldon. *A Historical Atlas of the Jewish People: From the Time of the Patriarchs to the Present.* (Schocken Books, 1995)

Bellow, Saul. *Herzog.* (Penguin USA, 1996)

—. *Ravelstein.* (Penguin USA, 2001)

Blackman, Philip. *The Mishna.* (Judaica Press, 1990)

Blavin, Nehemiah. *The Owner's Manual to the Soul: A Modern Guide to Spirituality from Ancient Jewish Sources.* (Jason Aronson, 2000)

Blech, Benjamin. *Understanding Judaism: The Basics of Deed and Creed.* (Jason Aronson, 1992)

Borowitz, Eugene B. *Renewing the Covenant: A Theology for the Postmodern Jew.* (Jewish Publication Society, 1998)

Bright, John. *A History of Israel.* (Westminster John Knox Press, 2000)

Brownstein, Rita Milos. *Jewish Holiday Style: A Beautiful Guide to Celebrating the Jewish Rituals in Style.* (Simon & Schuster, 1999)

Buber, Martin. *I and Thou.* (Scribner, 1974)

—. *Between Man and Man.* (Macmillan Publishing Company, 1985)

—. *Tales of the Hasidim.* (Schocken Books, 1991)

—. *Good and Evil.* (Prentice Hall College Division, 1980)

Cahill, Thomas. *Gifts of the Jews: How a Tribe of Desert Nomads Changed the Way Everyone Thinks and Feels.* (Anchor Books, 1999)

Carmichael, Joel. *The Satanizing of the Jews.* (Fromm International, 1992)

Cassway, Esta. *The Five Books of Moses for Young People.* (Jason Aronson, 1995)

Chabon, Michael. *The Amazing Adventures of Kavalier & Clay.* (Picador USA, 2001)

Chazan, Robert. *In the Year 1096: The First Crusade and the Jews.* (Jewish Publication Society, 1997)

Citron, Sterna. *Why the Baal Shem Tov Laughed: Fifty-two Stories about Our Great Chasidic Rabbis.* (Jason Aronson, 1993)

Cohen, Abraham. *Everyman's Talmud.* (Schocken Books, 1995)

Cohen, Edward. *The Peddler's Grandson: Growing up Jewish in Mississippi.* (Dell Books, 2002)

Cohen, Rich. *The Avengers: A Jewish War Story.* (Knopf, 2000)

Cooper, David A. *God Is a Verb: Kabbalah and the Practice of Jewish Mysticism.* (Penguin USA, 1998)

Cretzmeyer, Stacy. *Your Name Is Renee: Ruth Kapp Hartz's Story as a Hidden Child in Nazi-Occupied France.* (Oxford University Press Children's Books, 1999)

Dan, Joseph. *Jewish Mysticism.* (Ktav Publishing House, 1996)

Dawn, Marva J. *Keeping the Sabbath Wholly: Ceasing, Resting, Embracing, Feasting.* (Wm. B. Eerdmans Publishing Company, 1989)

Dershowitz, Alan M. *The Vanishing American Jew.* (Touchstone Books, 1998)

Dever, William G. *What Did the Biblical Writers Know and When Did They Know It?: What Archaeology Can Tell Us about the Reality of Ancient Israel.* (Wm. B. Eerdmans Publishing Company, 2001)

Diamant, Anita. *The Red Tent.* (Picador USA, 1998)

—. *Good Harbor.* (Scribner, 2001)

Diamant, Anita and Howard Cooper. *Living a Jewish Life: Jewish Traditions, Customs, and Values for Today's Families.* (HarperCollins, 1996)

Dinnerstein, Leonard. *Anti-Semitism in America.* (Oxford University Press on Demand, 1995)

Dipple, John. *Bound upon a Wheel of Fire: Why So Many German Jews Made the Tragic Decision to Remain in Nazi Germany.* (Basic Books, 1996)

Donin, Rabbi Hayim Halevy. *To Be a Jew: A Guide to Jewish Observance.* (Basic Books, 1991)

—. *To Pray as a Jew: A Guide to the Prayerbook and Synagogue Service.* (Basic Books, 1991)

Drob, Sanford. *Symbols of the Kabbalah: Philosophical and Psychological Perspectives.* (Jason Aronson, 2000)

Ducovny, Amram. *Coney.* (Overlook Press, 2001)

Duron, Pichas. *Rashi's Torah Commentary.* (Jason Aronson, 2000)

Einstein, Albert. *Ideas and Opinions.* (Bonanza Books, 1988)

—. *Out of My Later Years.* (Outlet, 1993)

—. *Essays on Humanism.* (Philosophical Library, 1978)

Einstein, Stephen J. and Lydia Kukoff. *Every Person's Guide to Judaism.* (Union of American Hebrew Congregations, 1989)

Eisenberg, Robert. *Boychiks in the Hood.* (Harper San Francisco, 1996)

Elon, Ari, Naomi Hyman, and Arthur Waskow. *Trees, Earth and Torah: A Tu B'Shvat Anthology.* (Jewish Publication Society, 1999)

Elon, Menachem. *Jewish Law: History, Sources, Principles.* (Jewish Publication Society, 1994)

Englander, Nathaniel. *For the Relief of Unbearable Urges.* (Vintage Books, 2000)

Epstein, Lawrence. *The Story of Jewish Comedians in America.* (Public Affairs, 2001)

Epstein, Lawrence J. *Conversion to Judaism: A Guidebook.* (Jason Aronson, 1997)

Fackenheim, Emil L. *Encounters Between Judaism and Modern Philosophy.* (Jason Aronson, 1995)

Feiler, Bruce. *Walking the Bible: A Journey by Land Through the Five Books of Moses.* (Harper Perennial, 2002)

Finkel, Avraham Yoakov. *Ein Yoakov: The Ethical and Inspirational Teachings of the Talmud.* (Jason Aronson, 1999)

Fishman, Cathy Goldberg. *On Rosh Hashanah and Yom Kippur.* (Aladdin Paperbacks, 2000)

Frank, Anne. *The Diary of a Young Girl.* (Prentice Hall, 1993)

Frankiel, Tamar. *The Gift of Kabbalah: Discover the Secrets of Heaven, Renewing Your Life on Earth.* (Jewish Lights Publishing, 2001)

Frankl, Viktor. *Man's Search for Meaning.* (Washington Square Press, 1998)

Freedman, Samuel G. *Jew vs. Jew: Inside the Civil Wars of American Jewry.* (Simon & Schuster, 2000)

Freud, Sigmund. *Moses and Monotheism.* (Random House, 1997)

Friedland, Ronnie and Edmund Case. *The Guide to Jewish Interfaith Family Life.* (Jewish Lights Publishing, 2001)

Friedman, Richard Elliot. *Commentary on the Torah.* (Harper San Francisco, 2001)

Gay, Peter. *My German Question.* (Yale University Press, 1999)

Gefen, Nan Fink. *Discovering Jewish Meditation: A Beginner's Guide to an Ancient Spiritual Practice.* (Jewish Lights Publishing, 1999)

Gerstein, Mordecai. *Queen Esther the Morning Star.* (Simon & Schuster, 2000)

Gillman, Neil. *Sacred Fragments: Recovering Theology for the Modern Jew.* (Jewish Publication Society, 1992)

Ginzberg, Louis. *Legends of the Bible.* (Jewish Publication Society, 1992)

Glickman, Elaine Rose. *Haman and the Jews: A Portrait from Rabbinic Literature.* (Jason Aronson, 1999)

Gold, Alison Leslie. *Memories of Anne Frank: Recollections of a Childhood Friend.* (Scholastic Paperbacks, 1999)

Goldberg, Myla. *The Bee Season.* (Knopf, 2001)

Goldberg, Rabbi Nathan. *Passover Haggadah.* (Ktav Publishing House, 1987)

Goldhagen, Daniel. *Hitler's Willing Executioners: Ordinary Germans and the Holocaust.* (Vintage Books, 1997)

Goldman, Ari L. *Being Jewish: The Spiritual and Cultural Practice of Judaism Today.* (Simon & Schuster, 2001)

Goldman, Marcy. *A Treasury of Jewish Holiday Baking.* (Doubleday, 1998)

Gonsher-Vinik, Debra. *Embracing Judaism: Personal Narratives of Renewed Faith.* (Jason Aronson, 1999)

Goodman, Allegra. *The Family Markowitz.* (Washington Square Press, 1997)

—. *Kaaterskill Falls.* (Delta, 1999)

—. *Paradise Park.* (Delta, 2002)

Goodman, Philip. *The Passover Anthology.* (Jewish Publication Society, 1994)

Gordis, Daniel. *Becoming a Jewish Parent: How to Add Wonder and Spirituality to Your Child's Life.* (Three Rivers Press, 2000)

Green, Arthur. *These Are My Words: A Vocabulary of Jewish Spiritual Life.* (Jewish Lights Publishing, 2001)

—. *World of Jewish Spirituality.* (Crossroad/Herder & Herder, 1989)

Greenberg, Blu. *How to Run a Traditional Jewish Household.* (Simon & Schuster, 1985)

Greenberg, Gary. *The Bible Myth: The African Origins of the Jewish People.* (Citadel Press, 1998)

Greenberg, Irving. *The Jewish Way: Living the Holidays.* (Touchstone Books, 1993)

Greenberg, Rabbi Sydney and Pamela Roth. *In Every Generation: A Treasury of Inspiration for Passover and the Seder.* (Jason Aronson, 1998)

Grossman, David. *See Under: Love.* (Noonday Press, 1997)

Ha-Levi, Yossi Klein. *At the Entrance to the Garden of Eden.* (William Morrow & Co., 2001)

—. *Memoirs of a Jewish Extremist.* (Little Brown & Company, 1995)

Hammer, Jill. *Sisters at Sinai: New Tales of Biblical Women.* (Jewish Publication Society, 2001)

Hammer, Reuven. *Entering the High Holy Days.* (Jewish Publication Society, 1998)

—. *Entering Jewish Prayer: A Guide to Personal Devotion and the Worship Service.* (Schocken Books, 1995)

Harris, Mark Jonathon, Deborah Oppenheimer, David Cesarani, and Richard Attenborough. *Into the Arms of Strangers: Stories of the Kindertransport.* (Bloomsbury Pub. USA, 2001)

Hazony, Yoram. *Jewish State: The Struggle for Israel's Soul.* (Basic Books, 2001)

Heller, David. *We Gave the World Moses and Bagels: Art and Wisdom of Jewish Children.* (Jewish Publication Society, 2000)

Heller, Joseph. *Catch-22.* (Scribner, 1996)

—. *Good as Gold.* (Scribner, 1997)

—. *God Knows.* (Outlet, 1984)

Hertz, J. H. *Pentateuch and Haftorahs.* (Soncino Press, 1960)

Heschel, Abraham Joshua. *God in Search of Man.* (Noonday Press, 1997)

—. *Man Is Not Alone.* (Noonday, 1997)

Heschel, Susannah. *On Being a Jewish Feminist.* (Schocken Books, 1983)

Hoffman, Ethel. *Everyday Cooking for the Jewish Home.* (HarperCollins, 1997)

Hoffman, Rabbi Lawrence A. *My People's Prayer Book: Traditional Prayer, Modern Commentaries.* (Jewish Lights Publishing, 2001)

Howe, Irving and Elizabeth Greenberg. *Voices from the Yiddish.* (University of Michigan Press, 1972)

Ibry, David. *Exodus to Humanism: Jewish Identity Without Religion.* (Prometheus Books, 1999)

Isaacs, Ronald H. *Every Person's Guide to Shabbat.* (Jason Aronson, 1998)

—. *Every Person's Guide to Dying in the Jewish Tradition.* (Jason Aronson, 1999)

—. *Jewish Music: Its History, People and Song.* (Jason Aronson, 1997)

Jaspers, Karl. *Spinoza.* (Harvest Books, 1974)

Jewish Publication Society of America. *TANAKH. The JPS Hebrew-English Tanakh: The Traditional Hebrew Text and the New JPS Translation.* (Jewish Publication Society, 1999)

Kalechofsky, Roberta. *Vegetarian Judaism: A Guide for Everyone.* (Micah Publications, 1998)

Kaplan, Mordecai. *The Meaning of God in Modern Jewish Thought.* (Wayne State University Press, 1995)

Karp, Abraham. *A History of the Jews in America.* (Jason Aronson, 1997)

Kedar, Rabbi Karyn D. *The Dance of the Dolphin: Finding Prayer, Perspective and Meaning in the Stories of Our Lives.* (Jewish Lights Publishing, 2001)

Keneally, Thomas. *Schindler's List.* (Simon & Schuster, 1994)

Kimmel, Eric A. *The Chanukkah Guest.* (Holiday House, 1992)

—. *Zigazak! A Magical Hannukah Night.* (Doubleday, 2001)

Kimmelman, Leslie. *Hanukkah Lights, Hannukkah Nights.* (HarperFestival, 1999)

Kirsch, Jonathon. *Moses: A Life.* (Ballantine Books, 1999)

Klemperer, Victor. *I Will Bear Witness: 1933–1941, A Diary of the Nazi Years.* (Modern Library, 1999)

—. *I Will Bear Witness: 1941–1945, A Diary of the Nazi Years.* (Modern Library, 2001)

Kolatch, Alfred. *The Jewish Book of Why.* (Jonathan David Publishers, 1981)

—. *What Jews Say About God: From Biblical Times to the Present.* (Jonathan David Publishers, 1999)

—. *A Child's First Book of Jewish Holidays.* (Jonathan David Publishers, 1997)

Kreisel, Howard. *Maimonides' Political Thought: Studies in Ethics, Law and the Human Ideal.* (State University of New York Press, 1999)

Kremer, Lillian. *Women's Holocaust Writing.* (University of Nebraska Press, 2001)

Kurzweil, Arthur. *From Generation to Generation: How to Trace Your Jewish*

Genealogy and Family History. (Jason Aronson, 2001)

Kushner, Harold S. *To Life: A Celebration of Jewish Being and Thinking.* (Warner Books, 1994)

—. *When Children Ask About God: A Guide for Parents Who Don't Always Have All the Answers.* (Schocken Books, 1995)

Lamm, Norman. *The Shema: Spirituality and Law in Judaism.* (Jewish Publication Society, 1998)

Lapin, Daniel. *Buried Treasure: Hidden Wisdom from the Hebrew Language.* (Multnomah Publishers, 2001)

Laquer, Walter and Barry Robin. *Israeli-Arab Reader: A Documentary History of the Middle East Conflict.* (Penguin USA, 2001)

Latner, Helen. *The Everything® Jewish Wedding Book.* (Adams Media Corporation, 1997)

Leibowitz, Nehama. *New Studies in the Bible.* (World Zionist Organization, 1986)

Leonard, Leah W. *Jewish Cookery.* (Crown Publications, 1989)

Lerner, Michael. *Jewish Renewal: A Path to Healing and Transformation.* (Harper Perennial, 1995)

—. *Best Contemporary Jewish Writings.* (Jossey-Bass, 2001)

Levenson, Alan T. *Modern Jewish Thinkers: An Introduction.* (Jason Aronson, 2000)

Levi, Primo. *Survival in Auschwitz.* (Scribner, 1995)

—. *If This Is a Man.* (Viking Press, 1979)

Levine, Joseph A. *Rise and Be Seated: The Ups and Downs of Jewish Worship.* (Jason Aronson, 2001)

Levy, Alan. *The Wiesenthal File.* (Carroll & Graf, 2002)

Levy, Faye. *1,000 Jewish Recipes.* (Hungry Minds, 2000)

Lew, Alan and Sherri Jaffe. *One God Clapping: The Spiritual Path of a Zen Rabbi.* (Jewish Lights Publishing, 2001)

Mack, Stan. *The Story of the Jews: A 4,000-Year Adventure.* (Jewish Lights Publishing, 2001)

Maimonides, Moses. *The Guide for the Perplexed.* (University of Chicago Press, 1974)

Malamud, Bernard. *The Fixer.* (Penguin USA, 1994)

—. *The Tenants.* (Farrar, Straus & Giroux, 1971)

—. *The Assistant.* (Harper Perennial, 2000)

Manukin, Fran. *Miriam's Cup: A Passover Story.* (Scholastic Trade, 1998)

Matt, Daniel C. *Essential Kabalah.* (HarperSanFrancisco, 1996)

Metzker, Isaac. *A Bintel Brief.* (Schocken Books, 1990)

Millgram, Abraham. *Jewish Worship.* (Jewish Publication Society, 2001)

Muller, Filip. *Eyewitness Auschwitz: Three Years in the Gas Chambers.* (Ivan R. Dee, 1999)

Musleah, Rachel. *Why on This Night? A Passover Hagaddah for Family Celebration.* (Simon & Schuster, 2000)

Nathan, Joan. *Jewish Cooking in America.* (Random House, 1998)

Novak, William and Moshe Waldoks. *The Big Book of Jewish Humor.* (HarperCollins, 1981)

Novick, Peter. *The Holocaust in American Life.* (Houghton Mifflin, 2000)

Nulman, Macy. *The Encyclopedia of Jewish Prayer: Ashkenazic and Sephardic Rites.* (Jason Aronson, 1995)

Orlinsky, Harry M. *The Torah: The Five Books of Moses.* (Jewish Publication Society, 1992)

Oz, Amos. *Unto Death.* (Harvest Books, 1985)

—. *To Know a Woman.* (Harvest Books, 1992)

—. *Fima.* (Harvest Books, 1994)

Ozick, Cynthia. *The Shawl.* (Knopf, 1989)

—. *The Pagan Rabbi.* (Syracuse University Press, 1995)

—. *The Puttermesser Papers.* (Knopf, 1997)

Peres, Shimon and Robert Litell. *For the Future of Israel.* (Johns Hopkins University Press, 1998)

Peretz, I. L. *Selected Stories.* (Schocken Books, 1975)

Pies, Ronald W. *The Ethics of the Sages: An Interfaith Commentary on Pirkei Avot.* (Jason Aronson, 1995)

Plaskow, Judith. *Standing Again at Sinai: Judaism from a Feminist Perspective.* (HarperSanFrancisco, 1991)

Postema, Don H. *Catch Your Breath: God's Invitation to Sabbath Rest.* (CRC Publications, 1997)

Potok, Chaim. *The Promise.* (Fawcett Books, 1990)

—. *The Chosen.* (Fawcett Books, 1995)

Rabinovich, Itamar. *Waging Peace: Israel and the Arabs at the End of the Century.* (Farrar, Straus & Giroux, 1999)

Rabinowicz, Harry, M. *Hasidism: The Movements and Its Masters.* (Jason Aronson, 1988)

Rand, Robert. *My Suburban Shtetl: A Novel about Life in a Twentieth-Century American Village.* (Syracuse University Press, 2001)

Raphael, Simcha Paull. *Jewish Views of the Afterlife.* (Jason Aronson, 1996)

Richler, Mordecai. *The Apprenticeship of Duddy Kravitz.* (McClelland & Stewart, 1989)

—. *Joshua Then and Now.* (Penguin USA, 1991)

—. *Solomon Gursky Was Here.* (Penguin USA, 1991)

Riskin, Shiomo. *Passover Haggadah with a Traditional and Contemporary Commentary.* (Ktav Publishing House, 1984)

Robinson, George. *Essential Judaism: A Complete Guide to Beliefs, Customs, and Rituals.* (Pocket Books, 2000)

Roden, Claudia. *The Book of Jewish Food.* (Knopf, 1996)

Rosenbaum, Thane. *Elijah Visible.* (St. Martin's Press, 1996)

—. *Second Hand Smoke.* (Griffin Trade Paperback, 2000)

—. *The Golems of Gotham.* (HarperCollins, 2002)

Rosenberg, Shelley Kapnek. *Adoption and the Jewish Family: Contemporary Perspectives.* (Jewish Publication Society, 1998)

Rosten, Leo Calvin. *The New Joys of Yiddish.* (Crown Publications, 2001)

Roth, Henry. *Call It Sleep.* (Cooper Square Press, 1934)

—. *Mercy of a Rude Stream.* (St. Martin's Press, 1994)

Roth, Philip. *Portnoy's Complaint.* (Random House, 2002)

—. *The Counterlife.* (Farrar, Straus & Giroux, 1989)

—. *I Married a Communist.* (Houghton Mifflin, 1998)

—. *Patrimony.* (Simon & Schuster, 1991)

Rottenberg, Dan. *Middletown Jews: The Tenuous Survival of an American Jewish Community.* (Indiana University Press, 1997)

Rozenberg, Martin and Bernard M. Zlotowitz, editors. *The Book of Psalms: The New Translation and Commentary.* (Jason Aronson, 2000)

Sachar, Howard M. *A History of Israel: From the Rise of Zionism to Our Time.* (Oxford University Press, 1987)

Sarna, Nahum M. *Studies in Biblical Interpretation: JPS Scholars of Distinction Series.* (Jewish Publication Society, 2000)

Scheindlin, Raymond P. *A Short History of the Jewish People: From Legendary Times to Modern Statehood.* (Hungry Minds, 2000)

—. *The Chronicles of the Jewish People.* (Jonathan David, 1996)

Scherman, Rabbi Nosson, translator. *Family Haggadah.* (Mesorah Publications, 1981)

Scholem, Gershom. *Major Trends in Jewish Mysticism.* (Schocken Books, 1995)

—. *Origins of the Kabbalah.* (Princeton University Press, 1987)

Schram, Peninnah and Howard Schwartz. *Stories Within Stories: From the Jewish Oral Tradition.* (Jason Aronson, 2000)

Schram, Peninnah, Barbara Goldin, Gloria Goldreich, and Daniel Sperber. *The 40 Greatest Jewish Stories Ever Told.* (Pitspopany Press, 2001)

Segev, Tom. *1949: The First Israelis.* (Free Press, 1986)

Seid, Judith. *God-Optional Judaism: Alternatives for Cultural Jews Who Love Their History, Heritage and Community.* (Citadel Press, 2001)

Shanks, Hershel. *101 Best Jewish Jokes.* (Biblical Archaeology Society, 1999)

Shapiro, Rabbi Rami. *Minyan: Ten Principles for Living a Life of Integrity.* (Bell Tower, 1997)

Shevrin, Aliza. *Treasury of Sholom Aleichem's Children Stories.* (Jason Aronson, 1996)

Sidi, Smadar Shir. *The Complete Book of Hebrew Baby Names.* (HarperSanFrancisco, 1989)

Siegman, Joseph. *Jewish Sports Legends: The International Jewish Sports Hall of Fame.* (Jewish Publication Society, 1997)

Singer, Isaac Bashevis. *In My Father's Court.* (Farrar, Straus & Giroux, 1966)

—. *Satan in Goray.* (Noonday Press, 1996)

—. *The Family Moskat.* (Noonday Press, 1988)

—. *The Manor.* (Noonday Press, 1987)

—. *A Crown of Feathers and Other Stories.* (Farrar, Straus & Giroux, 1973)

Singer, Israel J. *Brothers Ashkenazi.* (Random House, 1936)

Slater, Elinor and Robert Slater. *Great Jewish Women.* (Jonathan David, 1998)

Solomon, Aryeh and Louis David Solomon. *The Educational Teachings of Rabbi Menachem M. Schneerson.* (Jason Aronson, 2000)

Solomon, Lewis. *The Jewish Book of Living and Dying.* (Jason Aronson, 1999)

Soloveitchik, Rabbi Joseph B. *Halakhic Man.* (Jewish Publication Society, 1984)

Sonsino, Rifat and Daniel B. Syme. *Finding God: Ten Jewish Responses.* (Jason Aronson, 1993)

Sorosky, Marlene, Debbie Shahvar, and Joanne Newman. *Fast and Festive Meals for the Jewish Holidays: Complete Menus, Rituals, and Party-Planning Ideas for Every Holiday of the Year.* (William Morrow & Co., 1997)

Spinoza, Baruch. *The Ethics of Spinoza.* (Citadel Press, 2000)

Spitz, Elie Kaplan. *Does the Soul Survive? A Jewish Journey to Belief in Afterlife, Past Lives, and Living with Purpose.* (Jewish Lights Publishing, 2000).

Steiner, Jean-Francois. *Treblinka: The Inspiring Story of 600 Jews Who Revolted Against Their Murderers and Burned a Nazi Death Camp to the Ground.* (Meridian Books, 1994)

Steinsaltz, Adin. *The Essential Talmud.* (Jason Aronson, 1992)

—. *Teshuvah: A Guide for the Newly Observant Jew.* (Jason Aronson, 1997)

—. *A Guide to Jewish Prayer.* (Schocken Books, 2000)

Strassfeld, Michael and Arnold M. Eisen. *The Jewish Holidays: A Guide and Commentary.* (HarperCollins, 1985)

Telushkin, Joseph. *Jewish Literacy: The Most Important Things to Know About the Jewish Religion, Its People and Its History.* (William Morrow & Co., 1991)

—. *Jewish Humor: What the Best Jokes Say about the Jews.* (William Morrow & Co., 1992)

Tigay, Alan M., editor. *Jewish Traveler: The Hadassah Magazine's Guide to the World's Jewish Communities and Sights.* (Doubleday, 1987)

Trachtenberg, Joshua. *The Devil and the Jews: The Medieval Concept of the Jew and Its Relation to Modern Anti-Semitism.* (Jewish Publication Society, 1989)

Troller, Norbet. *Theresienstadt: Hitler's Gift to the Jews.* (University of North Carolina Press, 1991)

Tye, Larry. *Home Lands: Portrait of the New Jewish Diaspora.* (Henry Holt, 2001)

Uris, Leon. *Exodus.* (Random House, 2000)

—. *Mila 18.* (Doubleday, 1961)

—. *Mitla Pass.* (Doubleday, 1988)

Wagner, Jordan Lee. *The Synagogue Survival Kit.* (Jason Aronson, 1997)

Waskow, Rabbi Arthur. *Down-to-Earth Judaism: Food, Money, Sex and the Rest of Life.* (William Morrow & Co., 1997)

—. *Torah of the Earth: Exploring 4,000 years of Ecology in Jewish Thought.* (Jewish Lights Publishing, 2000)

Wiesel, Elie. *The Night Trilogy: Night, Dawn, the Accident.* (Noonday Press, 1994)

—. *The Town Beyond the Wall.* (Henry Holt, 1964)

—. *Souls on Fire: Portraits and Legends of Hasidic Masters*. (Jason Aronson, 1993)

—. *The Fifth Son*. (Summit Books, 1985)

Wiesel, Elie and Mark Podwal. *A Passover Haggadah*. (Simon & Schuster, 1993)

Wineman, Aryeh. *The Hasidic Parable: An Anthology with Commentary*. (Jewish Publication Society, 2001)

—. *Mystic Tales from the Zohar*. (Jewish Publication Society, 1997)

—. *Ethical Tales from the Kabbalah*. (Jewish Publication Society, 1999)

Wolf, Laibl. *Practical Kabbalah: A Guide to Jewish Wisdom for Everyday Life*. (Three Rivers Press, 1999)

Wouk, Herman. *This is My God: The Jewish Way of Life*. (Little Brown & Company, 1988)

Wyman, David S. *The Abandonment of the Jews: America and the Holocaust, 1941–1945*. (Pantheon Books, 1984)

Yahil, Leni. *The Holocaust: the Fate of European Jewry*. (Oxford University Press, 1991)

Yehoshua, A. B. *Mr. Mani*. (Doubleday, 1992)

—. *A Journey to the End of the Millennium*. (Doubleday, 1999)

—. *The Five Seasons*. (Doubleday, 1989)

Yezierska, Anzia. *Bread Givers*. (Persea Books, 1999)

—. *Salome of the Tenements*. (University of Illinois Press, 1996)

Zetter, Kim. *Simple Kabbalah*. (Conari Press, 2000)

Periodicals

Agada. Fiction, poetry, and essays pertaining to the Jewish experience.

Amit. Articles with general Jewish themes focusing on Israel, travel, and holidays. This magazine is directed to a readership consisting mainly of Jewish women.

The B'nai Brith International Jewish Monthly. Articles concerning Jewish affairs and news of B'nai Brith International.

Congress Monthly. The official publication of the American Jewish Congress, this periodical covers topics of interest to the American Jewish community.

Forward. Originally a daily Yiddish newspaper, it is now a weekly publication that covers international, national, and local (New York) news of Jewish interest.

Hadassah Magazine. The official magazine of Hadassah that includes a wide range of articles of Jewish interest.

Inside. A quarterly magazine of Jewish life and style published by the Jewish Federation of Greater Philadelphia.

Israel Horizons, Progressive Zionist Quarterly. Subject matter includes Israel and American Jewish society.

Jerusalem Post. An Israeli daily with an international English-language edition that you can subscribe to in the United States. Also available online.

Jewish Currents. Published by the Association for Promotion of Jewish Secularism, with an emphasis on Jewish culture, history, and Yiddishkeit.

Midstream. A monthly Jewish review published by the Theodor Herzl Foundation. This journal provides a medium for independent opinion and creative cultural expression.

Moment, The Magazine of Jewish Culture and Opinion. An independent periodical encompassing Jewish culture, politics, and religion.

Reconstructionist. Official publication of the Jewish Reconstructionist Federation.

Reform Judaism. Official magazine of the Union of American Hebrew Congregations.

The Reporter. Published by Women's American ORT (Organization for Educational Resources and Technological Training), this periodical covers a wide array of Jewish topics.

Sh'ma, A Publication of Jewish Family and Life. Articles and essays of Jewish subject matter.

Tikkun. A Jewish critique of politics, culture, and society, often from the point of view of the Jewish Renewal movement.

United Synagogue Review. Official publication of the United Synagogue of Conservative Judaism.

Web Sites

A World of Jewish Singles
  www.worldofsingles.com
American Jewish Historical Society
  www.ajhs.org
A Haggadah for the American Family
  www.americanhaggadah.com
An American Jewish History
  www.borisamericanjews.com

The Anti-Defamation League
  www.adl.org
Aleph: Alliance for Jewish Renewal
  www.aleph.org
Bang It Out.com: Jewish Comedy, Culture and Classifieds
  www.bangitout.com
Being Jewish
  www.beingjewish.com
Beth-Din of America
  www.bethdin.org
Bibliodrama: Dedicated to Jewish Education and the Creation of Midrash
  www.crosswinds.net
"Bnei Baruch"—World Center for Kabbalah Studies
  www.kabalah-web.org
Chanukah on the Net
  www.holidays.net
COEJL: Coalition of the Environment and Jewish Life
  www.coejl.org
Council for Jewish Elderly
  www.cje.net
FAQ: Kosher Food
  www.cyber-kitchen.com
Fun Jewish Jewelry
  www.funjewishjewlry.com
Gates to Jewish Heritage
  www.jewishgates.org
High Holy Days on the Net
  www.holidays.net
Jewish-American History on the Web
  www.jewish-history.com

Jewish Burial Society
✍ *www.jewishburial.org*

Jewish Celebrations—the Jewish Wedding Resources and Planning
✍ *www.mazomet.com*

Jewish Community Online's Internet Resources
✍ *www.jewish.com*

Jewish Cuisine—Jewish Holidays, Food, and More!
✍ *www.jewishcuisine.com*

Jewish Culture and History
✍ *www.apc.org*

Jewish Deaf Singles Registry
✍ *www.jdsr.org*

Jewishfamily.com
✍ *www.jewishfamily.com*

Jewish Family Life and Homepage
✍ *www.jewishfamily.com*

Jewishfilm.com
✍ *www.jewishfilm.com*

Jewish Food Recipes Archives
✍ *www.jewishfood.org*

Jewish Holiday and Festivals on the Net
✍ *www.melizo.com*

Jewish Holiday Kitchen
✍ *www.epicurious.com*

Jewish Holocaust Web Sites
✍ *www.sjwar.org*

Jewish Jobs
✍ *www.jewishjobs.com*

Jewish Law
✍ *www.jlaw.com*

Jewish Music
✍ *www.jewishmusic.com*

Jewish Music Resources—Zamir Chorale
✍ *www.zamir.org*

Jewish Online Studies, Torah, Kabbalah, Talmud, Laws
✍ *www.foreveryjew.com*

Jewish Outreach Institute
✍ *www.joi.org*

Jewish Reconstructionist Federation
✍ *www.jrf.org*

Jewish Renewal Life Center
✍ *www.jewishrenewallifecenter.org*

Jewish Singles Beshert Introductions for Jewish Professionals
✍ *www.beshert.com*

Jewish Source
✍ *www.jewishsource.com*

Jewish Travel
✍ *www.jewishtravel.com*

The Jewish Vegan Lifestyle
✍ *www.jewishvegan.com*

Jewish Women International
✍ *www.jewishwomen.org*

Jewish Women's Archive
✍ *www.jwa.org*

Jewish World Center
✍ *www.jewishworldcenter.com*

Jewish World Review
✍ *www.jewishworldreview.com*

JStudies.Org—Our Jewish Studies Site
✍ *www.jstudies.org*

Judaism and Jewish Resources
✍ *www.shamash.org*

Judaism 101
✍ *www.jewfaq.org*

Klezmerica Jewish Music Home Page
✍ *www.frozenchozen.com*

Lights along the Path: Jewish Folklore for the
Children of Today
✎ *www.thirdside.com*

Mazon: A Jewish Response to Hunger
✎ *www.mazon.org*

National Jewish Outreach Program
✎ *www.njop.org*

Rosh Hashanah and Yom Kippur
✎ *www.ohr.org*

Single Jew: Jewish Singles Dating Site
with Photos
✎ *www.singlejew.com*

The American Israel Public Affairs Committee
✎ *www.aipac.org*

The Coalition for the Advancement of
Jewish Education
✎ *www.caje.org*

The Jewish Bride and More!
✎ *www.jewishbride.com*

The Jewish New Year
✎ *www.jewishnewyear.com*

The National Yiddish Book Center
✎ *www.yiddishbooks.com*

The Source for Everything Jewish
✎ *www.jewishsource.com*

The Virtual Beit Midrash—Torah Web Yeshiva
✎ *www.vbm-torah.org*

Union of Orthodox Jewish Congregations
of America
✎ *www.ou.org*

United Synagogue of Conservative Judaism
✎ *www.uscj.org*

World Congress of Gay and Lesbian
Jewish Organizations
✎ *www.vwc.edu*

World Jewish Congress
✎ *www.wjc.org*

Index

THE EVERYTHING SERIES!

BUSINESS

Everything® **Business Planning Book**
Everything® **Coaching and Mentoring Book**
Everything® **Fundraising Book**
Everything® **Home-Based Business Book**
Everything® **Leadership Book**
Everything® **Managing People Book**
Everything® **Network Marketing Book**
Everything® **Online Business Book**
Everything® **Project Management Book**
Everything® **Selling Book**
Everything® **Start Your Own Business Book**
Everything® **Time Management Book**

COMPUTERS

Everything® **Build Your Own Home Page Book**
Everything® **Computer Book**
Everything® **Internet Book**
Everything® **Microsoft® Word 2000 Book**

COOKBOOKS

Everything® **Barbecue Cookbook**
Everything® **Bartender's Book, $9.95**
Everything® **Chinese Cookbook**
Everything® **Chocolate Cookbook**
Everything® **Cookbook**
Everything® **Dessert Cookbook**
Everything® **Diabetes Cookbook**
Everything® **Indian Cookbook**
Everything® **Low-Carb Cookbook**
Everything® **Low-Fat High-Flavor Cookbook**

Everything® **Low-Salt Cookbook**
Everything® **Mediterranean Cookbook**
Everything® **Mexican Cookbook**
Everything® **One-Pot Cookbook**
Everything® **Pasta Book**
Everything® **Quick Meals Cookbook**
Everything® **Slow Cooker Cookbook**
Everything® **Soup Cookbook**
Everything® **Thai Cookbook**
Everything® **Vegetarian Cookbook**
Everything® **Wine Book**

HEALTH

Everything® **Alzheimer's Book**
Everything® **Anti-Aging Book**
Everything® **Diabetes Book**
Everything® **Dieting Book**
Everything® **Herbal Remedies Book**
Everything® **Hypnosis Book**
Everything® **Massage Book**
Everything® **Menopause Book**
Everything® **Nutrition Book**
Everything® **Reflexology Book**
Everything® **Reiki Book**
Everything® **Stress Management Book**
Everything® **Vitamins, Minerals, and Nutritional Supplements Book**

HISTORY

Everything® **American Government Book**
Everything® **American History Book**
Everything® **Civil War Book**
Everything® **Irish History & Heritage Book**

Everything® **Mafia Book**
Everything® **Middle East Book**
Everything® **World War II Book**

HOBBIES & GAMES

Everything® **Bridge Book**
Everything® **Candlemaking Book**
Everything® **Casino Gambling Book**
Everything® **Chess Basics Book**
Everything® **Collectibles Book**
Everything® **Crossword and Puzzle Book**
Everything® **Digital Photography Book**
Everything® **Easy Crosswords Book**
Everything® **Family Tree Book**
Everything® **Games Book**
Everything® **Knitting Book**
Everything® **Magic Book**
Everything® **Motorcycle Book**
Everything® **Online Genealogy Book**
Everything® **Photography Book**
Everything® **Pool & Billiards Book**
Everything® **Quilting Book**
Everything® **Scrapbooking Book**
Everything® **Sewing Book**
Everything® **Soapmaking Book**

HOME IMPROVEMENT

Everything® **Feng Shui Book**
Everything® **Feng Shui Decluttering Book, $9.95 ($15.95 CAN)**
Everything® **Fix-It Book**
Everything® **Gardening Book**
Everything® **Homebuilding Book**

All Everything® books are priced at $12.95 or $14.95, unless otherwise stated. Prices subject to change without notice.
Canadian prices range from $11.95–$31.95, and are subject to change without notice.

Everything® **Home Decorating Book**
Everything® **Landscaping Book**
Everything® **Lawn Care Book**
Everything® **Organize Your Home Book**

EVERYTHING®
KIDS' BOOKS

All titles are $6.95

Everything® **Kids' Baseball Book,
    3rd Ed.** ($10.95 CAN)
Everything® **Kids' Bible Trivia Book**
    ($10.95 CAN)
Everything® **Kids' Bugs Book** ($10.95 CAN)
Everything® **Kids' Christmas Puzzle &
    Activity Book** ($10.95 CAN)
Everything® **Kids' Cookbook** ($10.95 CAN)
Everything® **Kids' Halloween Puzzle &
    Activity Book** ($10.95 CAN)
Everything® **Kids' Joke Book** ($10.95 CAN)
Everything® **Kids' Math Puzzles Book**
    ($10.95 CAN)
Everything® **Kids' Mazes Book**
    ($10.95 CAN)
Everything® **Kids' Money Book**
    ($11.95 CAN)
Everything® **Kids' Monsters Book**
    ($10.95 CAN)
Everything® **Kids' Nature Book**
    ($11.95 CAN)
Everything® **Kids' Puzzle Book**
    ($10.95 CAN)
Everything® **Kids' Riddles & Brain
    Teasers Book** ($10.95 CAN)
Everything® **Kids' Science Experiments
    Book** ($10.95 CAN)
Everything® **Kids' Soccer Book**
    ($10.95 CAN)
Everything® **Kids' Travel Activity Book**
    ($10.95 CAN)

KIDS' STORY BOOKS

Everything® **Bedtime Story Book**
Everything® **Bible Stories Book**
Everything® **Fairy Tales Book**
Everything® **Mother Goose Book**

LANGUAGE

Everything® **Inglés Book**
Everything® **Learning French Book**
Everything® **Learning German Book**
Everything® **Learning Italian Book**
Everything® **Learning Latin Book**
Everything® **Learning Spanish Book**
Everything® **Sign Language Book**
Everything® **Spanish Phrase Book,**
    $9.95 ($15.95 CAN)

MUSIC

Everything® **Drums Book (with CD),**
    $19.95 ($31.95 CAN)
Everything® **Guitar Book**
Everything® **Playing Piano and
    Keyboards Book**
Everything® **Rock & Blues Guitar
    Book (with CD), $19.95**
    ($31.95 CAN)
Everything® **Songwriting Book**

NEW AGE

Everything® **Astrology Book**
Everything® **Divining the Future Book**
Everything® **Dreams Book**
Everything® **Ghost Book**
Everything® **Love Signs Book, $9.95**
    ($15.95 CAN)
Everything® **Meditation Book**
Everything® **Numerology Book**
Everything® **Palmistry Book**
Everything® **Psychic Book**
Everything® **Spells & Charms Book**
Everything® **Tarot Book**
Everything® **Wicca and Witchcraft Book**

PARENTING

Everything® **Baby Names Book**
Everything® **Baby Shower Book**
Everything® **Baby's First Food Book**
Everything® **Baby's First Year Book**
Everything® **Breastfeeding Book**

Everything® **Father-to-Be Book**
Everything® **Get Ready for Baby Book**
Everything® **Getting Pregnant Book**
Everything® **Homeschooling Book**
Everything® **Parent's Guide to
    Children with Autism**
Everything® **Parent's Guide to Positive
    Discipline**
Everything® **Parent's Guide to Raising
    a Successful Child**
Everything® **Parenting a Teenager Book**
Everything® **Potty Training Book,**
    $9.95 ($15.95 CAN)
Everything® **Pregnancy Book, 2nd Ed.**
Everything® **Pregnancy Fitness Book**
Everything® **Pregnancy Organizer,**
    $15.00 ($22.95 CAN)
Everything® **Toddler Book**
Everything® **Tween Book**

PERSONAL FINANCE

Everything® **Budgeting Book**
Everything® **Get Out of Debt Book**
Everything® **Get Rich Book**
Everything® **Homebuying Book, 2nd Ed.**
Everything® **Homeselling Book**
Everything® **Investing Book**
Everything® **Money Book**
Everything® **Mutual Funds Book**
Everything® **Online Investing Book**
Everything® **Personal Finance Book**
Everything® **Personal Finance in Your
    20s & 30s Book**
Everything® **Wills & Estate Planning
    Book**

PETS

Everything® **Cat Book**
Everything® **Dog Book**
Everything® **Dog Training and Tricks
    Book**
Everything® **Golden Retriever Book**
Everything® **Horse Book**
Everything® **Labrador Retriever Book**
Everything® **Puppy Book**
Everything® **Tropical Fish Book**

All Everything® books are priced at $12.95 or $14.95, unless otherwise stated. Prices subject to change without notice.
Canadian prices range from $11.95–$31.95, and are subject to change without notice.

REFERENCE

Everything® **Astronomy Book**
Everything® **Car Care Book**
Everything® **Christmas Book, $15.00**
   ($21.95 CAN)
Everything® **Classical Mythology Book**
Everything® **Einstein Book**
Everything® **Etiquette Book**
Everything® **Great Thinkers Book**
Everything® **Philosophy Book**
Everything® **Psychology Book**
Everything® **Shakespeare Book**
Everything® **Tall Tales, Legends, &**
   Other Outrageous
   Lies Book
Everything® **Toasts Book**
Everything® **Trivia Book**
Everything® **Weather Book**

RELIGION

Everything® **Angels Book**
Everything® **Bible Book**
Everything® **Buddhism Book**
Everything® **Catholicism Book**
Everything® **Christianity Book**
Everything® **Jewish History &**
   Heritage Book
Everything® **Judaism Book**
Everything® **Prayer Book**
Everything® **Saints Book**
Everything® **Understanding Islam**
   Book
Everything® **World's Religions Book**
Everything® **Zen Book**

SCHOOL & CAREERS

Everything® **After College Book**
Everything® **Alternative Careers Book**
Everything® **College Survival Book**
Everything® **Cover Letter Book**
Everything® **Get-a-Job Book**
Everything® **Hot Careers Book**

Everything® **Job Interview Book**
Everything® **New Teacher Book**
Everything® **Online Job Search Book**
Everything® **Resume Book, 2nd Ed.**
Everything® **Study Book**

SELF-HELP/ RELATIONSHIPS

Everything® **Dating Book**
Everything® **Divorce Book**
Everything® **Great Marriage Book**
Everything® **Great Sex Book**
Everything® **Kama Sutra Book**
Everything® **Romance Book**
Everything® **Self-Esteem Book**
Everything® **Success Book**

SPORTS & FITNESS

Everything® **Body Shaping Book**
Everything® **Fishing Book**
Everything® **Fly-Fishing Book**
Everything® **Golf Book**
Everything® **Golf Instruction Book**
Everything® **Knots Book**
Everything® **Pilates Book**
Everything® **Running Book**
Everything® **Sailing Book, 2nd Ed.**
Everything® **T'ai Chi and QiGong Book**
Everything® **Total Fitness Book**
Everything® **Weight Training Book**
Everything® **Yoga Book**

TRAVEL

Everything® **Family Guide to Hawaii**
Everything® **Guide to Las Vegas**
Everything® **Guide to New England**
Everything® **Guide to New York City**
Everything® **Guide to Washington D.C.**
Everything® **Travel Guide to The**
   Disneyland Resort®,
   California Adventure®,

Universal Studios®, and
   the Anaheim Area
Everything® **Travel Guide to the Walt**
   Disney World Resort®,
   Universal Studios®, and
   Greater Orlando, 3rd Ed.

WEDDINGS

Everything® **Bachelorette Party Book,**
   $9.95 ($15.95 CAN)
Everything® **Bridesmaid Book, $9.95**
   ($15.95 CAN)
Everything® **Creative Wedding Ideas**
   Book
Everything® **Elopement Book, $9.95**
   ($15.95 CAN)
Everything® **Groom Book**
Everything® **Jewish Wedding Book**
Everything® **Wedding Book, 2nd Ed.**
Everything® **Wedding Checklist,**
   $7.95 ($11.95 CAN)
Everything® **Wedding Etiquette Book,**
   $7.95 ($11.95 CAN)
Everything® **Wedding Organizer,**
   $15.00 ($22.95 CAN)
Everything® **Wedding Shower Book,**
   $7.95 ($12.95 CAN)
Everything® **Wedding Vows Book,**
   $7.95 ($11.95 CAN)
Everything® **Weddings on a Budget**
   Book, $9.95 ($15.95 CAN)

WRITING

Everything® **Creative Writing Book**
Everything® **Get Published Book**
Everything® **Grammar and Style Book**
Everything® **Grant Writing Book**
Everything® **Guide to Writing**
   Children's Books
Everything® **Screenwriting Book**
Everything® **Writing Well Book**

Available wherever books are sold!
To order, call 800-872-5627, or visit us at everything.com

Everything® and everything.com® are registered trademarks of F+W Publications, Inc.